Toronto

NO MEAN CITY

Toronto

NO MEAN CITY

Eric Arthur

University of Toronto Press

But Paul said, I am a man which am a Jew of Tarsus, a city in Cilicia, a citizen of no mean city ... Acts 21:39

To my grandson
Eric Arthur Leach

Foreword

Too little has been written about the early development of Toronto and the reasons for its growth. When my grandfathers came to live here about one hundred years ago, one from Scotland, the other from what was once known as Lower Canada, Toronto was a city of some sixty or seventy thousand people. At the beginning of that century, it was nothing but a frontier village of no more than four or five hundred inhabitants. Today the population exceeds one and a half million and there is no end in sight.

In writing this book, it was not Eric Arthur's purpose to explain why Toronto has grown so big, so quickly, or to guess what may happen to it in the years that lie ahead. However, in providing us with this record of the things our predecessors built, often with difficulty and with limited resources, he has given some insight to their characters. Torontonians have been noted for their drive, energy, and ambition, for a materialistic urge to get ahead. In the process they found time to create some things that were handsome, even beautiful. It is these that should be preserved.

Toronto is no longer exclusively British or colonial in outlook. It is now a cosmopolitan city whose people have come from all corners of the earth. This makes it a much more lively and interesting place to live in, and provides an atmosphere in which the arts can flourish and develop. Nevertheless, the same characteristics of drive, energy, and ambition are still very much in evidence. We would not wish it to be otherwise.

Some years ago, Professor Arthur told me of his plans to write this book about the origins and early architecture of Toronto. He asked me to write a Foreword. As one who was born and brought up in Toronto, I was pleased that a man of Professor Arthur's talents was going to write a book about our city. And I was flattered at the thought of being associated with it even in a minor way.

However, our conversation proved to be one of the most expensive experiences I have ever had. Professor Arthur had expressed the wish to include illustrations of the building at 15 Wellington Street West owned by the firm of which, at the time, I was the senior partner. Shortly after our conversation, the building was inspected and found to be unsafe. We were ordered to vacate it. Some of my partners thought the building should be demolished to make way for a more modern structure. Others felt this might spoil Professor Arthur's book on which he had been working for some years. They said if I were to write the Foreword, the only decent thing for us to do would be to renovate the building. This argument prevailed and the old Commercial Bank building at 15 Wellington Street West has been completely rebuilt from the inside out. It was a costly undertaking.

However, it is a lovely building. Now it will be preserved for many years, and not only within the pages of this book. I am sure all my former partners are pleased with the decision that was taken for there cannot be many chartered accountants who, in Professor Arthur's words, occupy "A truly fine building which cannot help but evoke thoughts of Greece and of Byron, Shelley, Keats and others."

I hope his labours will inspire others to preserve some of the few architectural gems of earlier times that still remain. One of these is St. Lawrence Hall on King Street at Jarvis. A building of a much later period renovated recently is Saint Anne's Church on Gladstone Avenue, north of Dundas. The interior of this church was decorated by local artists who later became famous as the Group of Seven. In a pulsating, vital metropolis like Toronto with its ever changing population, there is a need to be reminded of the things that were created by those who went before us. Professor Arthur's book meets this need admirably.

31 December, 1963

W. R. Gordon

For a quarter of a century or more, this study of Toronto has never been far from my thoughts, and it is inevitable, however much I regret it, that many acquaintances and some old friends who provided information will be forgotten in these acknowledgments. We may have met by chance at dinner, on the street or in a bus, and, rather like the subversive characters about whom one reads in the newspapers, an address has been given, a snapshot or a letter has changed hands, and we have parted. The number of such encounters, if not legion, must number hundreds, and they have led more than once to old books, old photographic collections, and not least, to old people.

It has been my good fortune to make my investigations into old Toronto at a time when many who are still living remember with enviable clarity the buildings and people of the later 19th century which are of vital importance in the story of the city. So many of our ancient landmarks are lost that the architectural historian of even so recent a period as the 19th century must frequently feel that he is concerned with some ancient civilization like Pompeii or Herculaneum. Fortunately, he can be brought back to reality by meeting older citizens like Mr. William Wadsworth, Q.C., who remembers vividly having Sunday tea with his mother at the house of her uncle, Col. Frederick Cumberland, the designer of St. James' Cathedral. Even more impressive and more indicative of the youthfulness of Toronto are Mr. Wadsworth's records of his great-grandfather Thomas Ridout who came to Toronto when the population was only fifty. For the interviewer, Max Beerbohm's phrase, "the intruder from posterity," cannot help but come to mind.

Few who recall the seemingly venerable walls of old Trinity (1851) on Queen Street would believe that many now living knew its architect, Mr. Kivas Tully, who died in 1905. I myself knew and greatly admired Mr. W. A. Langton and his brother Hugh, the distinguished sons of the great Vice-Chancellor of the University, John Langton, who acted as intermediary between Cumberland, the architect, and Sir Edmund Head in the building of University College in 1856. It is with rather special pride that I can count the late Dr. Needler as colleague and friend. He fought in the Riel Rebellion, and was a youth when the Metropolitan Church was built. For him, the melancholy story of Mrs. Anna Jameson who died in 1860 seemed that of a near and dear friend rather than of a figure who appeared briefly on the Toronto stage and left, never to return, in 1837. These are but a few of the men and women in that ever diminishing band whose memories, only slightly dimmed, recall the buildings and the people of the past century.

Fortunately for the architectural historian, there were others, actually living in the 19th century, whose love of buildings was second only to their interest in their neighbours. Where they lived, where they worshipped and where they worked have been the study of several works. Chief, of course, was Dr. Henry Scadding's *Toronto of Old*, followed by the monumental records of John Ross Robertson in his *Landmarks of Toronto*. To both of them, I am bound to acknowledge my profound obligations. There are other sources of material which may be read in the Bibliography elsewhere in this volume, but I should like to pay special tribute to the late Mr. Percy Robinson whose *Toronto during the French Régime* first introduced me to a period that I found far from negligible in the evolution of Toronto's urban pattern.

But to return to the present. Many have gone, but there are still Torontonians with no personal memories of the 19th century, who, perhaps, by reason of their closeness to it as children, have made a study of early buildings and people of that period the habit of a lifetime. From them, the most notable contribution was that of the late Mr. T. A. Reed who published little, but left a sizeable collection of photographs to complement the Ross Robertson sketches in the Public Library. Mr. Reed was not only an eager collector of Canadiana, he ranked second to none in his love of Toronto.

Less well known, but one who has been tireless in research on my behalf has been Mr. John Songhurst. Mr. Songhurst has been long a resident of Toronto, and can remember his first interest in buildings as a messenger boy seventy years ago. At the age of seven he received the first volume of the *Landmarks*, and it has been a constant companion every since. His wife shares his interest, as well she might, having been born in St. Lawrence Hall of parents who, like her grandparents, had the custody of the Hall in the days of its dignity in the life of the community.

I am particularly indebted to Mr. Hugh Robertson, the photographer. His skill is apparent in his work, but had it not been for his interest in the subject and his willingness to work at odd and critical times, many buildings would have perished without record. At various times, foundations and friends have contributed towards the cost of photography, and I am happy to express my gratitude to the Architectural Conservancy of Ontario, the Flavelle Foundation, and Mr. Harry Kohl.

I am very much obliged to Mr. Wallace Bonner of the Toronto Public Library for bringing to life by photography many old maps and hardly discernible pictures, to Mr. Uno Prii and Mr. Vyt Kvedaris, two young architects, for sketches of similar material, and to Mrs. Howard Garfield and Mrs. G. E. Edgar for the typing and retyping of these pages.

Professor John Russell of Winnipeg has been a source of inspiration and encouragement over most of the years when this book was in preparation and I can only hope that the book, itself, may be some sort of requital for his kindness.

I am under various obligations to friends who have provided information on matters of art, technology, or history: to Mr. F. de Rege, the Consul General of Italy; His Excellency, Mr. Leo Maynard, the Canadian Ambassador to Italy; Dr. Emilio Goggio, Mr. Alan Jarvis, Mr. Wm. Colgate, Mrs. Marion Fowler, Mr. R. E. Chadwick, Mr. L. J. McGowan, Mr. George Grainger, and Mr. W. E. Fleury.

Finally, there are people and institutions without whom this study of old Toronto would, in all probability, not have been made. I am chiefly indebted to the President and Board of Governors of the University of Toronto for allowing me sabbatical leave in 1958–59, and to the Canada Council for a very welcome senior grant directed particularly to research into the early architecture of Toronto. I should be remiss if I did not include in these thanks my colleagues in the School of Architecture whose labours, one must assume, were not lightened by my absence.

The basic material on the origin of street names comes from John Ross Robertson and T. A. Reed, but even their lists left many streets of doubtful or unknown origin. Some yet remain uncertain, but the gap in our knowledge has been greatly narrowed. It is my hope that the publication of the origin of Toronto street names will bring more people to the defence of ancient names when they are attacked by those for whom history has no meaning or importance. Until recently, Ann and McGill Streets were not unromantic reminders of Ann McGill who became the wife of Bishop Strachan, but Ann became Granby as a concession to a long-held Toronto belief that a change of name would raise the tone of a street both socially and morally. Granby, of course, was a marquis. The fact that, in 1834, Strachan purchased twenty-five acres north of Gerrard Street out of which he gave the land to the city for Ann, McGill, and part of Carlton Streets carried no weight with Judge Parker who granted the change. Guy Carleton Wood was Mrs. Strachan's brother, and Carlton is misspelled.

I am very aware that there is some presumption in a person of antipodean birth and English education following in the footsteps of Scadding, Robertson, and Robinson as a recorder of old Toronto. My excuse is that the story might well be told again through the eyes of an architect, aided, as his predecessors were not, by photography and the clarity of the modern printed page. At the same time, I am very conscious of the fact that the story of its architecture is part of the social history of Toronto and cannot be told without a knowledge of the political and economic history that, through war and peace, boom and depression, gave it character and life.

In that area of knowledge, I must confess my own inadequacy and my very real debt to Miss Edith Firth. She must be held blameless for any of the errors that must, inevitably, appear in these pages. The period in which she is an authority covers the early years of York, Upper Canada; I, with the innocence of a fairly new Canadian and an audacity which, at times, must have left her breathless, have not hesitated to explore the Toronto scene from Louis XIV to Edward VII. Her painstaking reading of manuscripts and her frequent suggestion of clues which led to English architects like Fowler and Soane can never be repaid.

For many years, Mrs. Harry Davidson has been a tireless research worker and collaborator in the preparation of the material for this book. Many of the illustrations would have remained hidden but for her zeal in pursuing them in odd places, and the section on street names owes much to her patience and persistence. My very sincere thanks go to her.

The writing of a book makes many inroads on the family and social life of the author, and my thanks go to my wife for her sympathetic understanding of the many problems the work imposed.

Last, but by no means least, is my grateful acknowledgment of the generosity of the J. S. McLean and the Laidlaw Foundations which have helped to make the publication of this book possible.

E. A.

For the purposes of the second edition, the information in the captions has been brought up to date wherever possible but no attempt has been made to adjust the text. ERIC ARTHUR, NOVEMBER 1973

Contents

This architectural history of Toronto has been in the mind of the writer since the time, many years ago, when he first made it a habit of wandering with no fixed objective through the streets of the old town. Thirty-five years ago, one could enjoy many thoroughfares that still had about them an air of colonial Upper Canada—a quiet Georgian peace created, in part, by the low horizontal lines of the two-storeyed, terraced houses. Those streets are now slums or ruins and can be enjoyed, like Ruth Draper with her imaginary garden, only in memory.

But, if the architecture is gone, a few individual buildings of an older time remain. The visitor to Paris knows what it is to turn a corner and see a famous monument like the Madeleine for the first time. It is not necessary to leave Toronto to have the same emotional experience; one may have it when one looks north on John from Queen and sees the Grange for the first, or even the tenth time. Osgoode Hall at the head of York, and Sir William Campbell's house closing so beautifully the vista of Frederick Street, are not easily forgotten.

The newcomer to Toronto from Europe or Great Britain has, probably, left a city that was rich in those ancient landmarks which give colour and meaning to history. And there are other newcomers—our own children—for whom the city of Toronto shows few visible signs of its ancient origins, or of the various cultural influences which have shaped our architecture since Simcoe chose his capital in York.

In the march of progress, we have ruthlessly destroyed almost all our older architecture; street names cherished for a hundred years or more have been altered to suit the whims of the people on the street, and even our most treasured buildings, Fort York, going back to the beginnings of British settlement, have recently been threatened because the historic soil on which they stood interfered with the curvature of a modern expressway. In our defence, it must be said that the loss of a great deal of early building can be laid to more than one disastrous fire in the days when water pressure was inadequate and fire-fighting equipment was primitive. Whatever the reasons for the destruction of our early architecture, the sad fact remains that the buildings worthy of record from the 19th century are, for the most part, churches and university buildings whose safety can be reasonably assured. The rest have disappeared, some without trace.

It would not be the wish of this writer to condone the destruction of our early buildings, but it would be unfair to compare the interest of the people of London or Edinburgh in the preservation of their ancient monuments with the apparent lack of interest of the citizens of Toronto in theirs. Toronto is a growing city under a pressure that could hardly be conceived in a city in the United Kingdom where half-timbered houses can stand on High Holborn in London from Jacobean times, and Georgian squares remain untouched by the speculative builder or the financial institution. It has not been so here. What has been saved from wanton destruction or from fire in the last hundred and fifty years is extremely vulnerable in a period of unprecedented growth. As a result, the few idealists who tried to save the Cawthra house at King and Bay knew that they stood little chance against the millions of the Bank of Nova Scotia which required the site for a new head office. We may regret the loss, but we may feel less humiliated if we think of the chances of survival had the same old house stood at the corner of the Haymarket and Piccadilly.

It was partly the architectural gaps in our history that posed for me the question whether to show only buildings of unquestioned merit, or whether to demonstrate the taste of the century more truthfully by showing a greater number of buildings of unequal architectural quality. The decision to do the latter was supported also by the fact that not every reader has access to the Ross Robertson *Landmarks*, and that many would be interested in illustrations of historic houses, churches, and other buildings that, on a strictly architectural selection, would be discarded.

I have suggested that we in Toronto are curiously apathetic towards our history in terms of landmarks, street names and the like; indeed surely no city in the world with a background of three hundred years does so little to make that background known. Our children are brought up to take pride in the British beginnings of the city, but they have a limited knowledge of that vastly more exciting period when the Senecas had a village on the site, when black-robed priests and French noblemen dwelt at times at the mouth of the Humber and wrote glowing letters home to France of the potentialities of Toronto as a settlement in the empire of Louis XIV. No pageants recall the great events that took place under the French régime: 1959 passed with little comment on the destruction of Fort Rouillé in 1759, and yet, in the opinion of historians, this was the birthplace of a metropolis that now boasts a million and a half souls. M. Pierre Roy, the Quebec archivist, was moved to say of Fort Rouillé, "this is the great city of Toronto in embryo—Paris did not have a more glorious beginning." In Mr. J. E. Middleton's three-

1 Davenport Road. Davenport Road is on the line of an old Indian trail which followed the shore line of ancient Lake Iroquois. It became a road about 1800, running north from Lake Ontario on the east side of Parliament Street. South of the present Bloor Street, it turned northwest intersecting Yonge at the Potter's Field, just north of Bloor and opposite the Red Lion Inn. It was first called New Road or New Pinery Road because of the pine woods through which it passed.

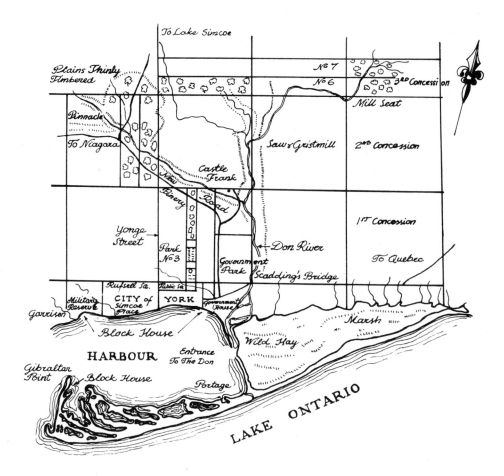

volume work on the *Municipality of Toronto*, the French period enjoys a mere ten pages out of a total of over a thousand.

I hope to show in the early part of this book on Toronto that its beginnings are based on use and a road pattern, to my mind, far more important than that isolated monument, Fort Rouillé, housing less than a dozen men. It has become popular to speak disparagingly, or to speak not at all, of the so-called "pre-history" of Toronto, but from that neglected period, we can make more valid comparisons with the birth of Paris in Roman Lutetia and of London in Londinium than that made by M. Roy.

The comparison, at first sight far-fetched, is between the effect of Roman planning on Paris and London, and our present-day use of the location of the old trails. That they are by no means insignificant can be gathered merely from their names—the Don Valley Parkway, the Frederick Gardiner Expressway, and Davenport Road. The most important and the oldest of the old trails followed the Humber. It has disappeared, but its value as a highway to the north has not changed in several hundred years. We replaced it by Highway 400. The monotony of the rest of our street pattern, the gridiron, is a technique of planning that we received as a legacy from Rome via Mr. Alexander Aitkin in 1793. It is for these reasons, very real to the architect and the town planner, that the pre-Simcoe period in our history is discussed in some detail.

There is, of course, another reason and that is the inaccessibility of information for those new and old Canadians who would like to be more familiar with the earliest period. It is to be found chiefly in *Toronto during the French Régime* by Mr. Percy Robinson—a book issued first in a limited edition, for many years out of print. In 1697, Father Hennepin dedicated his book on the *New Discovery of a Large Country in America* to "His Most Excellent Majesty William III," which Mr. Robinson rather slyly suggests "will not be without significance to those who recall the subsequent devotion of the city of Toronto to that Monarch." It may well be asked whether our continued devotion to the memory of the House of Orange has not blinded us to the beauty, the tragedy, and the high adventure of the period under the kings of France—the centuries that saw brave men and women bringing civilization into the wilderness, as well as gentlemen explorers, both French and English, with names that rank high in the histories of both countries. They saw, too, the arrival of quite a number of rascals of many races, and of dedicated Catholic priests, some of whom were to die at the stake for their faith. All these people knew by reputation the village at the mouth of the Humber and the trails from the north, the east, and the west that led to it. A surprising number knew the site of Toronto from actual experience and left records of their impressions.

NOTE
Throughout the book, the date given for a building usually indicates the year in which it was begun.

Toronto
NO MEAN CITY

The pre-British story of Toronto is stimulating enough for the people of Canada, but it is a moving, almost a personal one for those of us who call Toronto home. We can still tread the principal path of the great explorers. It is broken, it is true, and is no longer a trail, but the basic elements remain unchanged. With eyes closed to the structures that have appeared only in this century, we can stand where Etienne Brulé stood on a September morning in 1615. To the south he would look on the great lake, its waves sparkling in the autumn sunshine, its farther shore remote and invisible. To that lonely traveller, the first of his race to set eyes on Lake Ontario, the sight must have been no less awe-inspiring than that which Cortez saw from his peak in Darien. More so, indeed, because Brulé was alone except for twelve Hurons, and the vast waters stretching to the far horizon had to be crossed or circumnavigated by canoe.

Behind him as he gazed across the lake was the Humber, meandering as it still does between swamps and high clay banks. It was autumn and the ducks, without the blessing of sanctuary that they enjoy today, would be getting ready with the red-winged blackbirds to follow Brulé to the south.

Half a century goes by, and we find people living in a village on the east bank of the Humber within sight of what we know today as the Old Mill. The village, the first settlement of people in the Toronto area, was called Teiaiagon. Its inhabitants were first Senecas and later Missisaugas, but its population would frequently be swelled by white men, most of whom would be free traders. The rest were soldiers and administrators under orders to enrich the coffers of the kings of France and to extend the borders of their empire; and that smaller band who were soldiers of Christ—Jesuits, Sulpicians, and Récollets—dedicated to the goal of the extension of God's Kingdom in the wilderness.

Teiaiagon was a trading post, a meeting place for three trade routes—the Indians from the north, the French from the east, and the English from the south. But, more important as it affected the development of Canada, was its strategic location at the southern end of "le passage de Toronto,"[1] or, to give it its other name, the Toronto Carrying Place, through which travellers went on journeys to the Georgian Bay and the Great Lakes—even to the far Mississippi. The Carrying Place was, therefore, not a "place" so much as a well-defined portage. "The Carrying Place possessed a permanence very different from casual paths through the forest. It was as old as human life in America."[2] Canoes and equipment had to be carried from Teiaiagon to the west branch of the Holland River which provided a storm-free and navigable waterway into Lake Simcoe. The last lap in the Carrying Place between Lake Simcoe and the vast open water of the Great Lakes was the Rivière Toronto which we now call the Severn.

Traders . . . of every description knew the mouth of the Humber and bargained here for the precious peltries; Dutchmen from the Hudson before the French themselves had gained access to Lake Ontario; French traders from Fort Frontenac; English freebooters from Albany, they all knew the Carrying Place, and with or without license robbed the poor Indian. How various and picturesque they were, these rascals from the Hudson and these lawless *coureurs-de-bois* from the St. Lawrence, wild hearts and children of the wilderness as truly as the aborigines whom they beguiled. To-day, there is a dance-hall on the bank of the Humber on a knoll overlooking the lake [burned in 1962]; it stands at the foot of the Carrying Place; below it is a cove where hundreds of these gentry landed for their nefarious trade. Time has shifted the scene.

1: The Village and the Ancient Trails

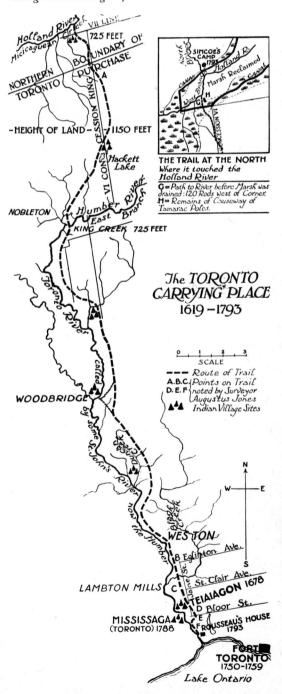

2 Map showing the Toronto Carrying Place or the *passage de Toronto* (from Percy J. Robinson's *Toronto during the French Régime*).

Here, too, in sombre contrast with the war-paint of the savages and the gay garments of the *coureurs-de-bois* were seen the black robes of the Jesuits and the less gloomy garb of the Récollets and Sulpicians. Hennepin was here, and Raffeix mapped the shore and traced the course of the Don as early as 1688; and Fénelon and d'Urfé came from the mouth of the Rouge to preach at Teiaiagon.

Du Lhut and Péré, Tonti and La Forest, Henry and Frobisher, and many of the French pioneers of the West passed this way. None of whom stand out so vividly as the great explorer of the Mississippi with his crowd of Shawanoes and his great canoes, three feet wide, to be carried over the long portage and the "high mountains" between Teiaiagon and *Lac* Toronto. Great days those for the old trail when the dream of empire was maturing in the brain of La Salle, a dream which in the end was to expel the French from America![3]

Of lesser importance than Teiaiagon was another village not too distant to be considered with the site of metropolitan Toronto. It was called Ganatsekwyagon by the Senecas who inhabited it, and is shown on the east bank of the Rouge in Charlevoix–Bellin's map of 1744. The same map shows a trail from the mouth of the Rouge connecting with the Carrying Place. This, however, is not the first time the village appears in history because the two Sulpician priests, the Abbé Fénelon and Father d'Urfé, spent the winter there in 1669–71. The name, Frenchman's Bay, would hardly suggest to the reader the dignity of a Sulpician mission in the reign of Louis XIV, but by that name for the inlet and community near the mouth of the Rouge we do give rather grudging recognition of the presence of two French priests nearly three hundred years ago. The river itself got its name from the deposit of red clay brought down from the banks.

In a study of the origins of Toronto, the town planner would be greatly interested in the fact that, for centuries, communities existed at the mouths of the Humber, the Don, and the Rouge. The Don, which we know today as a sluggish, sewage-laden stream, was once a magnificent river, navigable by canoe for at least five miles and famous, like the Credit and the Humber, for its salmon. From her eyrie on the Castle Frank ridge overlooking the Don, Mrs. Simcoe wrote in her diary of the colour and mystery of the scene as the Indian braves speared salmon from canoes at night by the light of flares. Deer abounded in the area, but the fishing, apart from trade, would be additional justification for the settlements of Teiaiagon and Ganatsekwyagon, and, between the two, there must have been considerable traffic by trail and canoe.[4] The harbour is still there, and great ships come from the far corners of the earth just as, at another time, the *bateaux* of the French explorers came from Quebec.

As we travel at speed over expressways on Front Street and the banks of the Don, we are likely to forget that we are riding on the ancient "road" system of the Indians, the *coureurs-de-bois*, and the traders. These were only trails, but how sensible they were in their use of the terrain. Much more sensible indeed than was Aitkin whose gridiron was imposed on the site of Toronto in 1793, ignoring completely the traffic problems to be faced on hills, or the unique town-planning possibilities of the ravines. The Indians could have shown Mr. Aitkin a simpler way of climbing the Avenue Road hill than by charging it head on.

If, to the above, we add Davenport Road and Indian Road (an old trail, but laid out as a road by John G. Howard), and allow ourselves the not unreasonable exaggeration of including Highway 400 as the successor to the "passage de Toronto," we have a network of trails that are built into the fabric of metropolitan

Toronto. For that reason, this writer would not accept for the birth of Toronto the building of Fort Rouillé in 1750—a little structure with a lifetime of nine years that, in 1754, had a population of one officer, two sergeants, four soldiers, and a storekeeper. That would be an insignificant and transitory landmark on which to base the foundation of a great city—transitory indeed compared with the immemorial trails. London has its Watling Street as a reminder of the Roman occupation of Londinium, Paris has its Rue St. Jacques, and posterity may yet realize its debt to those aborigines who blazed the trails of Front Street, Davenport, and the Don.

Teiaiagon does not appear again in this story of Toronto, but it will surprise many to know that the location of the village and the Humber are engraved indelibly on a terrestrial globe that once rested in state in the Grand Salon of the Doge's Palace in Venice. It was there in 1875 when Mr. Barlow Cumberland reported its existence to Dr. Scadding, but has since been moved to the Biblioteca

3, 4 The Coronelli Globe, 1683. The detail (**3**) shows "Toiougon" at the end of the "portage" and "L. Taronto."

5

Nazionale Marciana in the Piazetta S. Marco. The globe was made in 1683 for Louis XIV by the geographer Coronelli. It is 3 ft. 6 in. in diameter, and "Toiougon" is distinctly marked along with the words "portage" and "L. Taronto." It requires no great stretch of the imagination to see the Grand Monarque seated in Versailles reading letters from his administrators in Canada concerning the state of affairs at the "passage de Toronto," and turning to see its location on the globe. When the poet Thomas Moore wrote in 1804

> Where the blue hills of old Toronto shed
> Their evening shadows o'er Ontario's bed

he may not have known how truly "old" was the settlement that he visited.[5] He saw it with the discerning eye of the poet, and he felt instinctively its venerability where contemporary visitors saw only its newness.

Sufficient proof has already been given of the antiquity of the settlement at Toronto, a name which, by 1726, had superseded the old "fort du lac Ontario" and remained in use till Governor Simcoe decided on the more English title of York. But, in addition to antiquity, the settlement can also boast of continuous occupation except for the gap between 1759 and 1793 which will be referred to later. The first actual building by methods familiar to western eyes was the construction of a blockhouse or *Magasin Royal* at, or near, the mouth of the Humber in 1720. It was one of several at key points on Lake Ontario designed by the French to eliminate competition in their trade with the Indians. The one at Toronto was built by the Sieur Douville, and, according to Robinson, was similar to one at Lewiston on the Niagara River. The Lewiston blockhouse was, presumably, of wood with embrasures for musket fire, and was forty feet by thirty within a palisade. The building of magazines provided the French with only a precarious monopoly in the fur trade and for only a brief period. But for a time it was so successful that profits of the trade at New York declined almost one-half,[6] to the great chagrin of the English who countered by building a stone fort at Oswego (1726). The French, in turn, strengthened their position on the lake by completing Fort Niagara, the stone fortress we admire today at the mouth of the river opposite Niagara-on-the-Lake.

5 Map showing position of the three French posts at Toronto (from Percy J. Robinson's *Toronto during the French Régime*).

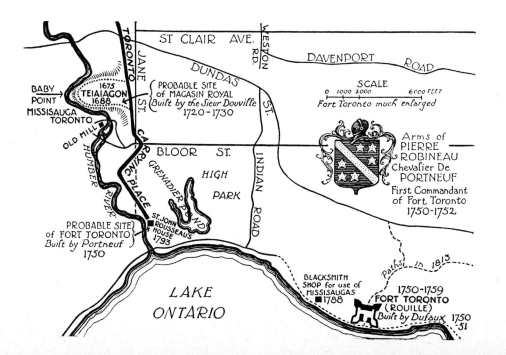

In the feverish competition of the time, "le poste de Toronto" proved to be not a serious contender for the fur trade compared with Oswego, and, in 1750, the French were forced to reply with a Fort Toronto erected by the Chevalier de Portneuf. It stood near the mouth on the east bank of the Humber, and in the short space of one year proved so successful that a second fort was found necessary.

In August 1750, the Governor of Quebec, the Marquis de la Jonquière, wrote M. Rouillé, the Minister of Marine and Colonies in Paris, that the "house" which the Sieur Portneuf had built at Toronto was too small, and that the garrison could easily be overpowered by the Indians, let alone the English. He asked and received permission to build another and larger fort which he would call Fort Rouillé. And so, in 1751, we see the last of the French forts at the site of Toronto. Its location was three miles east of that of Portneuf's on the Humber, and was marked, in 1887, by a monument which stands, today, in the grounds of the Canadian National Exhibition. In keeping with La Jonquière's flattering suggestion to his Minister in Paris, a plaque identifies the Fort as Rouillé. It was, however, generally described as Fort Toronto, or with its full title of "le fort royal de Toronto."

By the fall of 1759, Canada had ceased to be a battlefield in the Seven Years' War between England and France. Fort Frontenac had already fallen, and the bastion at Niagara fell to the forces of Sir William Johnson on July 25, 1759, after a siege of nineteen days. The Governor-General, Vaudreuil, had given orders for the evacuation and destruction of Fort Toronto if it were likely to fall into British hands, and, sometime during the siege of Niagara, his orders were carried out by Captain Douville in charge of the fort. Dr. Scadding remarks: "All that the English or any one else on approaching Toronto, would discover of the once flourishing trading post there would be five heaps of charred timber and planks, with a low chimney stack of coarse brick and a shattered flooring at its foot, made of flagstones from the adjoining beach, the whole surrounded on the inland side by three lines of cedar pickets more or less broken down and scathed by fire."[7]

It is customary to think of the next thirty years as a blank in the historical continuity of Toronto as a trading centre. Officially, certainly, it had ceased to exist. The French had gone, and the English were slow to realize its potentialities as a site. General Gage, the British Commander at Montreal, issued a proclamation in 1762, declaring the fur trade free to all, but forbidding the export of peltries to France. Passes seem to have been issued from Montreal much like licences today to hunt or to trap, and, among those enjoying such privileges at Toronto, was a "Monsieur Baby," one of a well-known family from Detroit who had been engaged in the fur trade long before the conquest. A descendant became the Honourable James Baby who built a house for himself on the banks of the Humber, and gave his name to the modern district surrounding Baby Point.

Then there was the family of Rousseau who help fill in the gap between the burning of Fort Rouillé and the arrival of Governor Simcoe. We hear of one St. Jean Rousseau living in Montreal being granted (1770) a licence for one year "to pass unmolested with one canoe and six men from Montreal to Toronto, with liberty to dispose of his goods and effects as he should occasionally find a market in his passage." His merchandise consisted of "eighty gallons of rum and brandy, sixteen gallons of wine" and gun powder, shot and balls amounting in value to

£300 lawful money. No wonder that Gage wrote "Complaints have been made here from Michilimackinac that the traders of Toronto debauch all the Indians from those quarters by selling them rum...."[8]

At the time of the founding of York, the Rousseaus had been established in Toronto for at least twenty-five years. Even the Toronto River in contemporary accounts became known as the St. John River. Assumed to be the son of St. Jean Rousseau the trader, was that Jean Baptiste Rousseau who lived in a house near Teiaiagon, and who, as pilot on the *Mississaga*, had the distinction of bringing Governor Simcoe, his wife and party safe to harbour on the historic occasion of the founding of York. We remember him in St. John's Road in the City of Toronto. Mr. Percy Robinson remarks: "The last Frenchman of Toronto was to welcome a governor who proceeded at once to wipe out all the traditions of the French régime."[9]

When one studies the late 18th century history of Toronto, it is clear that two men played a great part in guiding the destiny of the future city. They were Sir Guy Carleton, the first Lord Dorchester, and Lt.-Col. John Graves Simcoe. History has shone a bright light on the latter, and someone in Toronto daily recalls him in Simcoe Street (once Graves) and John Street, but it was Lord Dorchester as Governor-in-Chief of Canada who arranged the Toronto Purchase, the first step in the negotiations for a site for the future capital of Ontario. Even if his preference was for Kingston, and Toronto came about only as a compromise, the first step was a significant one. In 1787, Dorchester arranged a meeting between three Missisauga chiefs and his Deputy Surveyor-General Collins for the purchase of a rather vaguely described area of land amounting, in the final settlement, to 250,880 acres. The meeting was held at another Carrying Place, the one on that narrow neck of land between the mainland and what is now Prince Edward County. There, without pressure or hard bargaining as far as one may learn, the site of Toronto was bought for £1,700 along with some barrels of cloth, some axes and odds and ends "dear to the heart of the simple savage"—"In witness whereof, we have hereunto set our hands and seals the day and date above mentioned [September 23, 1787] Wabukanyne, Neace, Pakquan (chiefs) Witness present John Collins, Louis Protle, Nathnl Lines *Interpr.*"[1]

Eighteen years went by and another meeting was held, not from any qualms of conscience that the former deal was unjust or that the constitutional owners of the land had been deceived, but that the earlier instrument was "defective and imperfect." In the interim, Neace had died and Wabukanyne had been murdered by a Queen's Ranger in York in 1796. Pakquan did not sign the 1805 treaty, but another Wabukanyne, probably a son, was there to sign with seven chiefs. The treaty was witnessed by J. W. Williams, Jno. Blackenbury, Ens. 49th Reg., P. Selby and J. B. Rousseaux. The date of this historic meeting was August 1, 1805, and the place, the mouth of the River Credit in Ontario.

The year following the Toronto Purchase of 1787 is not without interest in the story of Toronto. In July of that year, Lord Dorchester gave orders for a survey to be made of the land acquired from the Missisaugas, including a site for a new town. The significance of this survey lies in the fact that at so early a date, and some five years before Lieutenant-Governor Simcoe went "a city-hunting," the Governor in Quebec had decided on the strategic value of Toronto as a town site. His interest in the area arose from a general plan to open up again the "passage de Toronto" from the Humber mouth to Lake Huron, and both Robinson and Middleton agree that, had it not been for the strong views held by the Governor-in-Chief on this matter, the capital of Upper Canada would, today, be on Simcoe's chosen site, the forks of the Thames.[2]

1788 is also the date of a quite remarkable plan made by Capt. Gother Mann commanding the Royal Engineers in Upper Canada. He calls it "Plan of Torento [*sic*] Harbour, with the proposed Town and Part of the Settlement." As will be seen in the illustration, the plan includes a central square containing military and government buildings surrounded by a common which, in turn, is enclosed to the north, east and west by a residential area. The whole territory is bounded by the modern High Park, Broadview Avenue and Bloor Street. The old Carrying Place

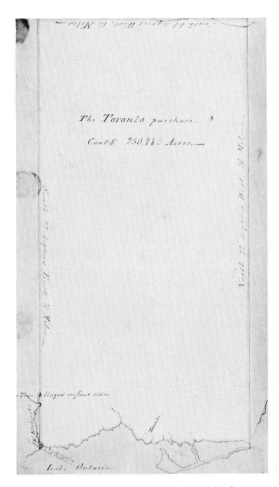

6 The Toronto Purchase (1787). On the lake front, it extended east from the mouth of the Etobicoke River a distance of 14 miles. Northwards the property extended 28 miles. The total area was 250,880 acres.

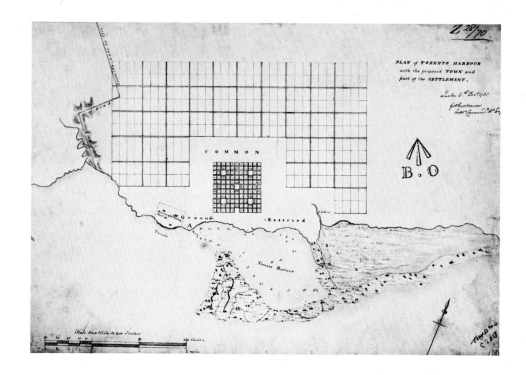

is there, but shown as a road leading to Lake la Clie, a misspelling of Lac aux Claies, the name usually given to Lake Simcoe as the former Lac Toronto fell into disuse.

The plan is what one might expect of a military engineer, and may go back in origin to the gridiron settlements which Roman engineers designed for coloni, or pensioned veterans in garrison towns. In Roman terms, Mann's square of public buildings becomes a forum and the residential squares a setting for the houses of the discharged soldiers. Had his plan been designed for a level site like that of Timgad in North Africa, it might, with some stretch of the imagination, be thought to have merit. The idea of public buildings in a neat British square separated in perpetuity from the residential area by a green common with shade trees and sheep quietly grazing is quite delightful, but fantastic and unrealistic when one considers the rising terrain and the deeply penetrating ravines. These topographical problems would hardly be appreciated in London where Mann's plan of "Torento" was forwarded with the colonial correspondence in 1790.

As we approach the last decade of the 18th century, several factors emerge that were to affect profoundly the future of Canada and the ultimate decision for the site of Toronto. Until the end of the Seven Years' War (1763), Canada had been predominantly French, and it was only with the American War of Independence that the racial balance of population was to change. Canada then became the natural refuge for those colonists who preferred the British Crown to life in the Republic. An estimate of the United Empire Loyalists who came north has never been accurately determined, but their numbers may have reached 40,000. It was obvious under the circumstances that the government of Canada could expect nothing but unrest and dissatisfaction if the French criminal and civil codes were to be imposed on people with a background of British law and culture. By 1791, there were already thriving Loyalist settlements in Ontario—on the St. Lawrence River,

Kingston, Prince Edward County, the Niagara Peninsula and the Detroit River, and agitation for representative government and English law from these settlers had much to do with the Constitutional Act which separated Canada into two parts at the Ottawa River. Lower Canada, largely French, retained the old system of laws with "representative institutions added," while Upper Canada followed the English model.

In 1791, Col. John Graves Simcoe was appointed Lieutenant-Governor of Upper Canada, and, in September of that year, he sailed from Weymouth to Quebec in the ship *Triton*, 21 guns, accompanied by his wife and two children and "a Lieutenant Talbot." (This was the Talbot who, as Colonel Talbot, was so active in the settlement of southwestern Ontario.) Niagara, across the mouth of the river from the old French fortress, became the temporary capital of the Province, and here the Lieutenant-Governor summoned his first parliament on September 17, 1792.

What impresses the reader of contemporary accounts of this period and of the principal actors was their calm acceptance of a mode of life completely foreign, at any rate for Mrs. Simcoe and the children, to that to which they had been accustomed. Plagues of flies of all kinds were encountered inside as well as outside their house because several windows were unglazed. But Mrs. Simcoe's diary, far from giving the impression of boredom or suffering for a wife suddenly transferred from a stately home in Devon to the rigours of an encampment in the wilderness, speaks rather of lively dinner parties, gay balls, the joys of riding and the pleasures of sketching in water colour. Elizabeth Posthuma Simcoe was an unusual woman, and an ideal wife for a soldier and proconsul. Only a soldier's wife, and an exceptional one at that, could write from Niagara-on-the-Lake with such equanimity: "The Governor set out to walk to Burlington Bay [Hamilton], at the head of Lake Ontario, about fifty miles from hence." "I sat up all night to read poems of Louis Velez de Guevara, the Spanish poet and dramatist (1570–1644), and the history of Prince Ctesiphon, and some pages of Don Quixote; went to bed in my clothes at six, rose at nine, dressed, breakfasted at ten."[3] There must have been many unusual women in early Canada, but few who, like Mrs. Simcoe, took comfort from Sir Joshua Reynolds' *Discourses*, or the five volumes of Palladio.

One of the Governor's chief concerns was, of course, to find a site for the capital city of Upper Canada. Niagara would not do, if for no other reason than, in the Governor's words, "Under the guns of an enemy's fort is not the place for the capital of a British province." It would appear that when Simcoe went on his next exploratory trip, he had already made up his mind from available maps as to the most desirable site for the capital. He travelled through the western end of the province covering the sites of the modern cities of Brantford, Chatham, London and Detroit. As early as January 8, 1791, he had written in England: "I propose that the Site of the Colony should be in that Great Peninsula between the Lakes Huron, Erie, and Ontario, a Spot destined by Nature sooner or later, to govern the interior World. I mean to establish a Capital in the very heart of the Country, upon the River La Tranche, which is navigable for batteaux for 150 miles. . . . The Capital I mean to call Georgina."[4] All he needed was proof on the ground itself, and he returned to Niagara convinced.

This is not the place to discuss at length the constant friction between the Lieutenant-Governor of Upper Canada and the Governor-General of Canada, Lord Dorchester—a state of affairs that brought about "the resignation of both of their respective commands in the usual form of 'leave of absence.'" Nevertheless, this incompatibility of the Lieutenant-Governor in Niagara and the Governor-General in Quebec had a direct bearing on the choice of a site for Toronto. We have seen that as early as the survey of 1788, Dorchester had shown an interest in Toronto, and, by the time of Simcoe's arrival, was supporting Kingston. He would have nothing to do with Georgina on La Tranche, and the blow to Simcoe's enthusiasm and pride can be imagined.

It was in May 1793 that Simcoe, accompanied by seven officers, set off from Niagara in a *bateau* on a new search for a capital. The party followed the shore line to the head of the Lake after which they sailed eastwards to arrive at last in the Bay of Toronto. Writing in 1832, Bouchette, who surveyed the harbour in 1793, remarked of it: "I still distinctly recollect the untamed aspect which the country exhibited when first I entered the beautiful basin. . . . Dense and trackless forests lined the margin of the lake, and reflected their inverted images in its glassy surface. . . . the bay and neighbouring marshes were the hitherto uninvaded haunts of immense coveys of wild fowl."[5]

Mrs. Simcoe records in her diary of May 13, 1793, "Coll Simcoe returned from Toronto, & speaks in praise of the harbour, & a fine spot near it covered with large Oak which he intends to fix upon as a scite for a Town. I am going to send you some beautiful Butterflies."[6] The people of Toronto are often accused of taking themselves too seriously, and indeed, there may be some who would resent a light-hearted reference to butterflies in the same note that heralded the birth of the present proud metropolis. It is usually omitted from her famous first comment on Toronto.

From contemporary accounts, we learn that the site of Toronto, if we may consider it from the Humber to the Don, was covered with a bush made up, in general, of hardwood trees and poplar with some clumps of evergreen, cedars and pine. There were, also, beaver meadows and much swampy ground through which ran a network of streams that are now submerged in the sewer system of the city. Two, to survive into this century, were the Garrison Creek and the Taddle which flowed behind the university library and is perpetuated in name by Taddle Creek Road in the University of Toronto grounds.

In the fascinating diary of Mrs. Simcoe, there are few items as important in the long story of Toronto as the one where she describes the departure from Niagara, and the arrival of the official party in Toronto.

29th of July   We were prepared to sail for Toronto this morng. but the wind changed suddenly, we dined with the Chief Justice [Osgoode] & were recalled from a walk at 9 oclock this Eveng as the wind was become fair—we embarked on board the Mississaga the band playing in the Ship—it was dark so I went to bed & slept till 8 oclock the next morning when I found myself in the Harbour of Toronto, we had gone under an easy sail all night for as no person on board had ever been at Toronto Mr. Bouchette was afraid to enter the Harbour till day light when St John Rousseau an Indian trader who lives near came in a Boat to pilot us.[7]

One would have thought that the first duty of the Queen's Rangers would have been the erection of Government House, but that awaited the arrival of the family.

"Government House" deserves a mention as much for its previous history as its unsuitability as the official residence of His Majesty's representative in Upper Canada. Before leaving London, Colonel Simcoe purchased three or four large and small tents which were among the effects of the late navigator Captain James Cook, and one of these, known as the "canvas house," became the Simcoe home for a whole summer and the following winter. Its location "on rising ground" was close to the Queen's Wharf at the foot of the present Bathurst Street, and not far from what we call the "Old Fort." The Honourable Peter Russell[8] was there in August 1793, and wrote his sister in Niagara:

The Governor & Mrs. Simcoe received me very graciously—but you can have no conception of the Misery in which they live—The Canvas house being their only residence—in one room of which they lie & see company—& in the other are the Nurse & Children squalling &c—an open Bower covers us at Dinner—& a tent with a small Table & three Chairs serves us for a Council Room.[9]

It is no wonder that Mrs. Simcoe found life more congenial among her old friends at Niagara which she visited as often as she could.

The year of their arrival in Toronto was an active one for the Simcoes, and a momentous one for the future city. Of major importance was the preparation and official approval of Surveyor Aitkin's plan for Toronto, a plan with which we have

8 Alexander Aitkin's "Plan of York Harbour," surveyed by order of Lieutenant-Governor Simcoe, 1793. (Published with the permission of the Public Record Office, London.)

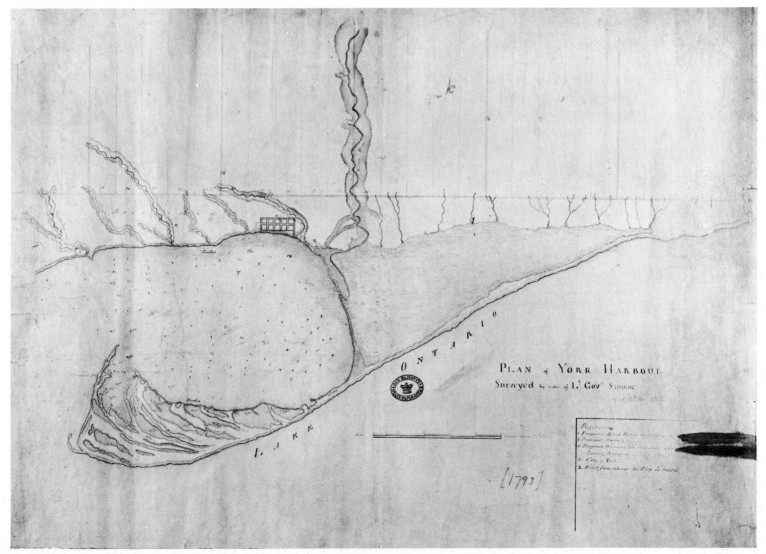

had to cope for one hundred and seventy years, and with which posterity will have to deal till the end of time. It was, of course, the surveyor's gridiron which like Captain Gother Mann's and Lord Dorchester's plans ignored completely the very features that give character and beauty to Toronto—the hill and the wooded ravines. But there the comparison ends. Where the two plans of 1788 were grandiose and impractical, Aitkin's was practical, but indescribably mean and unimaginative. It consisted of ten square "city" blocks bounded by George, Parliament, Duke and Front Streets, with the areas from Parliament to the Don and from Peter to the Humber, set aside for government and military purposes. North of the future Queen Street, Simcoe laid out a "range of 100 acre lots which were to be granted as 'douceurs' to the officials as compensation for having to come to York."[10] Lord Selkirk was not alone in suggesting in 1803 that Simcoe had two reasons for preferring York to Kingston—it was partly because Dorchester favoured the latter town and partly because "York had the advantage of being able to afford lots for all his friends round it."[11] Miss Firth describes this as an "ill natured rumour," but if true, it would be an unique and unflattering foundation for a great city.

It will be seen that in other matters Simcoe was not without imagination, and one wonders whether he ever dreamed that his little plan would some day spread over several thousand acres, that it would climb hills and leap ravines. One can be sure that he did not.

A minor, though a colourful event was the changing of the name by royal proclamation from Toronto to York. The sound of twenty-one guns reverberated among the hills, and what shipping in the harbour mounted cannon added to the joyful noise. It was August 27, 1793, and the capital still contained not a single house.[12]

The newcomer to Ontario must wonder at the number of English names that mark our counties and our townships far beyond Tiny, Tay, and Flos which immortalize Lady Sarah Maitland's dogs. It was that "abhorrence of Indian names" (T. A. Reed) or "the infelicitous mania for tautology of his generation" (P. Robinson) that caused His Excellency to change Niagara to Newark, Toronto to York, and so anglicize the map of Upper Canada as to leave no doubt of his loyalty to His Majesty, King George III. Yet one has to admit that, sometimes, the Governor showed good judgment in his search for English names. There is still romance in the quiet flowing Don at dusk or moonlight, but very little in the Nechengquakekonk at any time of day.

It was not until 1834, when York became a city, that the ancient name of Toronto, the "meeting place of the waters," was restored. Various writers have suggested that it was changed because, as far back as 1799, the Duke of York, whom Simcoe sought to honour, had ceased to be an heroic figure and was leading British troops from one disaster to another. It was not a popular change, tempers were aroused in council debates, and William Lyon Mackenzie himself was quite opposed to a return to the old name. It is probable that the choice was finally made because of objections to the town's being called "Little York" to distinguish it from New York.

The last years of the century saw much activity in clearing land and road building, but rather less in house building. In 1795, the Duke de la Rochefoucauld-Liancourt reported only twelve cottages in York, all of them near the Don.[13] Quite the best known one was that built by the Governor as a summer house. Little realizing that he would be leaving Canada in 1796, Colonel Simcoe obtained in the name of his son Francis two hundred acres of land including a ridge on the west bank of the Don with a superb view to the south down the valley of the river. On it, at what is now the northern end of Parliament Street, he built the clapboard-covered log house which he named for his son, Castle Frank. Mrs. Simcoe rightly describes the "cottage" as "built on the plan of a Grecian Temple," and to her sketch one looks eagerly for columns that might be Ionic or Doric. They were neither the one nor the other, but were vertical logs 16 feet high; and the "cottage" itself was large—50 feet long by 30 feet wide. Fundamentally Greek as it was in design, its simple construction would make the five volumes of Palladio a rather superfluous reference.

In 1795 Castle Frank was the only "official" house, and what few cottages existed to the south in York were hastily constructed of round log. It was to be many years in York before the building of houses became a pleasant experience or an economical venture for the home owner. Labour and materials were in such short supply that in 1803, £1,065 (New York Currency) was the cost of a two-storey house with four modest rooms on the ground floor. In that year there were only 75 houses in York. By 1809, there were 14 round log cottages, 11 one-storey and 27 two-storey houses had squared timbers, and 55 houses were clapboarded.[14]

As early as 1800, however, a house was built as the official residence of the King's representative in Upper Canada. It was of frame construction to the design of Captain Robert Pilkington, and its first occupant was the second Lieutenant-Governor, General Peter Hunter. Government House was an unostentatious one-

10 House of the Hon. William Dummer Powell on the site of the present Royal York Hotel (c. 1800). The design with its double-decker verandah was more common among the inns and country stores than for a private house. It was also very sensible when one remembers the proximity of the house to the water, the view of the harbour and the Island. The Powells came of an old Welsh family of Ap Howell with an estate at Caer-Howell.

9 Castle Frank. A sketch by Mrs. Simcoe in 1796.

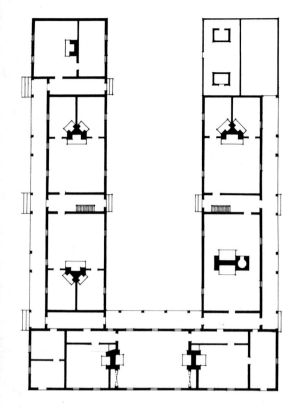

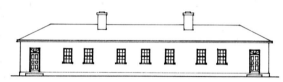

11 Plan and front elevation of the Lieutenant-Governor's house, erected by Capt. Pilkington in 1800 (redrawn from a faded drawing). Rooms are not named on the original, and only the kitchen and bake oven (right of plan) can be identified with certainty.

storey structure which served successive governors until 1813 when it vanished in the explosion of the nearby powder magazine. A new Government House was secured by the purchase of Elmsley House (built in 1798) at the southwest corner of King and Simcoe Streets, and it in turn was succeeded many years later by a third Government House on the same site.

In spite of expense and labour shortage, there are records of at least five fine private houses of which one, that of Mr. D. W. Smith, the Surveyor-General, was hardly surpassed in design by any in the following century. Others were those of Major John Small, Mr. Peter Russell, and Government House. The fifth was the House of Parliament.

It is little short of a miracle that we have complete records of the Smith house, Maryville Lodge. For over a hundred and sixty years, they have passed through wars, fire, and flood and, today, have a permanent and secure resting place in the Toronto Public Library. Maryville was really an estate of a size in keeping with

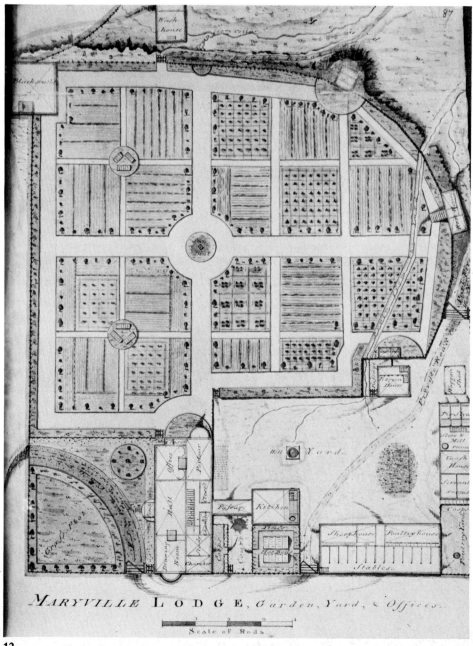

MARYVILLE LODGE, Garden, Yard, & Offices.
Scale of Rods

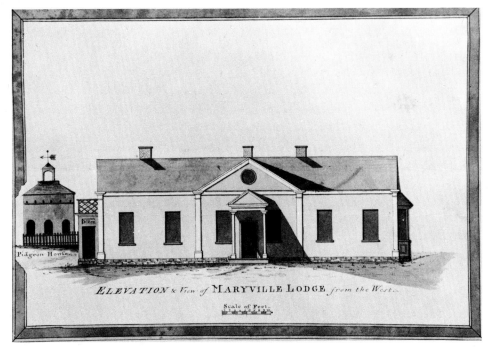

13

12–14 Maryville Lodge shows how a wealthy gentleman lived in York in 1794. On the north side of his estate (**12**) are his orchards and vegetable gardens, and to the east his animals, with servants' quarters off the coach house. The elevation of the Lodge appears in **13** and the first-floor plan in **14**.

the social position of so large a landowner. The Honourable D. W. Smith owned 916¼ acres in the township of York of which 116¼ acres were south of the modern Bloor Street. Both house and grounds were charming. Several plans of the property exist, the one illustrated being the most highly developed. The curving driveway off Ontario Street appears in each as does the formal garden about the house, but, in what must be an earlier plan, the landscaping is less formal. The formality of the first plan was offset by a curving road to the large "well yard," and by a lively "rivulet" on its way to Lake Ontario. In the final plan the road

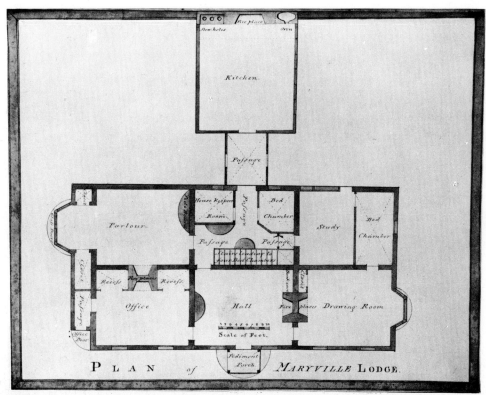

14

follows the perimeter of the estate, and the "rivulet" goes underground.

The house was built of wood, possibly flush boarded, and painted so bright a yellow that the colour gave the house its local name. The design of house, pigeon loft, and out-buildings is so competent that it would be very interesting to know the name of its author. What evidence there is would point to Smith himself as the architect. Books of house designs from the United States would be available to him, and he was, after all, a draftsman and Surveyor-General of Upper Canada. In 1794, when Maryville was built, the architect, as a professional man, had hardly emerged from the building trades in the republic to the south, let alone in Canada. In Massachusetts at that time the architect was commonly called a housewright, and, even in 1805, a book was published in Boston under the joint authorship of "Asher Benjamin, architect and carpenter and Daniel Raynerd, architect and stucco worker."

In 1802, the Honourable D. W. Smith returned to England, and the Smith papers in the Toronto Public Library show that, two years later, he was trying to sell Maryville to C. B. Wyatt, his successor as Surveyor-General. In April 1805 he wrote Wyatt: "I know of no inconvenience my Cottage possesses, having built it at a great expence for my own comforts, and without the smallest view of ever selling it; yet you are not to find it a house finished in the style of Architecture, which is generally so good in England; I mean as to finish in point of Workman-ship and materials—tho' no part of it is ten years old. . . ." He then goes on to say the plans were not exact, and the Drawing Room "is a few inches out of the Square," and the "back part of the house" was different from the plans.

The second house of the 18th century of which we have a record was Major John Small's house, Berkeley House at no. 51 Berkeley Street, at the corner of King. Major Small came to Canada from Gloucestershire as Clerk of the Crown in the entourage of Colonel Simcoe. It is conceivable that he designed his own house which Scadding describes as "one of the usual low-looking domiciles of the country, with central portion and two gable wings, somewhat after the fashion of many an old country manor-house in England."[15] We know that the original building was of log construction, and it is almost certain that the windows were rectangular.

Berkeley House, in our illustration, was a substantial enlargement of the original, undertaken by Major Small's son Charles. During this reconstruction, the house was stuccoed and the fenestration carried out in the "Gothic mode" that was fashionable in England in the first quarter of the 19th century. Berkeley, in its hey-day, had thirteen rooms of which the dining room and the drawing room measured 18 feet by 45 feet. The fact that Major Small had killed the Attorney-General, John White, in a duel and was acquitted of murder was forgotten by the next generation, but was calamitous to the social pretensions of Mrs. Small. For a num-ber of years, the other ladies of York would not attend parties if she were known to be there, and even later when they did, her presence was marked by ugly little scenes, such as the refusal to shake hands.

During the lifetime of the son, Berkeley House was "one of the great social centres and few indeed are the members of the old aristocracy who have not danced or dined beneath its roof."[16] It will be remembered by some in the 20th

15 Berkeley House, at the corner of King and Berkeley streets. The illustration shows a Gothicized enlargement of a modest dwelling of log (1794) with rectangular windows. (Demolished)

century as derelict and forlorn with broken panes and peeling plaster until, shortly after the First World War, it fell before the crowbar of the wrecker.

Among the early houses of York was that of Mr. Peter Russell at the corner of Princess and Front Streets. No reliable record of its design is preserved, and, in any case, it was destroyed by fire during construction. It was, however, essential that a suitable residence should be built for the Honourable Peter Russell who, by 1796, following the departure of Colonel Simcoe, had become President or Administrator of Upper Canada. The new house was of frame construction, and is variously described as "pretentious," but not lacking in "elegance and taste." We have clues to what it looked like from three sources—a sketch by the builder Samuel Marther who built the house, a remote view of it in a contemporary painting of York, and a drawing in the *Landmarks*.[17] In the painting, the house is the last in the row, and all one can be sure of is that it was one storey in height with a flattish roof. This agrees in general with the drawing in the *Landmarks*, but not with the builder's sketch which shows a well-pitched roof with dormers. He shows plans that by no manner of means could fit the drawing. On the other hand, one may be

16 "York (Olim Toronto) the intended capital of Upper Canada, as it appeared in the autumn of 1803," by Surgeon Edward Walsh, 49th Regt. The houses are on Palace (Front) Street, from left to right: 1 Duncan Cameron (partly shown), 2 William Willcocks (here William Lyon Mackenzie published the *Colonial Advocate* in the 1820's), 3 William Allan, 4 Peter Russell (Russell Abbey), 5 the first Government buildings (to the right of the trees), 6 the town blockhouse. (William L. Clements Library, University of Michigan.)

17 Russell Abbey at the corner of Palace (now Front) and Princes (now Princess) streets (c. 1798), the house (now demolished) of the Hon. Peter Russell, President of Upper Canada. It is fairly certain that this house was one storey high, that the windows had pediments over them and that it was U- or H-shaped in plan. The illustration is the only sketch we have of any size, the pediments are poorly drawn and the glass sizes are both ill proportioned and larger than were available in the 18th century.

unfair to Marther who was endeavouring to show his client how old timbers and old walls, left by the fire, could work into the new house.

The striking similarity of form between the house in the painting and the one in the *Landmarks* would seem to settle the fact that Russell Abbey was one storey in height with a low roof. The house in the painting is too far off, and too small, to show any detail, but that is supplied us to an astonishing degree in the *Landmarks*. There we see a house that is U- or H-shaped in plan with large windows, each framed by an architrave and surmounted by a pediment, against a wall of flush clapboard. Where Ross Robertson got his information we do not know, but forgetting the crudities of the drawing (the glass panes were larger than would be available in 1797), the U-shaped plan and the Renaissance air created by the windows would undoubtedly account for contemporary descriptions such as "elegant" and "pretentious." As both the plan and the windows were classical in origin, one wonders why Robertson describes the design as "ecclesiastical," or why the house became known as Russell Abbey. Had the windows resembled those of Holland House, or had they label moulds at their heads like many a later house of the Gothic revival, the description "ecclesiastical" and the nostalgic reference to an abbey would have some meaning.

Dr. Scadding saw no connexion between the design of the house and the kind of architecture normally associated with an abbey, but offers in its place an ingenious, if fanciful, substitute. From Dr. W. W. Baldwin's sister, he learned that Russell Abbey got its name from *The Children of the Abbey* by R. M. Roche, first published in 1798. After the Honourable Peter Russell's death, Miss Elizabeth Russell often entertained "the youth and fashion of the day" and "It chanced that, on one of these occasions, the remark was sportively made that the assemblage strongly resembled a scene described in 'The Children of the Abbey,' a book then in great vogue whose contents were familiar to everyone. The remark was repeated and, at length, the term 'Children of the Abbey' came to be a playful synonym for the meetings at Miss Russell's home, and her house itself acquired, in the same way, the style and title of 'Russell Abbey.'"[18]

One would like to know more of the Abbey than the U shape which we must accept for its plan. Such a house would have rooms for entertaining in keeping with the position of the President of the Government of Upper Canada as well as out-buildings for horses, carriages and slaves. Robertson writes that "Peter Russell owned and traded in slaves, despite his vigorous protection of the Indians." Russell had six Negro servants, a slave Peggy, her free Negro husband and their four children who were also slaves. These were divided between the farm on his 100-acre park lot, and his town house. In the latter, he usually had two or three Negroes and the same number of white servants. In 1806, he advertised in the *Gazette and Oracle* "to be sold, a black woman named Peggy, aged 40 years, and a black boy, her son, named Jupiter, aged about 15 years, both of them the property of the subscriber. . . . They are each of them servants for life." Within the memory of many in John Ross Robertson's day "a pure negress called Amy Pompadour" lived in York who had been presented to "Mrs. Captain Denison" by the same Miss Elizabeth Russell who held the gay parties for the young in Russell Abbey.[19] To modern eyes, it would appear as retribution that the last owners of the Abbey were Negroes, a family of shoemakers called Truss. It is remembered, today, by a shabby by-water called Abbey Lane, off King Street between Princess and Sherbourne Streets.

Our last building of the 18th century, though not the last in date, is the first Parliament buildings of 1796, which once stood at the foot of Berkeley Street overlooking the Bay. The *Landmarks* describes them as "humble but commodious structures, of wood" with, at the same time, "some pretensions to elegance of design and construction."[20] The latter statement is correct, but the first legislative buildings were undoubtedly brick, on the evidence of the builder himself—David Thomson, the first settler in the Township of Scarborough. In his account book is this item: "July 16, 1796: Begun to wall the Government brick houses. 55,000 brick at 17/6 per thousand."

We first hear of the Legislative Buildings in a letter from Simcoe to the Duke of Portland, February 27, 1796:

I am preparing to erect such Buildings as may be necessary for the future meeting of the Legislature; the plan I have adopted is, to consider a future Government House, as a Center, & to construct the *Wings* as temporary Offices for the Legislature, purposing that so soon as the Province has sufficient Funds to erect its own Public Buildings, that They may be removed elsewhere.

But should the seat of Government be ultimately established on the River Thames . . . the *Wings* now erecting . . . may be hereafter sold. . . .[21]

In March 15, 1797, the Honourable Peter Russell describes the project in a letter to John McGill (Commissary, in charge of Government buildings):

Since my last I have had an Opportunity of speaking with Mr. Pilkington [Captain Robert Pilkington], and very much approve of the Alterations he proposes for the Government House.— By these, the two Wings will be 40 by 24 feet and joined to the Body of the House by something like a Colonade. . . . It is not my intention to Attempt more at present than the two Wings, as before they are finished I may expect to receive final Instructions from home, which will determine me respecting the propriety of entering into so large an Expence as the mansion will assuredly prove.—But these two wings by being joined by a temporary covered way to the two Buildings in their rear,—may be of great use for the present,—as Houses for the meeting of the Legislature, holding Councils[,] giving entertainments in, and back appartments for occasional lodgings. . . .

This letter may account for the oft-repeated story that the Parliament Buildings of Upper Canada were of wood. Simcoe would appear to have considered them so when he thought that the wings might be sold. Thomson, in his builder's account book, is evidence enough, but as a final word we have another letter from the Honourable Peter Russell, written in York to Colonel Simcoe in England on December 9, 1797.

The Two wings to the Government House are raised with Brick & completely covered in. The South One, being in the greatest forwardness I have directed to be fited up for a temporary Court House for the Kings Bench in the ensuing Term, and I hope they may both be in a condition to receive the Two Houses of Parliament in June next, I have not yet given directions for proceeding with the remainder of your Excellency's plan for the Government House, being alarmed at the magnitude of the expence which Captain Graham estimates at (£10,000) I shall however order a large Kiln of Bricks to be prepared in the Spring. . . .[22]

It was not until November 1805 that instructions were given for the construction of the covered way between the two houses. A colonnade suggests columns, and it is sad to record that the work ordered described the supports as "posts to be 8 feet high,"[23] with an east wall of frame construction. Missed by writers in the

18 The York Hotel on the south side of King Street between Berkeley and Princes (now Princess) streets (1801) (demolished). Sometimes called Jordan's Hotel, this was a famous hostelry in the early days of York. The Legislature of Upper Canada met there for one year in 1814, but by 1820 it was losing its patronage to the Mansion House not far away. In design, the building is the only one we know in old Toronto that is strikingly French in character. Mr. John Jordan, one of the early pew-holders of St. James, is not to be confused with that Jordan and Melinda Post after whom Jordan and Melinda streets were named (see Appendix B).

19th century who have shown the buildings as of a low, almost domestic, scale is a reference of November 22, 1806, describing the poor state of the buildings and the need to repair the "gallery and the portico,"[24] both of which suggest considerable height and a dignity appropriate to the Legislature of Upper Canada.

The subsequent history of the Legislature may be briefly told. Following the burning of the old buildings in 1813, the members met for one year in the ballroom of Jordan's Hotel, a well-known hostelry on King Street near Berkeley Street. They then moved to the charming low Georgian house of Chief Justice Draper at the northwest corner of Wellington and York, and there they sat until 1820 when a new House arose on the site of the old building of 1796. Its life, unhappily, was short and, where the armed might of the United States caused the destruction of the first legislature, an overheated flue marked the end of the second. The year was 1824. For the next five years, members occupied the York Hospital—an imposing institution of Georgian design with eight windows across its second storey. They had saved some of the House papers and all of the furniture and the library, but the interior was incompatible with the dignity of the government of Upper Canada, and the intrusion of the legislature on an institution dedicated to the ill in York could not be tolerated for long.

York had to wait until 1829 for a well-planned and up-to-date Legislative building. The old brick Houses, elegant as they may have been, and their successor were conceived as a symbol of democratic government in an outpost of Empire; the new Houses of 1829 were recognizable as public buildings in a young and progressive community. The forest seemed to envelope the old Legislature or was never far away; the setting for the new seemed urban and controlled.

Before the departure of the Simcoes for England in July 1796, York must have been a busy place. Under his leadership, the ground plan of a village destined to be a great metropolis had been carved out of the wilderness, and Simcoe himself had followed Yonge Street on a survey trip all the way to Lake Simcoe. He did much for Little York, but he was, in many ways, a visionary with projects in mind even before he left England to assume his post in Upper Canada. Seated in the comparative privacy of his tent, he must have been shocked by the realization of how phantom-like and remote for York were his nucleus of a public library, his society based on the Royal Society, a college and a botanical garden.

Such symbols of civilization were indeed remote, but in a zoning order of the governor we can detect a vision for York which, even in miniature, would seem to Simcoe to include some of the urbanity and dignity that distinguished cities of the old world like Bath and London. It was, of course, highly impractical and not without an element of snobbery, and is best given in a letter of 1793 (when the Simcoes were still under canvas) written by Richard Cartwright:

You will smile perhaps when I tell you that even at York, a Town Lot is to be granted in the Front Street only on Condition that you shall build a House of not less than 47 Feet Front, two Stories High & after a certain Order of Architecture; in the second Street, they may be somewhat less in Front, but the two Stories & mode of Architecture is indispensible; and it is only in the back Streets and Allies that the Tinkers and Taylors will be allowed to consult their own Taste and Circumstances in the Structure of their Habitations upon lots of 1/10 of an Acre. Seriously, our good Governor is a little wild in his projects. . . .[25]

Governor Simcoe was not there to see his zoning ordinance ignored, or the scattered community assume even the semblance of a village, but his faith in the future of the Province was a lasting one. On March 26, 1798, he wrote that Upper Canada "will be with proper & honorable support, the most valuable possession out of the British Seas, in population commerce & principle of the British Empire."[26]

The Honourable Peter Russell, the owner of Russell Abbey, who headed the government after Simcoe, has been completely overshadowed in the public mind by his distinguished predecessor. We do not think of him as the colourful proconsul, or associate him with the pomp of power or the salute of guns. Rather he was the sound administrator (which, indeed, was his title) working for the good of the community of which he considered himself a citizen. Under his wise government, speculators and non-residents were kept out of the town lots, and a form of zoning was inaugurated to keep the town compact in the face of a tendency, not unknown today, to sprawl in more than one direction.

His achievements are the more remarkable when one considers the isolation of York, the lack of communication except by boat in suitable weather, the reliance on travellers for the mails until 1800. Even then, the service between Montreal and York could count on only four couriers a month in winter and none in summer. "In 1797 there were no roads connecting York with the older communities in the Province. Thriving settlements were established along the St. Lawrence to Kingston, on the Bay of Quinte and in Prince Edward County, in the Niagara Peninsula and on the Detroit River, all separated from York by vast areas of unsettled bush." Yonge Street was there, and was indispensable to the farmers bordering it for the transportation of the essential provisions to York, but in spring and fall it was an impassable bog. Under such conditions, a not inconsiderable achievement of the Russell administration was the contract in 1799 with Asa Danforth for a road to the east as far as the Trent in the Bay of Quinte. At about the same time, a road was begun by the Queen's Rangers, westerly to the Head of the Lake.[27]

The year 1800 has been chosen to close a chapter in the architectural development of Toronto, and, to some extent, it has not the significance of later dates such as 1834, 1867 and 1900. It was not a year of any note in the government of Upper Canada, but in many ways it represented the end of an era and the beginning of a new one for York. The houses referred to in this section were all there by 1800, and the community had assumed the form of a village if not of a provincial capital. The population of the town was 403, and, while not all, by any means, of the property in Aitkin's ten blocks was occupied, there were enough buildings to give a recognizable pattern to the plan conceived in 1793. Writing in 1801, it was the opinion of John Bennett, the King's Printer of Upper Canada, that "York is just emerging from the woods, but bids fair to be a flourishing town. . . ."[28]

3: A Late Flowering Georgian

A grave weakness in Aitkin's plan was that it lacked a focus. Had there been provision for a school, a church or, more particularly, a village green, the plan of Toronto today would have been different. It also lacked direction so that when expansion became inevitable the town grew merely by adding more squares, a practice we have followed ever since except for the labyrinth of Rosedale. Before the original ten blocks had been occupied, it had become apparent that the site near the Don was undesirable for a residential district. Visitors to York and the correspondence of the early settlers all tell of the prevalence of the ague which seems to have been rightly attributed to the miasma rising from a thousand acres of swamp at the mouth of the river. It was also generally agreed that the disease was less frequent in the sparsely settled areas to the west, and was unknown on Yonge Street. Hardships and actual suffering can be imagined when it is remembered that until the War of 1812 there were only two qualified civilian doctors in York—Dr. W. W. Baldwin, who also practised law and, occasionally, architecture, and Dr. James Glennon.

It was therefore an escape from the "vapours" rather than the inducement of economic or other advantages that led to the movement of population to the west of Yonge Street. As Scadding put it, "The path of progress was like that of Empire, westward." It was eventually to be northward, and by 1812, many representatives of the gentry such as Russell, Elmsley, Givins, Shaw and McGill were sufficiently settled in York to take up their 100-acre farm lots.

By that time, too, much had been accomplished to give meaning and substance to the life of the town. The civilizing influences of religion, education, and entertainment were at last being enjoyed by a people who were still close to the almost intolerable harshness of life in the early days of York. In 1803, a market place was established on the site of the present St. Lawrence Hall; in 1800 the rector of York, the Rev. George Okill Stuart, was prepared to take pupils, and by 1807 he had established the Home District Grammar School in his house at George and King streets; the Church at York opened its doors for divine service on the site of the present St. James' Cathedral in 1807; and, in 1809, Mr. Quetton St. George opened a general store on the ground floor of his very striking house at King and Frederick streets. As early as 1810, York had a book store and a subscription library. On the much-needed side of entertainment and relaxation, there were several taverns, and we learn from the *Gazette and Oracle* that Mr. Daniel Tiers was in business with his "Beef Steak and Beer Houses."

The architecture of these buildings and their successors for the next thirty years or more was what, for want of a better word, we call Georgian. The great movement which produced the Georgian houses of England in the 18th century, and later adorned the towns and villages of eastern Canada and the United States, finally came to rest in Ontario. Visitors from Great Britain are always amazed to learn how late in date are some of our best old houses. Many were built at a time when taste in England was changing under the pressure of the industrial revolution, and a series of revivals were taking the place of the traditional manner with its background of three centuries.

We, too, have had our revivals, but for forty years after the establishment of York, we had the kind of architecture that, today, attracts tourists to Boston or

Baltimore, and is preserved in those cities by vigilance on the part of an enlightened citizenry. Compared with their ancient architecture, ours was modest in scale and interior fittings, and the area which it occupied was small and vulnerable.

Of the early buildings already mentioned, we have no very accurate record of the "Church at York" other than it was "a plain structure of wood, placed some yards back from the road. . . . Its dimensions were 50 by 40 feet. The sides of the building were pierced by two rows of ordinary windows four above and four below."[1] We can appreciate its simplicity in a contemporary American description—"a meeting house for Episcopalians." This primitive building served the community until 1818 when Dr. John Strachan, who had been its pastor since 1812, induced the congregation to enlarge the church. Tenders were called for lengthening the building east and west with an apse, but, for reasons not clear, the nave was widened with a gallery on three sides. The "new" church was painted an "azure blue" with white trim and quoins. Here "used to assemble, periodically, the little world of York: occasionally, a goodly proportion of the little world of all Upper Canada."[2] For the visitor, the church provided quite a few surprising features. For example, the ringing of the bell was sufficiently violent "sensibly to jar the whole building," and the habit of one of the early clerks, Mr. Hetherington, was "after giving out a psalm to play the air on a bassoon, and then to accompany with fantasias on the same instrument such vocalists as felt inclined to take part in the singing."[3]

If the interior of the church was unromantic in design, at least two of the worshippers made up the loss. Sir Peregrine Maitland, the Governor, and his wife had both been present on the occasion in Brussels when the latter's mother, the Duchess of Richmond, gave the famous ball whose "sounds of revelry by night" preceded the Battle of Waterloo. They were then unmarried, and their elopement in Paris, shortly after, outraged the feelings of the Duke and Duchess of Richmond. They were, finally, reconciled and Sir Peregrine's happiness and diplomatic future were assured. It is unnecessary to say that the occupants of the Governor's pew did not go unnoticed on Sunday mornings in York.

St. James' Church deserves a brief mention especially as it is the one of which, in December 1836, Mrs. Anna Jameson, the wife of the Attorney-General of Upper Canada,[4] spoke in such unflattering terms: "A little ill-built town on low land, at the bottom of a frozen bay, with one very ugly church, without tower or steeple. . . ."[5] As a matter of fact this "very ugly church" was built of stone and was by no means unpleasing in design. Unfortunately, the front was never finished, and all Mrs. Jameson saw was the rectangular box with the truncated tower. The church was destroyed by fire in 1839, Dr. Strachan standing by "whistling the while as a means of relieving his sorrow."[6] There was, of course, to be another and then a final St. James, the cathedral we know today, but that is later in the story of Toronto.

The decade after the War of 1812 saw churches built for Methodists, Presbyterians, Roman Catholics, and Baptists. From what we know of them from contemporary writers, and from sketches in the *Landmarks*, they would seem to have been unpretentious little meeting houses of no architectural significance. The Wesleyan Church was built in 1818, about the time of the enlargement of St. James. It stood facing King near Jordan, was 40 feet square, and, according to Scadding, the old Anglican church custom prevailed of making the sexes sit separate—the men sat on the east side and the women on the west.[7]

The priest in charge of the first church at York, and the one who preceded Dr. Strachan in that office, was the Rev. Dr. Okill Stuart. His pulpit delivery was curious, and was marked by "unexpected elevations and depressions of the voice irrespective of the matter, accompanied by long closings of the eyes, and then a sudden re-opening of the same."[8] We are, however, more interested in him as the popular and competent tutor to the children of the upper classes as early as 1800, and as the master of the Home District School (1807).

Still standing in 1873 when Dr. Scadding saw it was a little building at the corner of King and George streets—one that in its day had served as a school for the children of the earlier inhabitants of York, as the home of the first rector of St. James, as general store, and as an inn. The house consisted of two parts, the rectory with its huge bay window and walls of log covered by clapboard, and an appendage in stone "resembling a small root-house"[9] which was the Home District School. The *Landmarks* do not suggest that the bay window was not there from the beginning, but, as it was divided by the front door, it must have been more useful for the display of goods in its decline than for the enjoyment of the Stuarts at the turn of the century. The establishment continued to function as a centre of education and the home of the rector of St. James until the departure of Dr. Stuart for St. George's Cathedral in Kingston and the opening of the Blue School under Dr. John Strachan in 1813.

The house of Mr. Quetton St. George is one that we would wish to preserve if fate had permitted it to survive. Mr. Laurent Quetton was a Royalist officer in the French army who escaped to North America during the Revolution. Arriving on English soil on St. George's Day, 1796, he added St. George to his name in memory of that occasion. He prospered so mightily as a trader, with agents in Orillia and elsewhere, that by 1809 he was able to move into his "mansion" at the corner of King and Frederick streets.[10] Robertson stated that "for its construction he brought the first bricks ever seen in York from Oswego or Rochester,"[11] but he was incorrect. The first brick buildings in York, it will be remembered, were the Legislative buildings (1796).

As we see from the illustration, the Palladian window over the porch is well detailed, and the massive chimneys all give evidence of wide fireplaces and handsome mantels. We have no records of the interiors of houses in Toronto at so early a date, but Poplar Hall at Maitland (*circa* 1805) can show, today, mantels of exquisite design, chair rails in the better rooms, and finely proportioned panelled doors. The same can be said of the Barnum House at Grafton (1817) as well as a score of less well-known houses on the Niagara Peninsula. When the first Series of the *Landmarks* were published in 1894, the house still stood: "no building is better known, and its removal will take away a landmark from what was once the most important part of town."

Mr. Daniel Tiers was the owner of the Red Lion Inn, but it was a great deal more than a Beef Steak and Beer House. It stood, until 1888, on the east side of Yonge,

19 The Rectory of St. James' Church and an early school in York, at 61 King Street East (1807). This was the rectory of the Rev. George Okill Stuart, the second rector of St. James, and master of the Home District School. The house was part log and part clapboard with a stone appendage to the east which, in 1805, or before, was fitted up as the school.
We know the same house in 1833 when it became the general store of Mr. George Duggan as well as the house which he shared with his brother, Dr. Thomas. Col. George Duggan was known in the thirties as one of the real characters of York, a jovial fellow, who paradoxically was also the coroner. Paradoxically, too, he was that George Duggan who would rather ostentatiously leave the church when the Rev. Dr. Stuart, as a visiting cleric from St. George's Kingston, would rise to deliver the sermon.

20 The house and store of Mr. Quetton St. George (1807) at King and Frederick streets (demolished). In later years it served as the Canada Company building.

21 The Red Lion Inn, Yonge Street, near Bloor Street, an important social and political centre for many years (demolished).

just north of Bloor, on a piece of property that, originally, embraced some two hundred acres. We hear of Mr. Tiers as early as 1797 on the first list of inhabitants of York and, again, in 1802 when he subscribed to a fund for the improvement of Yonge Street. In 1808, he built his inn.

The building was 100 feet in length and had on the second floor a ballroom 40 by 20 feet with a barrel vaulted ceiling 18 feet high, and a fireplace at each end of the room. Looking at the site today, close to that of Mr. Britnell's bookshop on the east side of Yonge Street, north of Bloor, it is difficult to imagine its former isolation. As the years went by, it became a great rallying point for farmers; it was a post house for travellers two miles north of the town of York and the young and the brave would journey there from York and the neighbouring farms for the dancing to which nothing else in York compared. The condition of Yonge Street in spring and summer made driving a nightmare, and dancing was understandably more enjoyable in winter when parties came in sleighs. The fact that Potter's Field was across the street had no apparent effect on the popularity of the inn or its ball-room of which the author of the *Landmarks* observes in melancholy mood—"How many a couple, whose voices are now hushed in the tombs, have whispered soft words in this room."

The Red Lion was also well known as a rallying place for political meetings of which the most famous was that when Wm. Lyon Mackenzie was re-elected after his expulsion from the House. On that "tumultuous" occasion (Jan. 2, 1832) as many persons as the floor could hold were gathered in the ballroom to present Mr. Mackenzie with a gold medal and chain and an address. A great honour, too, for Mr. Tiers, but when he endeavoured to sell the Red Lion and 200 acres for $400, the amount was thought excessive and the offer declined. There is little doubt, as Mr. Robertson suggests, that the success of the Red Lion attracted other businesses, and that the Inn itself was the nucleus on which the village of Yorkville was built.

The Lighthouse at Gibraltar Point was begun in 1806 and finished in 1809. The Point got its name from Governor Simcoe who saw its location at the mouth of the harbour as being not dissimilar to that of the Rock at the entrance to the Mediter-ranean. Gibraltar Point, as well as Block House Bay which it shelters, are names that have fallen into disuse. The Lighthouse still stands, but mariners are no longer guided by its warning light as they were for well over a hundred years. The struc-ture is 82 feet to the top of the vane, and the walls are 6 feet thick at the base. A curious fact about the design is that the stone cap beneath the lantern which seems so integral and necessary a part of the shaft was an addition of 1832 in Kingston stone to the original in Queenston stone.

A house that, in 1888, was known as the oldest house in Toronto was that of Col. Givins. As a young lieutenant, Mr. Givins went on Governor Simcoe's famous journey to Detroit and, later, became his aide-de-camp. The house from the rear is much more picturesque than other houses of the first quarter of the 19th century. It was built shortly after the purchase of the property in 1802. The front, which is obscured by trees in the *Landmarks* sketch, shows a formal elevation with a low pitched roof, a high basement, and two windows on each side of the central door. Of interest to the youth of Toronto who had the privilege of knowing the house in the last century was that it vied with Holyrood Palace in having authentic blood

22 Gibraltar Point lighthouse at the entrance to Toronto Harbour (1806), now inland.

23 House of Col. James Givins (rear view), at the head of Givins Street off Queen Street West at the easterly end of no. 999 (1802) (demolished). This famous house ranks number one in the six-volume *Landmarks of Toronto*, ahead even of Castle Frank. When Robertson wrote in 1888, it was considered the oldest building in Toronto. A young lieutenant in the Queen's Rangers, Givins was A.D.C. to Lieutenant-Governor Simcoe, and was with him for the historic landing at the harbour of Toronto in 1793. In 1802 he purchased from Col. Joseph Bouchette one of the 28 park lots, each of 100 acres, and then, or shortly after, built his home.

stains in the floor. Perhaps, indeed, the blood of Rizzio is less authentic than that in the Givins' drawing room because we know of Mrs. Givins' "surgical skill" and the use of the house for the wounded in 1813. Col. Givins was a pew holder in St. James from its beginning and is buried in St. James' Cemetery.

Unfortunately, no reliable sketch exists of an even more famous house known as "Spadina," but Dr. W. W. Baldwin's description gives us a good idea of its plan and its symmetrical and generous arrangements. He writes in 1819:

I have a very commodious house in the Country. I have called the place Spadina, the Indian word for Hill or Mont. The house consists of two large parlours, hall and staircase on the first floor—four bed rooms and a small library on the 2d floor—and three Excellent bed rooms in attic storey or garret—with several closets on every storey, a Kitchen, dairy, root cellar, wine cellar and man's bed-room underground. I have cut an avenue through the woods all the way so that we can see the vessells [sic] passing up and down the bay. The house is completely finished with stable etc. and a tolerable good garden, the whole has cost about £1,500; the land you know was the gift of poor Mr. Willcocks.[12]

This house was destroyed by fire in 1835, when one of similar size and style was built on the same property. The site was a magnificent one, and lay just east and north of the steps which mark the boundary of the Casa Loma grounds (see p. 42).

It is unlikely that, in his later years, Dr. Baldwin ever climbed the slope that lay below the lofty escarpment on which the house was built. We can be sure that means were found to reach the house by horse-drawn vehicle on an easy gradient, and not at right angles to Davenport Road as we approach the site today. Even so, winter on such an eyrie in the 1830's must have represented a challenge to the fittest, and sometime between 1835 and 1844, when he died, we find Dr. Baldwin living at the northeast corner of Front and Bay in a house that may well be described as a mansion.

A photograph survives, and it will be noticed that the house is of quite traditional Georgian design except for the curious decision of its architect to put the parapet below the cornice, and to puncture it with windows. It was done as a whim on somebody's part because, in 1844, there were few laymen and surely no architects so unfamiliar with the elements of classic architecture that the impropriety of a balustrade in so subservient a position would not go unnoticed. As a matter of fact, it is almost certain that to the professions of law and medicine Dr. Baldwin added architecture in this and, at least, one other building.

The Spadina house of the Baldwins is long forgotten, but the busy thoroughfare of that name will forever be a reminder of a great Torontonian and a generous benefactor. He gave to the city Spadina Avenue from Bloor to Front Street. It is regrettable that the architecture of the modern street is generally poor and out of keeping with the magnificence of the gift and the Parisian scale on which Baldwin laid out the roadway as an approach to Spadina House. Less regrettable, though not greatly to our credit, is our inability to arrive at a common pronunciation for Spadina. Spad-eena is, I believe, correct, but there are others who prefer Spad-ina, and still others who distinguish between Spad-ina up to College and the more re-fined Spad-eena in the residential portion to the north.

In 1811, the loyal colony in Upper Canada would have followed with increasing concern Britain's struggle with France on the continent of Europe. At the same time, the fighting was a long way off, and people in York went about their busi-ness little thinking that, along with the rest of Canada, they would soon be at war with their neighbour to the south. Following a series of misunderstandings and difficulties, the United States declared war on Great Britain on June 18, 1812.

York was immediately affected, and the population was reduced from over 700 to 625. Lieutenant-Governor Gore, though highly respected in some quarters, was not a fighting man, and, as the war clouds gathered in late 1811, he returned to England on leave of absence "accompanied by his good amiable lady and her menagerie."[13] Fortunately, as has so often happened in crises in British history, a man with all the qualities of leadership was available to assume command. Major-General Brock could not be made Lieutenant-Governor as Gore was only "on leave," but he was appointed President of Upper Canada, with all the powers of the former office, as well as Commander-in-Chief of the forces.

August 17, 1812, was a gala day in York. General Brock had returned with his troops after receiving the surrender of General Hull's forces at Detroit; people cheered and flags flew from every window. But the guns were silent. When the good news reached London a few weeks later, the guns boomed from the Tower, but powder was too precious a commodity to be wasted on salutes in York. Such jubilation as there was, was short lived—the death of Brock at Queenston Heights on October 13 was the first major tragedy of the war, and more was to follow.

Historians of the War of 1812 make it abundantly clear that, where York was concerned, our military intelligence was poor, and even though Sheaffe, the new Commander-in-Chief, expected an attack in the spring of 1813, little notice, if any, was taken of the expeditionary force which was being assembled at Sackett's Har-bor on the north shore of Lake Ontario. The American fleet consisted of fourteen vessels mounting fifty guns and carrying some seventeen hundred troops and an undetermined number of marines.

If our intelligence was faulty so, also, was the enemy's. With a force of four

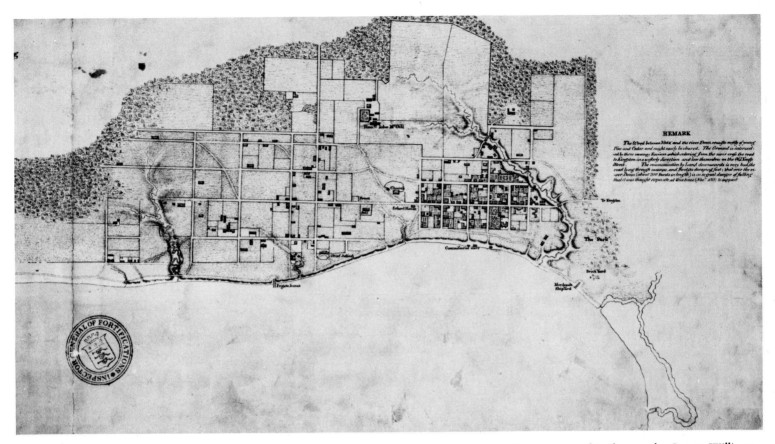

24 The Town of York, 1813, by George Williams. The boundaries of settlement were New (Jarvis) Street, on the east, to Ontario Street; and Palace (Front) Street to Duchess (Richmond) Street.

thousand in Sackett's Harbor, it was the original intention to take Kingston and then York, and thus seriously embarrass the British Lake Squadron. Happily for Kingston, a report reached American headquarters that the town was defended by some thousands of British regulars. It turned out to be quite unfounded, but was sufficient to divert attention from Kingston to York which, after all, was the capital of Upper Canada and not to be ignored in the military aims of the war.[14]

On the morning of April 26, 1813, the citizens of York went about their normal affairs quite oblivious of the plans for their capture by a powerful and fully armed enemy. The Rev. Dr. John Strachan performed the marriage ceremony for a young couple, merchants such as Mr. Quetton St. George attended the customers in their stores, and the farmers on the outskirts of the town were busy preparing the land for the spring sowing. There was to be a rude awakening. A lonely actor on the Toronto stage looked out that same evening over the bluffs at Scarborough, and there below him lay the enemy fleet at anchor.

The news was not long in reaching York where a state of emergency was immediately created by the firing of the signal gun, a summons to the militia that was heard as far away as Markham Township. As one would expect, people's reactions differed as widely as those of Major General Sir Roger Sheaffe, who thought that daylight would allow plenty of time for attack and defence, and of Dr. W. W. Baldwin who "bundled up his silver" and his black silk lawyer's gown and sent them out of town to a friend's barn. At dead of night, state papers and public money were put in strong boxes and taken to places of safety. We can imagine the frightened conversations between neighbours as to what was best to do—to stay, with the possibility of being a prey to an undisciplined victorious soldiery, or to go away with what valuables could be carried on foot. In the end it was the part of wisdom to stay and brave the enemy behind one's front door. The empty houses and stores were the ones that were looted.

Prideaux Selby, the Receiver-General of Upper Canada, had all the provincial public moneys in his keeping, and he lay dying on that fatal night. Many plans were made to save the public gold. Robertson records an elaborate plot, a scheme of Mrs. Selby and Mrs. Wm. Allan. According to this apocryphal tale, together they dressed one Billy Roe, the Secretary-General's confidential clerk, as an old woman and loaded him, with three bags of gold and a large sum in army bills, in a waggon pulled by an ancient horse. In this guise, he drove to the farm of Chief Justice Robinson on the Kingston Road east of the Don Bridge, and there he buried his treasure. After the departure of the Americans he recovered it, and delivered it intact before witnesses in the parlour of the Rev. John Strachan.[15] Unfortunately the reality is more prosaic: the gold was handed over to the Americans.

With daylight, a sleepless people looked out on the harbour and saw the American host, for such it must have seemed, lying at anchor "close to the south shore of the peninsula in front of the town."[16] Against the invaders York was practically defenceless. Sheaffe's forces consisted of two companies of the 8th (King's Regiment), a full company of the Royal Newfoundland Regiment, a company of the Glengarry Light Infantry, a bombardier, 12 gunners of the Royal Artillery, 100 Indians and 300 York militiamen: 700 in all.

The odds against York were too great, but the town capitulated only after a brave defence with loss of life on both sides. For eleven days, the citizens suffered the humiliation of seeing the Stars and Stripes fly over the town, and there was burning and looting.

Outstanding among the principals in this drama, a very David in defence of his people, was the master of the Blue School and parish priest, the Rev. Dr. John Strachan. We see him demanding an audience of the American commander to discuss the parade of captured militiamen and the care and feeding of the wounded; and when Major Allan was made a prisoner of war though under a flag of truce, a furious Strachan marched with him "to the centre of the town in the middle of an enemy column."[17]

There were others less conspicuous during the occupation, but significant in the story of Toronto either in their own right or as the ancestors of succeeding distinguished Torontonians. In the capitulation negotiations, John Beverley Robinson, the acting Attorney-General, was present to defend the legal rights of the community and Col. Wm. Chewett, the father of J. G. Chewett, the architect, played an important role at the same meeting. We hear also of Capt. John McGill. He was the owner of a park lot east of Yonge on which he built a house "on the southerly edge of the forest." The grounds were once known as McGill Square, but, whatever were the owner's intentions, the square was lost with the building of the Metropolitan Church in 1872. St. Michael's had occupied the northerly part since 1848, and Robertson suggests that that location was chosen with the expectation of a McGill Square in front as a distinguished and open park for the cathedral.

Accounts differ as to the actual losses in York either from fire or from looting, but Mr. Humphries' well-documented record does not leave the impression of anything like a conflagration or of a disorderly soldiery bent on destruction. Penelope Beikie whose charming house appears in the *Landmarks*, wrote: "I kept my castle when all the rest fled; and it was well for us I did so—our little property was saved by that means. Every house they found deserted was completely sacked. We have lost a few things which were carried off before our faces; but as we expected to lose all, we think ourselves well off."[18]

Jordan Post suffered minor losses, Elmsley House was plundered, and Dr. Strachan's appeal to General Dearborn on behalf of Angelica Givins failed to prevent the looting of her lovely house. In American eyes, the fact that her husband, Major Givins, commanded a party of Indians put him and his family beyond the pale. In spite of the terms of capitulation, several store keepers including Quetton St. George and Wm. Allan suffered serious losses. It seems certain that the Legislative buildings were deliberately burned, and this gave Strachan an opportunity to write an indignant letter to Thomas Jefferson in which he referred to the buildings as those "two elegant mansions." It is pleasing to see them so described because even the crudest sketches that have come down to us indicate something better than the "humble but commodious structures of wood."

There were other losses that were, by comparison, small in size, but their going was none the less grievous. Among them were the Speaker's mace and the carved lion above his chair. The mace was returned to Toronto at the centenary celebration in 1934. It was presented to His Honour the Lieutenant-Governor at the express desire of the President and Congress of the United States. An ignominy, hardly to be borne by a British colony, was the loss of the Royal Standard, which is now an exhibit at the U.S. Naval Academy at Annapolis, Maryland.

Its mission accomplished, the victorious flotilla left the harbour of York, and

25 Bellevue (1815) (demolished). The house gave its name to Bellevue Avenue which runs south from College to Denison Square. Its owner was Col. George Taylor Denison, whose son gave the site and built the church of St. Stephens-in-the-Fields at the corner of Bellevue and College. The porch may have been influenced in design by the somewhat older Quetton St. George house (see **20**), which it resembles. The sturdy chimneys indicate their function—the fireplaces beneath burnt logs as a source of heat as well as for the pleasure of the blazing fire.

some years later a street was named, perhaps in requital, for President Madison, the good neighbour.

Recovery was slow for York in the years immediately following the war. The population remained static right up to 1816, but from then on Canada, and indirectly York with it, was to be affected by the grave events in Great Britain which were an aftermath of the Napoleonic Wars. The mother country was then in the depths of an economic depression. Thousands were out of work, and the demobilization of four hundred thousand men had aggravated enormously an already desperate situation. Scotland suffered equally with England, and, to its already acute industrial dislocation, was added the eviction of the crofters by the great landowners. The conversion of much arable land to deer park was a disaster for the Highland crofters, and many a well-established family in Canada, Australia, or New Zealand traces its history to a family who left Scotland at that unhappy time. Immigration from the United Kingdom to British North America amounted in 1815 to 680; in 1816 to 3,370; in 1817 to 9,797; in 1818 to 15,136 and in 1819 to 23,534.

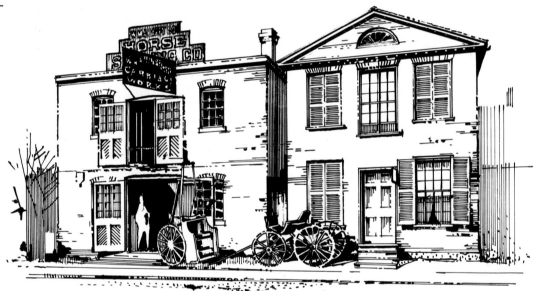

26 A smithy and the law office of Sir John Beverley Robinson at 156–158 Front Street (1816) (demolished). Before the advent of zoning, the juxtaposition of the noisy blacksmith and the office of the Attorney-General of Upper Canada was not thought odd except, one can be sure, by the Attorney-General.

The influx of immigrants must have caused considerable overcrowding in a community unused to, and unprepared for, such an emergency, and their lot was in many cases extremely hard. One immigrant in describing his first days in York (about 1819) speaks of sleeping in the upper storey of the Parliament Buildings with chalk marks on the floor to mark the area each family could occupy.

Yet the population figures for the years following the war of 1812 show that York was not much affected. The Town Clerk's records disclose only 703 persons in 1812; 691 in 1814; and 720 in 1816. In 1816, Strachan informed his bishop that there were 120 houses in York, and 710 inhabitants.

An attractive map showing the growth of the city by 1818 is that of Lieutenant George Phillpotts of the Royal Engineers. The old centre of population was then

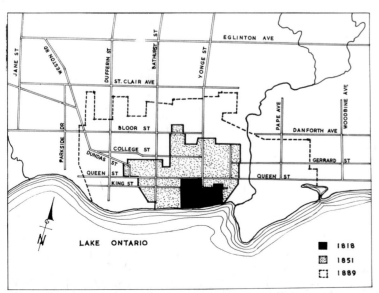

27 The Old Fort, Officers' Quarters (1816). Nothing extant, except the blockhouses, in Toronto is as old as this officers' mess. The majority of buildings in the old fort had a friendly domestic atmosphere like this mess building which could be an attractive farm house in any of the older parts of North America. The broad chimneys suggest the source of heat – logs in open grates.

28 Diagram imposed on the plan of Toronto showing three stages of growth: 1818, 1851 and 1889 (re-drawn from Griffith Taylor).

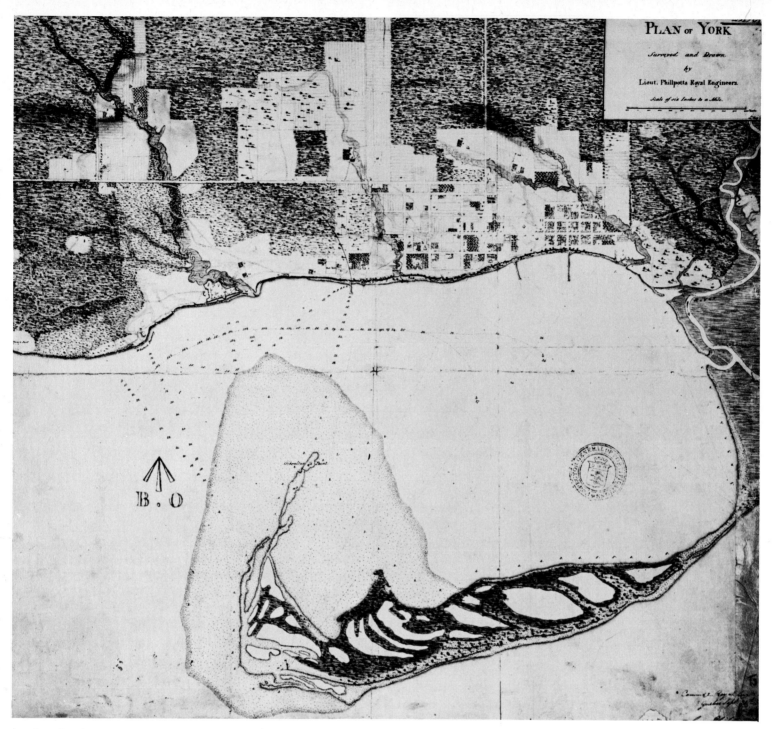

29 Plan of York surveyed and drawn by Lt. George Phillpotts, R.E. (1818). Phillpotts' map gives us a more realistic picture of York than anything left to us in written description or picture. Lot Street (Queen) strikes boldly off to the west from its junction with "Young" St. (Phillpotts' spelling), which passes through dense bush on its way to "Holland Landing." The street of real importance was, of course, King which goes on a diagonal to Kingston on what seems little better than a trail. Aitkin's gridiron had taken form in the checkerboard of houses near the mouth of the Don.

bounded by Berkeley, New (Jarvis), Palace (Front), and Duchess, but other sparsely settled streets had been laid out west of Yonge. The area between the present Jarvis and Yonge was largely swamp, though it contained a dozen or more houses and St. James' Church. Lot Street (Queen) was laid out as the northerly boundary and ran as far east as Parliament Street.

By 1818, York was only a city in miniature and by courtesy, but, at an even earlier date, the finest architect in England had been asked to prepare plans for a "Public Building." We read about it in a letter written by Wm. Halton, the provincial agent in London, to Sir Peregrine Maitland (Nov. 17, 1818). It seems that

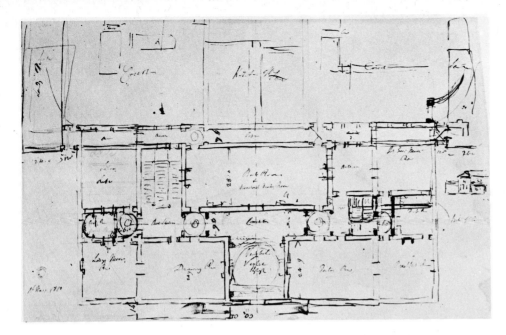

30 "A Public Building," a plan by Sir John Soane (1818). The fragment shown here was of Government House.

31 Residence of the Hon. and Rev. John Strachan, D.D. (1818), on a site that originally comprised the land bounded by York, Simcoe, Wellington, and Front streets (demolished). This residence was popularly called the Palace and one is not surprised at the question of Strachan's brother from Scotland: "I hope it's a' come by honestly, John?" From the underpaid schoolmaster and rector in 1813 to the owner of the "finest house in the town" who "gave entertainments that outshone those of the Lieutenant-Governor, and rode about in a grand coach with a hemispherical top," is an ecclesiastical success story that would remind one faintly of Cardinal Wolsey if one did not recall the Bishop's marriage to the well-to-do Mrs. McGill. When Robertson wrote in 1888, the Palace of the great bishop had degenerated into the Palace Boarding House, and its end came eight years later.

Mr. President Smith, Sir Peregrine's predecessor, had instructed Halton to send out two "plans," presumably for the same building. One was included with the letter. It has been lost, but the architect was a Mr. Laing who was known, particularly, for his designs for the London Customs House. In his letter, he offered to send one of his own men as supervisor of the work for £120 per annum. The other was promised: "the plan by Mr. Soane, R. A. and Architect to the Bank [of England] will follow." Sir John Soane was a most distinguished architect whose house in London has, since his death, been the Soane Museum. His commission was to design a residence for the governor and his family with a separate building for

32 The house of Chief Justice Sir William Campbell sat firmly on a site on Duke (Adelaide) Street at the head of Frederick Street from 1822 until 1972. In this latter year, many thousands turned out to see it on wheels as it was moved from Adelaide Street to a new and permanent resting place at the corner of Queen Street and University Avenue, just south of the Canada Life Building. This and the restoration of the house as to structure and furnishings have been made possible through a foundation formed by the Advocates Society of Ontario. Research on the ground and impressions on the brickwork indicated a semicircular porch with Tuscan columns and pilasters, much earlier than the Greek Doric which has been scrapped. Every effort will be made to make the house a living museum like its contemporary the Grange. It will be open to visitors at regular hours, but it is expected that it will be enjoyed by the Advocates when not in use by the general public. Architects, Marani, Rounthwaite and Dick.

the legislature. It is therefore with a feeling of keen disappointment that we read, a month later, that Soane had dropped the project. It is possible that the great man was unaccustomed to the North American atmosphere of designing under pressure of time, but he had not been idle. A sketch survives in the Soane Museum which tells the story of a possibly very great building that never left the drawing board. An awful sense of urgency on the client's part, followed by a period of vacillation and inaction, is not unknown in the professional life of an architect. In the case of the Legislature, eleven years were to elapse before an architect was again appointed.

In a story of Toronto building that recalls so much that is lost, it is a pleasure to be able to point to a house that still stands, even though it has suffered every kind of indignity, not excluding evisceration. The house is that of Chief Justice Sir William Campbell on Duke Street (1822). The writer has known this fine house for over thirty years, but from the beginning it was gutted of anything that would suggest its original use as the home of the Chief Justice of Upper Canada. During that time, a wing has been added to the west and a new railing built over the porch. Sir William came to America as a soldier in a Highland regiment, and was taken prisoner at Yorktown in 1781, but two years later was able to move north to Nova

33 King Street showing the Jail and the Court House with St. James' Church to the east, drawn by Thomas Young in 1835. This is one of a set of four lithographs of Toronto .(Fragments of the jail appear in **34**, a photograph of the rear of York Chambers.) According to Robertson (*Landmarks,* Series 1, page 83), the "plans" were drawn by Dr. Baldwin and Mr. Ewart. Sufficient credit has not been given to the planners who so arranged the two buildings between Toronto and Church streets that they formed a public space which, for many years, was called Court House Square. It is one of the earliest attempts in Toronto at civic design.

34 The Second Jail (1824), now part of York Chambers. The yard has grim memories because it was here that Lount and Matthews were executed, and, by a curious coincidence, two architectural families were involved–Storm, the builder of the scaffold, was the father of W. G. Storm, the architect, and Joseph Sheard, his foreman, refused on principle to assist in its construction. He, later, was the architect who designed the Cawthra house, and, in 1871–72, was Mayor of Toronto.

35, 36 Holland House, 63 Wellington Street West (1831) (demolished). It was built by the Hon. H. J. Boulton, the Attorney-General, who named it after that Holland House in Kensington, London, where he was born. He occupied it for only two years, and left Toronto to become Chief Justice of Newfoundland. The house, which originally faced on Front Street, is of architectural interest chiefly because it represents the transition from the colonial manner, which we see in windows and unbroken front (bottom), to the romantic, which is evident in porch, battlement and turrets. The rear, or garden view (top) resembles even more the castle in miniature with its circular keep and pointed arches. One would give much to know whether the furniture was contemporary with the medievalism of the exterior.

37 Ontario House, built as a house by Peter MacDougall, converted to a hotel in 1829, and becoming the Wellington Hotel in 1845, stood at the corner of Wellington and Church streets (demolished). The City Hotel, the Steamboat Hotel, Franks' and others were in business before 1834, and offered hospitality to travellers by land or water. Generally, they followed the design of the Ontario House, a pattern of balconies and columns, not infrequently seen in the United States. A good example still exists in the Collins Hotel at Dundas. The columns in Ontario House were pine logs peeled and planed. In 1837, the proprietor advertised that it was "newly and beautifully fitted up for the reception of ladies and gentlemen visiting Toronto. The spacious gallery and promenade render it particularly delightful as they overlook the harbour, city and environs. . . . the table will be supplied with the choicest of the market," the beds are double, and "it may not be amiss to state that they are warranted free from vermin or insects of any kind." The latest building on the site was the head office of the Bank of Toronto (demolished 1961).

37

Scotia where he studied law. At one time, he was Attorney-General for the Island of Cape Breton, a position he held for nine years until his promotion to a judgeship in Upper Canada where he became an eminent member of the bench.

It is doubtful whether the Chief Justice's bedroom can be identified in the skeletal interior of the house, but a story of his last days is irresistible. His physician, Dr. Henry, tells it. Sir William, on his death bed, was so weak that he could eat only tidbits; medicines proved unavailing and the doctor prescribed snipe! "At the point

35

36

of the sandy peninsula opposite the barracks, are a number of little pools and marshes, frequented by these delectable little birds, and, here," writes Dr. Henry, "I used to cross over in my skiff and pick up the Chief Justice's panacea. On this delicate food the poor old gentleman was supported for a couple of months: but the frost set in—the snipes flew away, and Sir W— died."[19] He was seventy-six and the date was 1834. Archdeacon John Strachan pronounced the funeral oration in the Church of St. James.

38

38 View of Ontario House from the Fish Market on Cooper's Wharf at the foot of Church Street (drawn by Bartlett in 1838). In 1845 the wharf was leased and improved by John Maitland. An exciting innovation was a paddle boat driven by four horses which for a sevenpence halfpenny return fare took passengers to the Island. "Privat, a Frenchman, had a large hotel on the Island where the water now runs through the eastern entrance."

39 Nos. 58, 60 and 62 Duke (Adelaide) Street (c. 1835) (demolished). No accurate date is available for these terraced houses, but the detail of the brackets would indicate a designer with less skill than the architect of the Latham House, 1837 (**83**) on the same street.

40 Nos. 23, 25 and 27 King Street West (c. 1835) (demolished). Mr. George Brown purchased this property, which occupied the site of the present Bank of Commerce, in 1850 on behalf of the *Globe*.

39

40

41 The second Spadina House, the home of Dr. W. W. Baldwin (1836). Like the first Spadina, it stood just east of the Casa Loma steps.

42, 43 The home of Dr. W. W. Baldwin, northeast corner of Front and Bay streets (*c.* 1837) (demolished). Rather extravagantly, one would think, the first-floor plan provides for three parlours, a library, and a large closet. All rooms are trimmed or panelled in walnut. The basement plan indicates a kitchen 25′×19′, a wine cellar 25′×10′ and a meat room 10′×10′. The only clue to dining arrangements is a dumbwaiter in the kitchen that served one of the parlours. On the outside, the balustrade beneath the cornice would be an unforgivable solecism to the purist. The sketches would indicate Dr. Baldwin was himself the designer, and he appears again as an amateur architect with the second jail (**34**).

42

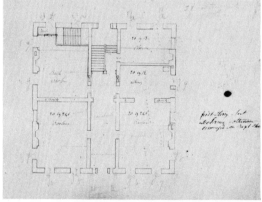

43

44 The second Scadding house (*c.* 1818) (demolished). This log house was built after John Scadding's return to York from England in 1818. It was located across the Don somewhat north of his first house (now in Exhibition Park) on a site approximately that of the present jail. It is said that John's distinguished son, Dr. Henry Scadding, used the lean-to on the right as a study while a school boy at Upper Canada College.

By 1823, the town had grown to 209 houses, 27 shops, and 5 store houses. It was not until 1828 that it passed the two thousand figure with a population of 2,235. By that time, York was but eleven years from its new dignity as a city. The establishment of the Bank of Upper Canada in 1822 and the opening of the Welland Canal in 1829 were concrete evidence of the growing maturity of Upper Canada, and trade and commerce were noticeably stimulated. Evidence of wealth in the hands of a few, and a new feeling of security in the province, was the building of houses of quite impressive size, and of smaller houses and terraces for those of moderate means. The frontier village with its scattered buildings was becoming a memory, and a cohesive community of dignified Georgian dwellings was taking its place.

45

45 Half-way House, Kingston Road at Scarborough (*c.* 1820). The writer remembers this ancient hostelry when it looked much as it did in the photograph. Parts of it are still there, but so eroded by shops and covered with signs as to be unrecognizable. It was halfway between Dunbarton and St. Lawrence Hall. In 1965 the Half-Way House was moved to Black Creek Pioneer Village by the Metropolitan Toronto Conservation Authority, and was restored as an inn.

47 House of Col. Joseph Wells, sometimes called Wells' Hill (1820), on the escarpment east of Bathurst and north of Davenport (demolished). Col. Wells was a hero of Badajos where Frank Simcoe lost his life. Details on this historic house suggest a period later than 1820, but fundamentally it is unchanged. Chimneys, dormers and window heads have been altered, to keep up with the Joneses of the time. The view of the Town of York from the lawn must have been unequalled.

46

47

46 Tecumseh Wigwam, northwest corner of Bloor and Avenue Road (1820) (demolished). The photograph was taken in 1870, and the fact that the site is now occupied by the Park Plaza Hotel shows how very close behind us is our past. Between 1820 and 1860 the house was famous as an inn and a drinking place for the bloods of York. For many years, it was kept by one King whose son George was hanged for the murder of a stagecoachman. The hitching posts in the photograph of 1870 indicate its former function as a stopping place for the stage and other equestrian visitors. The walls were log (visible behind the stoep), covered elsewhere with clapboard.

48–50 The Grange facing Grange Road at the head of
John Street (*c.* 1818). This well-known Toronto
house (**48**) was built for Mr. D'Arcy Boulton, but was
increased in size by Dr. Goldwin Smith following
his marriage to Mrs. W. H. Boulton in 1875.
Originally, the house stood on a 100-acre lot and for
many years enjoyed the proximity of the St. Leger race
track which ran from what is now Dundas Street to
the present College Street. The structural changes
made by Goldwin Smith are in marked contrast to the
taste of his time, and consisted chiefly of a new porch
in stone (**50**) which replaced one of wood, and a
library to the west (**49**) replacing the original
"grapery." The house which, until 1970, was the
administrative division of the Art Gallery of Ontario,
has undergone a complete restoration, done with
taste and care for its period. Furniture selected covers,
in general, the years 1830 to 1840. The house is open
to the public as a living museum without ropes or
other barriers to rooms. The cost of restoration will be
approximately $500,000. Architect, Peter John Stokes.

The building of the Parliament Buildings in 1829 was a reflection of the prosperity of the province and the stability of its institutions. Following the burning of the Legislature in 1813, the government of Upper Canada had moved from place to place rather like some of those governments in exile which "made do" with incongruous quarters in the late war. In York, following the fire, we find the legislature first in Jordan's Hotel (hardly in keeping with the dignity of the Crown, incompatible with 21 gun salutes, but not without its compensations), and, in 1820, in new buildings, soon to be destroyed by fire, on the site of the present gas works. This was followed by accommodation in the first Toronto General Hospital (or

51 The Millen Cottage, Bay Street (1826) (demolished). Robert Millen came from Belfast and bought himself a lot on the road which led to Teraulay Cottage, the home of Dr. Macaulay. In the course of time the dirt road became Teraulay Street and finally Bay; the cottage was demolished to make room for Shea's Hippodrome and it, in turn, was razed to make room for Nathan Phillips Square. Mr. Millen was a carpenter, and we must admire the loving care that has gone into his doorway (even if the cornice is heavy), and the battlemented rain-water heads. The huge chimney indicates the source of heat and the size of the logs that were burned. The builder of the cottage was, in fact, more than a carpenter, and we are told that the carving on the altar at St. Michael's Cathedral was his work.

second if we remember the use of the first St. James) and, when that was required for its original purpose, the legislature moved into the Court House.

The completion of the new Legislative buildings in 1832 on Front Street between John and Peter streets would, one would have thought, have terminated this peripatetic existence. However, in 1841 the provinces of Upper and Lower Canada were united and the seat of government was set up elsewhere. Between 1841 and 1849 the buildings were used for university purposes, and between 1849 and 1851 as an insane asylum. Their subsequent history included their use for sessions of the United Parliament, and as a barracks between 1861 and 1866; finally, the cycle is complete and we return to them as the Legislature of Ontario, 1867–1892.

52

· ELEVATION · OF · PORTION · OF · PORCH · RAILING · FORMER · BANK · OF · UPPER · CANADA ·
· DUKE · STREET · TORONTO ·

· PANEL · OF · GRAVE · RAILING ·
· ST. MARK'S · CHURCHYARD ·
· NIAGARA – ON – THE – LAKE ·

· FRONT · ELEVATION · OF · WINDOW · BALCONY ·
· HOUSE · AT · 56 · DUKE · STREET · TORONTO ·

· SIDE · ELEVATION ·

DETAILS OF

CAST

IRONWORK

· SCALE · FOR · DETAILS · OF · IRONWORK ·

· FRONT · ELEVATION · OF · PORCH · BANK · OF · UPPER · CANADA ·
· SHOWING · POSITION · OF · RAILING ·

· VIEW · LOOKING · DOWN ·
· SHOWING · GRATING ·

· METHOD · OF ·
· ATTACHING ·
· BRACKET ·

· SECTION ·

· VIEW · OF · TOP ·

DONALD J. REED MENS. ET DELT. 1931.

54

52, 53 Bank of Upper Canada (1822), northeast corner of Duke (Adelaide) and George streets. The old bank has suffered many vicissitudes and face liftings, and was once a school for boys (De la Salle). Within the writer's memory, it had a fine cast-iron railing on the cornice (see **54**). The sketch of the bank (**53**) is redrawn from the *Landmarks of Toronto*. The classic porch still stands forlorn on its podium; weeds grow in the eaves. Looking at the arrangement of windows in the façade, it is not difficult to contemplate its restoration, but at what cost and for what purpose?

54 Details of ironwork on the Bank of Upper Canada and a house at 56 Duke Street, drawn by students in the School of Architecture.

55 York's second market (1831), J. G. Chewett and Dr. W. W. Baldwin, architects (demolished). This building stood on the site of the present St. Lawrence Market. The upper room over the main entrance was used by City Council from 1834 to 1844.

55

56 York from Gibraltar Point, drawn by James Gray
in 1828.

57 Two houses on the east side of George Street (1829)
(demolished). From 1852 to 1860 the house on the
left, no. 28, was a school owned by Mrs. M. C.
Crombie. Houses like these can be matched with some
of the best in the Beacon Hill area of Boston, and we
know for a fact that there were many others, lost
to us now by fire or "progress." The adjoining house
was owned by Mr. Robert Manners, a relative of the
Duke of Rutland. In 1898, both dwellings were
standing, and it was the belief of the editor of the
Landmarks that they were good "for many years to
come."

57

48

58

The Legislative Buildings have gone, and with them the second market, a smaller structure, but one of at least equal significance in the story of Toronto. It was built under the authority of the magistrates in Quarter Sessions in 1831–33, a body always short of funds, but one which was the municipal government of the area before its incorporation as a city. Over this building, which housed both municipal government and market, the Quarter Sessions went heavily into debt— so much so that it became one of the chief reasons for incorporation and a major embarrassment to the new city government who inherited it. The market–cum–town hall was the last milestone in the chequered history of York. Only a year away were its new dignity as a city and a return to its old name of Toronto. There would be none then who could conceivably have forecast the greatness of its future.

59

58 The Legislative Buildings (1829) on Simcoe Place (Front Street West) between John and Peter Streets (demolished). J. G. Chewett was the architect. The lithograph by Currier of a drawing by Thomas Young shows a portico of four columns that was never built – unfortunately for the architect because its absence exposes a marked difference in scale between the doorways and the windows to the chamber.

59 The interior of the buildings of 1829, photographed c. 1892.

60 Plan of the Buildings as they were in 1857.

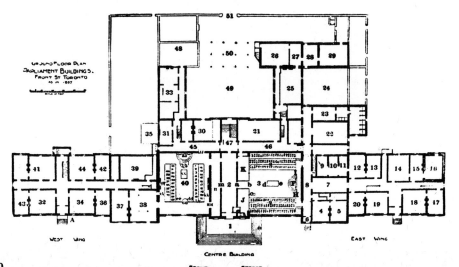

60

61 House near York Downs Golf Club (*c.* 1830). This house is typical of the farm houses of Upper Canada prior to 1850. It relies for its effect entirely on proportion, and the nice distribution of the windows. Its date may be indicated partly by the size of the chimneys and the smallness of the window panes.

62 "Drumsnab," or the Cayley House (1830), 5 Castle Frank Crescent. The original owner and builder was Mr. William Cayley who is mentioned by Mary Jarvis as a fellow passenger on a steamboat on the Georgian Bay in 1835. The present owner, Mr. M. F. Feheley, has restored the house (1966) with sensitivity and respect for the original. A storey has been added (*c.* 1860), and the wilderness that once surrounded "Drumsnab" is now Rosedale. In well over a century of change, only the Don has remained constant, and it is no longer that crystal stream in which the salmon leapt in the spring. A feature of the drawing room known to travellers like Sir James Alexander in 1847 was the mural decoration representing scenes from *Faust* in sgrafitto – drawn, we are told by Sir James, "with a bold and masterly hand by the proprietor." A recalcitrant fireplace gives a certain realism to the damnation of Faust whose features appear strangely through the murk.

61

62

63 69 and 71 Gerrard Street West. This photograph was taken when Gerrard Street was lined with horse chestnuts (like Elm Street) and the houses were still houses. Later, it became known as "the Village" and the home of silver workers, wood carvers, jewellers and other craftsmen. They gave place to gift shops and restaurants, and the houses were demolished in 1971.

63

64 No. 591 Jarvis Street and flanking houses. The centre house gives one an idea of a once charming little terrace, now marred by the monstrous dormers of the builder and the typical 20th century Toronto porch. A former owner who was ninety years of age, thirty years ago, remembered the rural setting of the terrace in her childhood, and the fact that "Bloor Street" did not exist. (demolished in 1966)

65 Upper Canada College, King Street West, in 1830 (demolished).

66 Some shops on the south side of King Street between George and Frederick streets (demolished). Their design would suggest that they were built about 1830.

67 Mud-block house which stood on Bathurst Street near York Downs Golf Club (*c.* 1840). This was once a not uncommon form of construction which provided a dwelling that was both warm in winter and cool in summer. Such houses abound in Ontario, but in Hogg's Hollow and Willowdale they came to light when moved some years ago for street widening. Moving shook the stucco or the wood siding which, one or the other, is essential as a protection to the mud. The writer once owned a mud block which measured 16″ × 16″ × 8″ and was reinforced with pea straw. The late Mr. C. W. Jefferys' house in Hogg's Hollow was built of mud block protected by 4 inches of brickwork (see also **87**).

68 House of the Hon. Wm. Allan (1830) in "Moss Park" on the west side of Sherbourne Street. William Allan came to York in Simcoe's time, and lived there till his death in 1853. From then on, Moss Park takes some colour from the activities of his son, George William Allan. Of him we read as Mayor of Toronto (1855), Speaker of the Senate, President of the Royal Canadian Institute, President of the Ontario Society of Artists, Chairman of the Art Union of Canada, President of the Upper Canada Bible Society. The present Allan Gardens owes its existence as a public park to his generosity. (house demolished)

4: Prosperity and Eclecticism

69 Wm. Lyon Mackenzie house (*c.* 1850), 82 Bond Street. The house is now a show piece and completely furnished. It must be remembered that a house like this never stood alone in old Toronto, but was part of a terrace.

Both politically and architecturally, the year 1834 was a significant one in the story of Toronto. The population had grown to 9,254, and a change had come over its building. There must have been some loyal souls who, in that year, would have thought of Toronto as "No mean city," but there were many who found it, in another sense, indescribably mean. Mrs. Jameson had this to say of it in 1836: ". . . most strangely mean and melancholy. A little ill-built town . . . some government offices, built of staring red brick, in the most tasteless, vulgar style imaginable; three feet of snow all around; and the gray, sullen, wintry lake, and the dark gloom of the pine forest bounding the prospect. . . ." "Two years ago" (she wrote in 1837), "we bought our books at the same shop where we bought our shoes, our spades, our sugar, and salt pork! Now," she had to acknowledge, "we have two good booksellers' shops, and at one of these a circulating library of two or three hundred volumes of common novels." She felt that a "reasonable person" might be happy in Toronto if he or she could tolerate the flies and frogs in summer and the "relentless iron winter." On another occasion, she wrote of the infrequency of the mails: "It is now seven weeks since the date of the last letters from my dear far-distant home. The archdeacon told me, by way of comfort, that when he came to settle in this country, there was only one mail-post from England in the course of a whole year, and it was called, as if in mockery, 'The Express'. . . ."[1] Mrs. Jameson was a highly educated, talented woman, but her views may have been prejudiced by her unhappy marriage to the Attorney-General of Upper Canada.

A sympathetic observer was Dr. Henry Scadding who recalled that, in the twenties, the intersection of the future Queen and Yonge was so remote from York that travellers found it difficult to locate the few houses in the area, and that it was quite possible to be lost in the surrounding woods and swamps.

Another critic was John Galt, the founder of Guelph and Commissioner of the Canada Company, who was inspired to say in his *Autobiography*: "Everyone who has ever been at Dover knows that it is one of the vilest blue-devil haunts on the face of the earth, except Little York in Upper Canada, when he has been there one day."[2]

One can have nothing but sympathy for those early critics who complained of the many disagreeable features that are inevitably associated with life in a primitive community—of inadequate heating, smells and lack of sanitation, of wooden sidewalks, muddy roads and a general lack of those amenities that went with an older and more settled way of life in Great Britain or Europe. These were all practical matters that disappeared with wealth, the organization of the municipality and the technological discoveries of the 19th century of which the water closet, designed originally by Sir John Harington for Queen Elizabeth in 1596, was not the least important.

A friendly visitor was Charles Dickens who, writing to John Forster in 1842, was able to say: "the town itself is full of life and motion, bustle, business and improvement. The streets are well paved,[3] and lighted with gas; the houses are large and good; the shops excellent . . . there are some which would do no discredit to the metropolis itself." On the obverse side, he was shocked into writing a friend "the wild and rabid Toryism of Toronto, is, I speak seriously, *appalling*."[4]

T. A. Reed has pointed out that, in the year prior to incorporation, King and

Yonge was still "far westward of the town proper, the venture of a store at the present Royal Bank corner in 1833 being described as 'wild and foolish.' The line of Lot Street (to be called Queen Street in 1842 in honour of Queen Victoria) was the northern boundary, all north of it being laid out in Park Lots, for gentlemen's villas, traces of which still exist in street names, such as Bleecker and Sherbourne, which reminds us of the Ridouts; Jarvis of Secretary Jarvis; James, Elizabeth, Hayter and Teraulay of Dr. James Macaulay and his wife, Elizabeth Hayter (Macaulay had been surgeon of Simcoe's 'Queen's Rangers'); Spadina, Robert, Sullivan, Willcocks, St. George and Baldwin of Dr. Wm. Warren Baldwin and his family; Denison, Bellevue, Borden, Lippincott, Ossington, Dovercourt, Hepbourne and Dewson of the Denisons, and many others of greater or less importance."[5]

On March 6, 1834, by royal assent, the title "York" was dropped, the ancient name of Toronto was restored and the village became an incorporated city. To the surprise of many and the disgust of the Tory opposition, the "rabid reformer," Mr. William Lyon Mackenzie, was declared Mayor. Five wards were created: St.

70 The attractive well-lit kitchen in the Mackenzie house with its superb stove – a view looking toward the dining room.

Lawrence in the neighbourhood of the market, and four others, St. George, St. Andrew, St. Patrick, and St. David, named after the patron saints of the United Kingdom. This nomenclature, with additions, represented the political divisions of the city until 1892, when the numerical system, still employed, was adopted.

When we think of the 153,402 acres covered today by Metropolitan Toronto, it is worth recalling the size of the city in 1834. Its boundaries formed a rectangle described by Parliament Street on the east, Bathurst on the west; the Bay Shore to

71 Two Breweries. Joseph Bloor was an Englishman who ran a very successful inn, the Farmers Arms, near the marketplace of York until 1830, when he sold out and moved to Yorkville. There he built a brewery (not illustrated) in the bottom of the ravine at the head of Huntley Street. His name is perpetuated in Bloor Street, and it was he and Sheriff Jarvis who, as a speculation, laid out the village of Yorkville.
A less important citizen with a much more important brewery (illustrated) was John Severn who moved to Yorkville in 1835. Robertson writes of the picturesque irregularity of the plant, and of the ingenious use of galleries on the "domestic portion" to take advantage of the "adjacent scenery." This wing was probably necessary as a staff house in the sparsely inhabited woods north of Bloor in 1835.

the south and a line four hundred yards north of Queen Street at, approximately, the present Dundas Street. Beyond these boundaries, growth must have seemed quite visionary, but an open area marked by the present Dufferin Street to the west and the concession line (Bloor Street) to the north was set aside for annexation when sufficiently populated. It was known as the "Liberties." The centre of the city was still in the neighbourhood of King and Frederick streets. Lot Street was unopened east of Victoria Street, and on Yonge Street there were few houses and no shops. Roads leading out of the city were still Dundas and Lakeshore on the west, Yonge on the north and the Kingston Road on the east.

T. A. Reed records also the dire effects of inadequate civic amenities:

There were neither sidewalks, drains nor sewers, no water supply except from wells, no attempt at street lighting, nothing indeed that placed the city above the average of any frontier town. When an enquiry was made into the causes of the cholera epidemic of 1832, a disaster that was repeated in 1834, these primitive conditions were blamed, together with the universal practice of allowing garbage to accumulate on the vacant lots and the curse of strong drink. During these epidemics, business came to a standstill, the streets were deserted, 25 per cent. of the population were attacked and one in ten died.[6]

It would seem paradoxical that a disease-ridden town plagued by flies, and the butt of visiting English of both sexes, would have had the energy and the foresight to press for recognition by the legislature as a city. The fact is that, behind this bleak frontier façade, were all those elements that are essential to the good life in an organized community. On the wholly physical side were firms in the iron foundry business, firms with steam sawmills and flour mills, and others who provided the inhabitants with soap and candles as well as "blue and Poland starch."

On the spiritual side were the churches of which there were ten; there were the Literary and Philosophical Society, several libraries and the enterprising Messrs. Daly and J. G. Howard who "aimed to cultivate the public taste" by arranging loan exhibitions of art.

The Masons had met as early as 1800, and by 1822 had a hall on Market Lane where they gathered "on every Thursday previous to the full moon." Several literary magazines appeared, and, like their successors for the next hundred years, had their little day and passed away. The Typographical Society was a union rather than a social group, but it was interested in the improvement of the craft and had regular dinners. Mr. Joseph Lawrence was its first president. When, to these activities, we add those groups inevitably connected with the affairs of the ten churches where they worshipped, we have a picture of life quite different from that seen through the eyes of that "haughty" hypochondriac, Mr. Galt, or the lonely and unhappy Mrs. Jameson. What we see, in fact, is the present-day great city of Toronto in all its cultural aspects, but in miniature. Even lecture-going, for which Toronto is notorious, was not unknown in 1834. Indeed, it had its own highly organized society under the distinguished sponsorship of Dr. Baldwin, Mr. Jarvis, Dr. Rolph, Mr. Worts and Mr. Ewart.

One name is missing from the list—that of Mr. John G. Howard whose gift of High Park to the City will be remembered long after his buildings have been

72 A scheme for a public building in Court House Square by John G. Howard, architect. In this grandiose scheme (probably for the Legislature) Mr. Howard anticipated all that was worst in the Chicago Exhibition of 1892. The second St. James, which burned in 1849, is on the right.

demolished and forgotten. His works will be referred to again, but here it is appropriate to include his efforts to influence the cultural life of York. So energetic a

73 Colborne Lodge in High Park (1836), John G.
Howard, architect. Colborne Lodge was the house of
the architect, named after his patron, Sir John Colborne.
It still stands on a knoll overlooking the lake in the
great estate that Mr. Howard left to the city as a
park. As Robertson says in the *Landmarks*, High Park
was "the most munificent gift ever made by a private
individual to the public in Upper Canada."
The house is a "cottage ornée," examples of which
appeared in many books of the 18th and 19th
centuries. Their publication met the demand for
designs for a house that represented rusticity, nature
and the simple life. The railings round the verandah
took the form of huge serpents and dragons with
glittering eyes and fiery mouths. The house is furnished
with many pieces that belonged to the Howards and
other furniture of the period. It is the responsibility
of the Toronto Historical Board and is open to the
public.

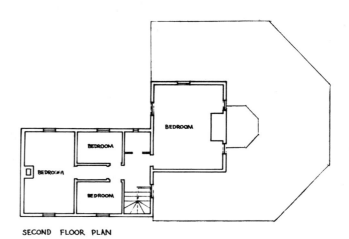

SECOND FLOOR PLAN

74 First and second floor plans of Colborne Lodge,
drawn by students in the School of Architecture.

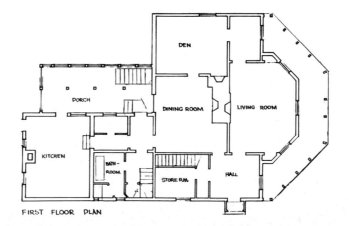

FIRST FLOOR PLAN

man was likely never depressed, but the contrast between London and York, so shocking to Mrs. Jameson, must have been equally so for him when he arrived in September 1832 after a journey from England that involved near shipwreck and mutiny with violence.

By 1833, he was the drawing master at Upper Canada College at a salary of £100 per annum, and, a year later, had sufficient support in the local community to organize the Society of Artists and Amateurs. The catalogue of the first exhibition is preserved in the Toronto Public Library, and there we learn that the new

75 Colborne Lodge, the Lantern. From its position, the lantern, known to us now only in a photograph, must have been used as a guide for visitors arriving at the house which, even today, can be missed in daylight on modern roads. It was designed at the height of the Greek Revival which saw such buildings as the York Magistrates' Court on Adelaide Street, and the Commercial Bank on Wellington Street (**100, 169**).

76 Design for a church by John G. Howard (*c.* 1840).

77 Plan for an inn by John G. Howard (*c.* 1840). The main entrance is to a hall with public room to the left and parlour to the right. Upstairs is an assembly room, used for dances and public meetings. The bar on the ground floor is accessible from public room and bar parlour. There was always, in the inn, a side door for those using the bar. Stabling and carriage shed were at the rear.

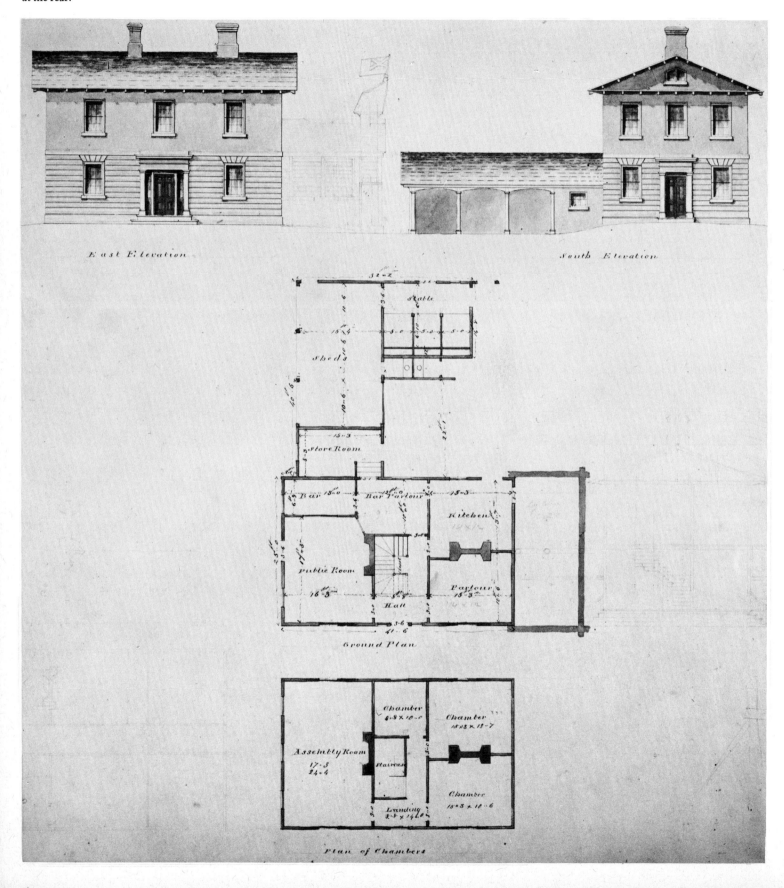

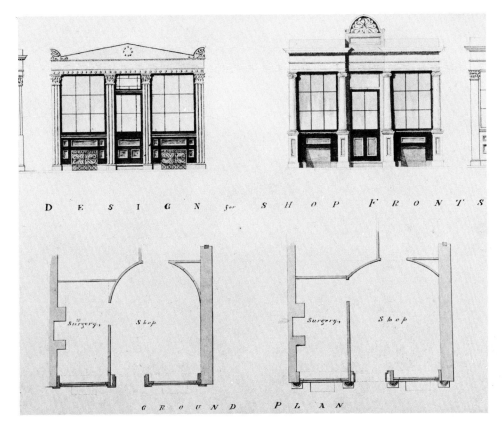

D E S I G N *for* S H O P F R O N T S

G R O U N D P L A N

78 Plan for a dentist's surgery and shop by John G. Howard (*c.* 1835). Until 1840, the apothecary or chemist served also as dentist – hence the surgery. A combination somewhat earlier than Howard was that of the barber-surgeon for whom the plan would be admirable.

79 Design for a labourer's cottage by John G. Howard (*c.* 1842). This design was one for a series of cottages built, presumably as a speculation, by Capt. Irving. Its rather quaint medievalism is carried out consistently in windows, door and many-sided chimney. A pump in the kitchen would supply water for dishes, cooking and washing. The earth closet would be somewhere in the back yard, though in "better" houses it was often indoors.

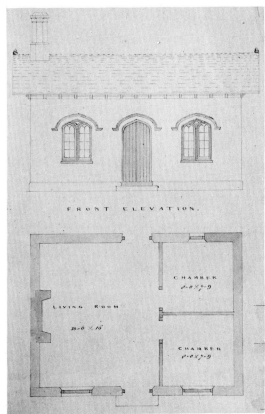

FRONT ELEVATION.

CHAMBER

LIVING ROOM

CHAMBER

society was under the distinguished patronage of Sir John Colborne and Archdeacon Strachan. Captain Richard Bonnycastle, R.E., was president. Rather in reverse of the English custom at cricket where amateurs are "gentlemen" and play "the rest," the professionals in this first society of artists in Toronto were named, but the "amateurs shall not be compelled to annex their names." The result was work by Paul Kane, Krieghoff, John G. Howard and others alongside a painting by "A Lady." Among the exhibits were "Lioness with Whelps" and, very daring, "An Idea in Perspective."

Toronto was apparently not ready for such a society, or the times were out of joint, because only two exhibitions were held between 1834 and 1837. In the latter year, Howard reorganized the Society under the title "The Toronto Society of Artists." Hardly more successful than its predecessor, the newly formed group held three exhibitions in the old City Hall before it, too, was dissolved in May 1848.

The theatre in Toronto has had a chequered career, but its roots go deep into the 19th century. The earliest recorded performance was in 1809 when an American strolling company put on *The School for Scandal* in a tavern ballroom. Just

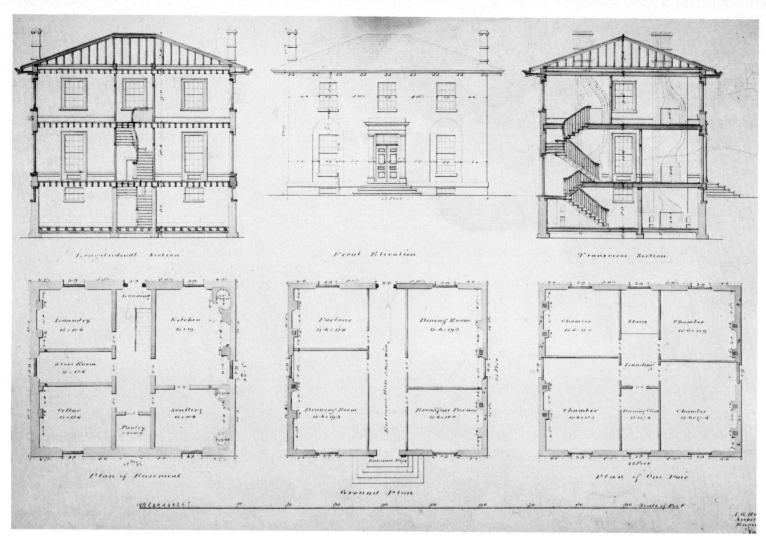

Longitudinal Section   Front Elevation   Transverse Section

Plan of Basement   Ground Plan   Plan of One Pair

80 Design for a house by John G. Howard (1833). A very elegant little house with all the elements of "gracious living" for Toronto in the 1830's including four rooms for entertaining on the first floor, good-sized bedrooms, and an ample wine cellar. The kitchen is 15′ × 19′ with a bake oven and fireplace 5′6″ in width. The two circular spaces in the scullery are "coppers."

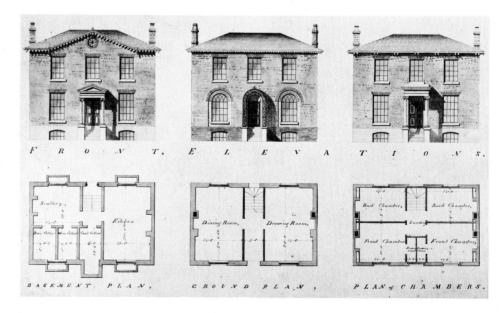

FRONT, ELEVATIONS.

BASEMENT, PLAN,   GROUND PLAN,   PLAN of CHAMBERS.

81 Three designs for a house by John G. Howard. One would assume that the dining and drawing rooms were intended for entertaining on a generous scale, and that the large kitchen (20′ × 13′) would serve as a family room for living and eating. By contrast, the four bedrooms were minimum in area. Heating was through coal-burning fireplaces, even to the basement scullery which was as big as a bedroom. There was no bathroom in the house, but each bedroom would have basin, water-jug, and chamber-pot.

before the War of 1812, the favourite place for such entertainments was a tavern known as O'Keefe's Assembly Rooms. We hear of strolling "Yankee" stock companies visiting York in the twenties, and "traditions exist of private theatricals in good style at Spadina House and the Garrison."

Robertson's sketches in the *Landmarks* of ten theatres, all built or "adapted" between 1820 and 1849, would indicate that the demand for theatrical performances, both amateur and professional, was a lively one. All except the ninth, the Royal Lyceum, were of frame construction and had been barns, a Wesleyan chapel, and a carpenter's shop, but only two were destroyed by fire in spite of lighting by candles and construction of a kind that would shock the most casual of building inspectors.

The change that came over the architecture of Toronto about the time of incorporation as a city had nothing to do with the new status of the community, nor was it something that can be fixed by a date. It was a change in taste brought about

82 Design for a house by John G. Howard (*c.* 1835). The design is unusual in that the high basement provides an extra habitable floor with living room convenient to the kitchen, wine and beer cellars. The "best bedroom" on the principal floor is also unusual, but often very useful. Small as the house is, it required seven fireplaces to heat it.

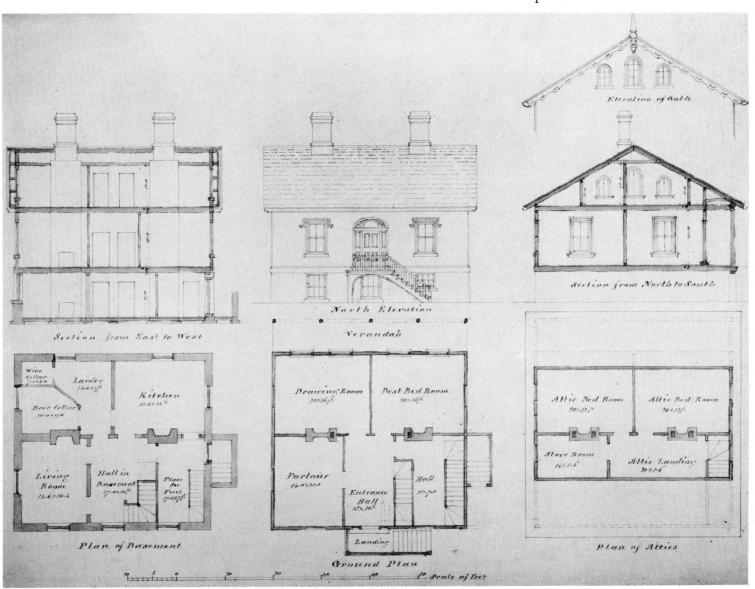

by the Romantic movement, a movement that was felt most strongly in the Western Hemisphere and left its mark on architecture as well as on literature, painting, and music. Romanticism has been said "to consist in a high development of poetic sensibility towards the remote, as such. It idealizes the distant, both of time and place. Its most typical form is the cult of the extinct."[7] We recognize it at this time in St. Andrew's church in the style of ancient Greece, and, before long, we shall see a Gothic St. James, and a Romanesque University College. Inspired by books dealing on the one hand with the new science of archaeology or, on the other, with the imagery and beauty of language of Byron, Keats and Shelley, the lure of Greece was irresistible even in a Presbyterian church. Yet in the confused aesthetic standards of the time, Ruskin and Pugin would have condemned the Greek as pagan and intolerable in a Christian church—only the Middle Ages provided the architecture that pointed to God in pinnacles and soaring spires. For most people, the architecture of the Middle Ages suggested piety and the feeling of reverence and awe that went with a dim Miltonian light; and elderly professors dreaming of home could find equally convincing arguments in favour of Gothic as the only style compatible with learning in the new land. We can imagine, also, the zeal

83 Three houses on Duke (Adelaide) Street near Parliament. The large house on the *left* shows old Toronto domestic architecture at its best. It was the house in 1837 of Jacob Latham, a prominent builder. The semi-circular Ionic porch and the balustraded fence contribute greatly to its charm. The *middle* house was built for Mr. Alexander Grant about 1859. The *end* house at the corner of Duke and Parliament streets was Mr. Obadiah Stafford's. It might well have been built in the twenties or earlier because Robertson notes that it "presented tokens of age" in 1833. (demolished)

84 St. Andrew's Church (1830), southwest corner of Church and Adelaide streets, John Ewart, architect/builder (demolished). It is quite possible that the designer of this church, the first Presbyterian church in Toronto, knew of the hold which the Greek revival had on the city of Edinburgh, still referred to as the Athens of the north. The design is heavy and the transition from the first stage to the next of the spire, which was added in 1850 by John G. Howard, is abrupt. As it was usual for Greek Revival architects to adhere closely to archaeological precedent, the problem of fenestration with no classical prototype was acute. Circular headed windows such as those on St. Andrew's would be definitely "against the rules."

85 Houses, 750 Bay Street, west side, south of College (demolished). Charming cottages, but high land costs and primitive sanitary conditions spelt the end of such housing in Toronto. This photograph was taken thirty years ago before Eaton's occupied the corner opposite.

with which they urged their not unwilling architects to give them buildings as remote as possible from the familiar present.

A factor of no little significance in the Toronto story was the arrival of the architect as a professional man. He appears first with the construction of the third Parliament Buildings in 1829 as Thomas Young and J. G. Chewett, and again, in the same year, with the erection of the east wing of Osgoode Hall by an architect

[*text continues page 80*]

86, 88 Beverley House, at the corner of Richmond and John streets (demolished). About the year 1816, John Beverley Robinson, Attorney-General of Upper Canada, acquired a one-storey brick cottage, formerly the property of Mr. D'Arcy Boulton, the future owner of the Grange. The site, bounded by John, Simcoe, Richmond and Queen streets, was out of all proportion to the house and the home of a distinguished lawyer, soon to become Chief Justice. In the changes that were made, a wing was added to the west and the cottage disappeared in a two-storey structure screened on the ground floor by a verandah. In the years 1839 and 1840, Beverley House became the residence of the Governor-General who took the title of Baron Sydenham of Sydenham in Kent and Toronto in Canada.

The curtain to the right of the mantel in the dining room (**88**) may still be seen in some Toronto houses of the period. It screened the comings and goings of the servants at dinner. The gaselier has been supplemented by a ring of naked electric bulbs.

86

87 House of Dr. Wm. Charles Gwynne at Dufferin Street and the Lake (*c.* 1840) (demolished). Dr. Gwynne was admitted to the practice of medicine in Upper Canada in 1832, and, later, became a highly respected surgeon on the staff of the Medical Faculty of the University of Toronto. The house is of a type not uncommon among Ontario farm houses though the French doors are unusual in this climate. The walls were built of sun-dried mud bricks protected by stucco.

88

89 Zion Congregational Church (1839), northeast corner of Adelaide and Bay streets, William Thomas, architect (demolished). This is a very classical little church (80′×40′) with its Doric columns *in antis* at the porch entrance. It was built of bricks covered with plaster "made of white marble dust" – a technique not unknown to the Greeks in 500 B.C., but undoubtedly rare in Upper Canada. It will be noted that the plaster was scored to simulate blocks of Cararra marble.

90 The former Paisley Shop at 927 Yonge Street (*c.* 1840) (demolished). It would be hard to imagine a shop that offered a more genuine invitation to the customer than did the Paisley Shop. When the photograph was taken the delicacy of the window detail and the cast iron columns at the entrance were matched by the elegance of the old silver and glass on display within. The 20th century has produced nothing to equal it in Toronto.

91, 92 The Third Jail (1840), John G. Howard, architect (demolished). The jail (**92**) was built overlooking the harbour on the bay side not far from the present corner of Front and Berkeley streets. The sketch shows only half the front with wings radiating to the rear from the central octagon. The windows in this grim prison remind one of a columbarium with its niches for urns. It was, if anything, more terrifying than old Newgate whose demolition in 1911 was the cause for rejoicing for the whole population of London.
The picture of a flogging in the Toronto Jail, 1879, was evidently thought to be entertaining as it was published in the *Canadian Illustrated News*. It is shown here only for the Piranesi-like character of the scene.

91

92

93, 94 The New Fort, known later as Stanley Barracks, in the C.N.E. grounds. Many will remember the group of grey military buildings which were demolished to provide space for the ever extending Canadian National Exhibition until by 1953 only the Officers' Quarters (1840), now the Marine Museum of the Inland Waters and the headquarters of the Toronto Historical Board, was left. A restaurant in a warm and comfortable basement room with a log fire serves lunches except on Saturdays. The photograph (**93**), taken many years ago, shows a comfortable mess room which has witnessed many colourful receptions and regimental dinners. The buildings that have gone were, except for the hospital (**94**), of little historical and still less architectural significance. The Exhibition Ground gates, made in England in 1839, are now the main entrance to Guildwood Village on Kingston Road.

93

94

95, 97, 98 A very complicated interlocking collection
of buildings grew on a property bounded by Front
and Wellington streets, west of Spadina. It began with
Vice-Chancellor Jameson's house (1837–1844),
which became part of "Lyndhurst," the house of Mr.
Frederick Widder (1844–1865). In 1860 the house
was bought by Loretto Abbey and many changes took
place (see **338** and **340**). The Vice-Chancellor's house
was unpretentious and quite the opposite of Lyndhurst
which was clearly built for entertainment and display.
It is likely, however, that the Jameson house will be
remembered for Mrs. Anna Jameson, the authoress,
long after the Widders are forgotten. She came to
York and her husband, the Attorney-General (later
Vice-Chancellor) in 1836, but their differences were
irreconcilable, and she left for England, never to

95

96 Topographical plan of the city and liberties of
Toronto (1842), surveyed, drawn and published by
James Cane.

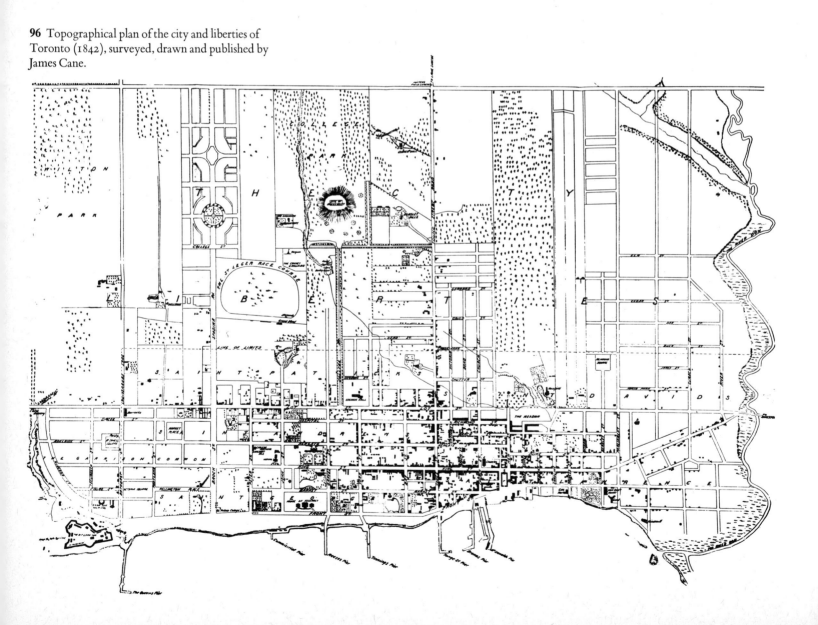

97

return, fifteen months later. The small parlour of unhappy memory for her existed until recently, and opened off the drawing room of the Widders. Mr. Frederick Widder came to Canada as Commissioner of the Canada Company in 1845. It is not clear why he decided to build Lyndhurst around a fragment of the Jameson house. One doesn't need to read contemporary accounts to know something of the hospitality of the Widders and of the lavish entertainments for which they became famous. The drawing room (**98**) itself suggests a mode of life rare in Upper Canada over a hundred years ago. Marble mantels, high ceilings, cornices and ornate columns help to confirm the stories of fancy dress balls and revellers like Edward, Prince of Wales. The dining room of Lyndhurst (**95**) is a room in a different scale, but with a mantel rich in detail. The female figures and the lyre are of iron. So also, of course, is the very beautiful rococo fender. The plant in a pot in a kind of embroidered plaster belongs to some forgotten period of interior decoration. **97** shows the lace-like iron of a radiator cover in the drawing room.

98

99

100

99–101 The Commercial Bank, 15 Wellington Street West (begun 1843), Wm. Thomas architect. In 1843, the cost of the land and building was $22,303. A long-time owner was the firm of Clarkson Gordon and Company who sold the building in November 1972 to the Canadian Imperial Bank of Commerce. The caduceus on the parapet (since removed) consists of the herald's staff with two snakes intertwined, the symbol of the messenger-god, Hermes: often, as here, associated with commerce. Interior mantels (99), doors (101), and window trim show that, for Thomas, the Greek Revival was not just something to give distinction to a façade, it permeated the building.

101

102, 103 The Commercial Bank (1843), details of the exterior and interior showing the Greek Revival influence. Drawings by students in the School of Architecture.

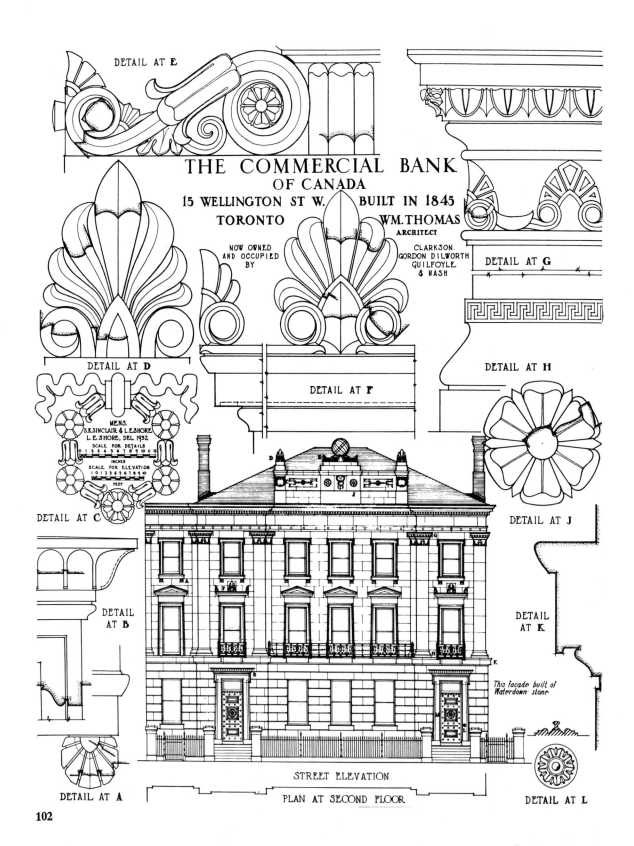

DETAIL AT E

THE COMMERCIAL BANK
OF CANADA
15 WELLINGTON ST W.   BUILT IN 1845
TORONTO   WM. THOMAS
ARCHITECT

NOW OWNED
AND OCCUPIED
BY

CLARKSON.
GORDON DILWORTH
GUILFOYLE
& NASH

DETAIL AT G

DETAIL AT D

DETAIL AT F

DETAIL AT H

ME.NS.
S.K.SINCLAIR & L.E.SHORE
L. E. SHORE, DEL. 1932
SCALE FOR DETAILS

INCHES
SCALE FOR ELEVATION

FEET

DETAIL AT C

DETAIL AT J

DETAIL
AT B

DETAIL
AT K

This facade built of
Waterdown stone

DETAIL AT A

STREET ELEVATION

PLAN AT SECOND FLOOR

DETAIL AT L

102

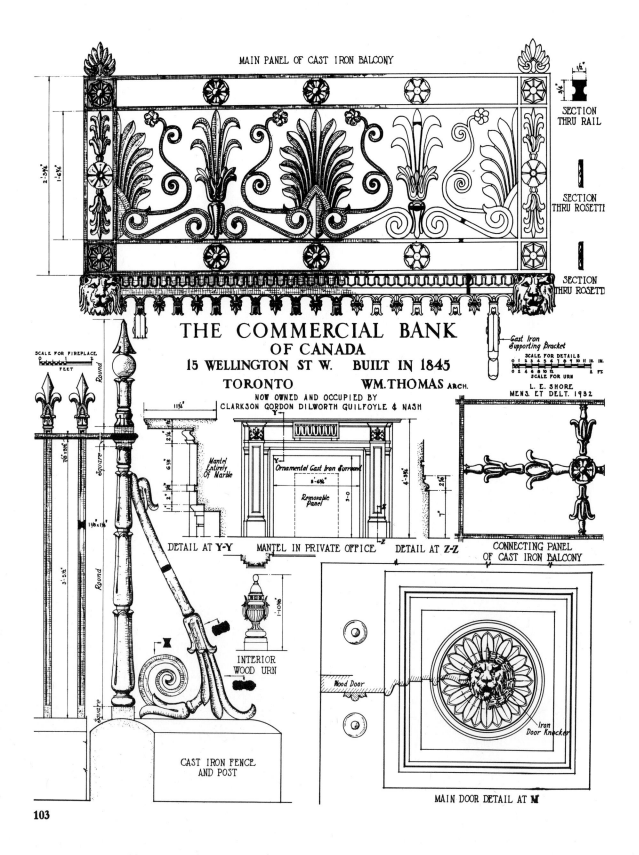

MAIN PANEL OF CAST IRON BALCONY

SECTION
THRU RAIL

SECTION
THRU ROSETTE

SECTION
THRU ROSETTE

Cast Iron
Supporting Bracket

THE COMMERCIAL BANK
OF CANADA
15 WELLINGTON ST W.   BUILT IN 1845
TORONTO   WM. THOMAS ARCH.

SCALE FOR DETAILS
SCALE FOR URN

NOW OWNED AND OCCUPIED BY
CLARKSON GORDON DILWORTH GUILFOYLE & NASH

L. E. SHORE
MENS. ET DELT. 1932

SCALE FOR FIREPLACE
FEET

Round

Square

Round

Square

Mantel
Entirely
Of Marble

Ornamental Cast Iron Surround

Removable
Panel

DETAIL AT Y-Y   MANTEL IN PRIVATE OFFICE   DETAIL AT Z-Z

CONNECTING PANEL
OF CAST IRON BALCONY

INTERIOR
WOOD URN

Wood Door

Iron
Door Knocker

CAST IRON FENCE
AND POST

MAIN DOOR DETAIL AT M

104 Methodist Church, south side of Richmond Street between Yonge and Bay (1844) (demolished). The Wesleyan Methodists were among the first to engage in religious instruction in York, and in 1801 we hear of Nathan Bangs as the first missionary. Reference has already been made to the first church of 1818 on King near Jordan where, it will be remembered, the sexes were separated by the centre aisle. That was the day of lanterns and poke bonnets, and it is interesting to read that to find their wives on dark nights, the men would cast the beam of the lantern down the funnel of the bonnet which was worn in front of the face. That, of course, was before the Richmond Street church, which was built on land purchased from Mr. Jesse Ketchum for $22,000. In rather dilapidated condition at the turn of the century, it was still referred to with respect, indeed with reverence, as the mother church of every Methodist congregation in the city.

105 Church of St. George the Martyr, John Street (1844), Henry Bower Lane, architect. Robertson describes St. George's as one of Toronto's oldest. It was built on land given by Mr. and Mrs. D'Arcy Boulton in the "first west end Anglican parish." The total cost was $24,000. A tragic fire in 1955 destroyed the church except for its graceful tower which stands today, alone on a green lawn, a picturesque reminder of old Toronto.

106 St. John's York Mills (1843), John G. Howard, architect. This church is not Howard at his best, but it stands on one of the most commanding sites in Toronto, and behind it, to the east, the "rude forefathers of the hamlet sleep." A change in the neighbourhood from simple village to expensive suburb finds an echo in the interior which is an interesting commentary on the taste of our time. Even so, when one stands at the front door looking west across the valley on a summer's evening, one seems to breathe the authentic air of Upper Canada when the bricks of St. John's were yellow, and the noise of horses' hoofs was barely audible in the dust of Yonge Street.

107 Bank of Montreal, northwest corner of Yonge and Front streets (1845), Kivas Tully, architect (demolished). To the left is the Customs House (1876). The bank was built in the manner of a London town house or gentleman's club. There would likely be a board room on the second floor in the very commodious quarters of the manager and his family. Its date coincides with the formation of the Toronto Board of Trade. Another Bank of Montreal occupies the same site. (see **310-12**)

108 Bank of British North America, corner of Yonge and Wellington streets (1845), J. G. Howard, architect, (demolished). This bank was greatly admired in its day, and its design, according to Scadding, was "preferred by the directors in London to those sent in by several architects there." The Royal Arms were copied from those on the Bank of England, and the scallop-shell on the parapet was a device introduced by Sir John Soane, the architect of the Bank in London, to suggest the "gold-digger's occupation."

109, 110 City Hall, corner of Front and Jarvis streets (1844), Henry Bower Lane, architect. A probable architect of Osgoode Hall in 1844, and the undoubted designer of the two Trinity churches, was the author of this old town hall, built at a cost of $52,000. It is true the west elevation bears no relation to the front, but few would agree with W. H. Smith in *Canada: Past, Present and Future*, "This is a very strange-looking building, and it is unfortunate for the reputation of the architect employed that he had not left the Province *before* he completed the design instead of *afterwards*." When a new City Hall was built in 1890, the old one became part of the Toronto market with some of the arches still visible on Front Street. The very fine south side, or rear (**110**) can still be seen from inside the market.

108

109

110

111 Nos. 25, 29, 31 and 33 Lowther Avenue. Yorkville is still a desirable and stable residential district, but nothing remains of the old village as typical as these houses. They do not demonstrate the qualities once found in our old terraces, qualities of rhythm and dignity that were achieved through continuity, but individually they are arresting on a street of rather nondescript houses.

111

whose present identity is shrouded in some mystery. He will be examined later. As the city grew in wealth and position, buildings arose that called for the skills of men who were not only master builders, but who were trained in the art of architecture. All were educated at the height of the Romantic movement which produced buildings in Britain as varied in style as the Houses of Parliament at Westminster which were Gothic, and the British Museum which was impeccably and, undeniably, Greek.

Nowadays, lack of conviction on the part of an architect is considered an unpardonable sin, but in Toronto from, say 1834, it was regarded, more than likely, as versatility and something to be commended. Whatever it was, it produced many delightful buildings of which not the least is Trinity Church, sometimes called Little Trinity, on King Street East.

When John Ross Robertson wrote of Trinity in 1898, he described it as weatherbeaten, and the walls "dingy with the dust and dirt of many years." Even then, the district had deteriorated. In our day, it has not improved, but one would go far to find a congregation more loyal to the church they love. Its congregation may not be as wealthy as that of Holy Trinity, but, in its great days, the Gooderham and Worts families were generous supporters, and the Chief Justice, John Beverley Robinson, gave a ten-acre lot on the Kingston Road for the rector's income.

An interesting tablet records the service of the first pastor, the Rev. Wm. Honeywood Ripley, who, for six years, served the church "without money and without price." He was also classical master at Upper Canada College, and died in 1849 in his thirty-fourth year. For economy's sake, the twenty-four burner gaselier used to be turned low during the sermon, putting the congregation "into the hazy mystery

112

112 The Schoolhouse (1848), the first free school in Toronto, was the gift of Enoch Turner, a wealthy brewer. It is situated on Trinity Street just south of Little Trinity Church. It was restored in 1972 and was officially opened by His Excellency the Rt. Hon. Roland Michener on 15 November 1972. Children from several Metro schools come five days a week, sitting on old benches, using old slates, and experiencing the atmosphere and teaching of a schoolroom of a century and a quarter ago. Instruction is by volunteers from the Junior League. Architects for the restoration were Nightingale and Quigley.

113, 114 Little Trinity, King Street East (1843), Henry Bower Lane, architect. This church can be compared with two other Gothic churches by Lane, St. George's (**105**) and Holy Trinity (**119, 120**). The large photograph (**113**) shows the main entrance on King Street; the date is carved in the two shields that act as terminals to the bold label mould.

114

113

115–117 Mental Asylum, 999 Queen Street West (1846–49), John Howard, architect; surrounding wall, F. W. Cumberland, architect. In 1844, architects were invited to compete for a prize of £30 for the new Lunatic Asylum. Mr. Howard was the successful competitor, and the building was built under his direction. His handwritten specifications are in the possession of the superintendent of the Asylum. Quite frightening in size today, this institution must have seemed enormous when seen from the lake front or from Queen St. in 1846 (see sketch **116**). Up to 1900, it was considered the best-ventilated mental institution in North America though it was a legend that a furnace in the dome drew air and odours from wards through vitreous tile pipes. Hardly visible in the interior of the dome (**117**) is the rim of an immense tank, but there is no sign of a furnace. One wonders why so striking a spiral stair was needed to reach the quite inhospitable cupola on the dome. It is really only a piece of theatrical scenery, but it has all the fascination of a set in which Orson Welles might have played a part. The building is now (1973) undergoing major reconstruction and nothing of Howard's façade or the dome and its fantastic stairs will remain. Present architects, Somerville, McMurrich and Oxley.

115

of semi-darkness, a condition very favourable for napping or little social amenities." The exterior is in the perpendicular Gothic manner with five aisle windows and a well-proportioned tower in no need of the spire originally intended for it.

A fire in 1960 nearly proved disastrous, and for a time many must have feared that Trinity would share the fate of St. George the Martyr on John St. One is happy to record that it is safe, and that the restoration was in the capable hands of Mr. F. Hilton Wilkes.

The Church of the Holy Trinity and its site on Trinity Square have a romantic history. The site was once occupied by Teraulay Cottage, the home of the family

116

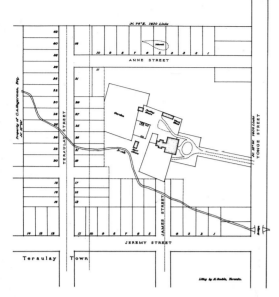

118 Property of the Hon. John Simcoe Macaulay, who gave the "most eligible site" in the district, known as Macaulay's fields, for Holy Trinity. The plan shows Teraulay Cottage and the building lots on adjacent streets in 1845. Anne Street became Alice and then Teraulay; Jeremy was a Macaulay family name.

119 Original plan of Holy Trinity, signed by H. B. Lane, architect (1846). It shows some alterations in pencil, particularly the extension of the chancel into the nave, which was done.

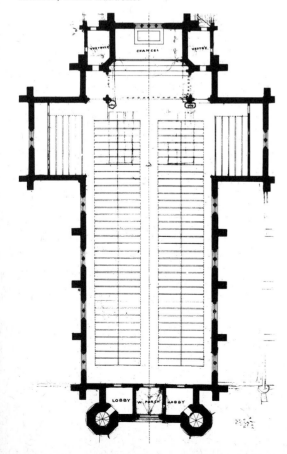

of Macaulay who have played no small part in the long history of Toronto, and the church was the gift of an anonymous lady who had never visited Toronto. But to begin with the site. In 1797, Dr. James Macaulay, surgeon of the Queen's Rangers, received a Crown grant of one hundred acres in an area where the principal boundaries were the west side of Yonge, Bloor, and Queen. Early in the century, he laid out the southerly portion as a residential subdivision and named it Macaulay town—a "suburb" of York far removed from the town proper. As a centre and focus of the community, he built Teraulay Cottage, a house that was to become famous in the social life of York, and was destined, nearly half a century later, to be moved bodily to make room for Holy Trinity.

The church was built in 1847, but, only twelve years earlier, the land south of Macaulay Lane (now Louisa) was known as the "fields," and behind, as far as the eye could see, were "treacherous swamps and tangled forest."[8] Scadding records that Mr. Justice Boulton travelling in his own vehicle took half a day to cover the distance between the Don and Teraulay Cottage. By 1847, when Col. John Simcoe Macaulay made a gift of the land necessary for the church, Teraulay Cottage was moved to the corner of Louisa and the present James Street.

It was in 1845 that Bishop Strachan received a gift of £5,000 for the building and maintenance of a church, the only stipulations being that it be called "the Church of the Holy Trinity," "the seats of which to be free and unappropriated forever." It was also stipulated that £3,000 was to be spent on the building and £2,000 on an investment for the incumbent. It was not until 1898 that the donor was known to be Mrs. Lambert Swale of Settle, near Ripon, in Yorkshire. During her lifetime, this unknown benefactress supplied the church with "silver sacramental plate for public use and smaller service for private ministration," as well as "a large supply of fair linen, a covering of Genoa velvet for the altar and surplices for the clergy."

In 1847, Bishop Strachan published a notice inviting "the poor families of the United Church of England and Ireland to make the church their own," and another announcing the opening for service of the "Parochial Church of the Poor of Toronto." In spite of what they say, these advertisements were not intended to restrict the congregation to a single financial or social group. It was merely that the deed of gift had to be observed, and the Church of the Holy Trinity became the first Anglican church in Toronto where pews were free. It has also been suggested that the character of Holy Trinity was determined from a fear that many good Anglicans, not appreciating the high pew rents of St. James or the social atmosphere which dominated the Cathedral, might have been driven into the bosom of the Presbyterian or Methodist church. In view of the political and emotional atmosphere in the Anglican church in the thirties and forties, one can imagine with what misgivings the congregation of Holy Trinity invited the pew-holders of St. James to worship with them after the disastrous fire to the Cathedral of 1849. This *mariage de convenance* lasted for two years, and was not without friction.

Henry Bower Lane was commissioned by the Bishop to design the church. He will be remembered in Toronto as the probable architect of part of Osgoode Hall, and as the undoubted author of Little Trinity, St. George's, and the City Hall of 1844. If, at first glance, one would not judge Holy Trinity to be his best work, one has to remember how different is the setting today. The main entrance to the west

120

121

120 Holy Trinity, in 1907, when excavations were being dug by hand for Eaton's mail order building.

121, 122 Home of Dr. Henry Scadding, 10 Trinity Square (*c.* 1861), Wm. Hay, architect. It was in this cheerful looking town house that Dr. Scadding wrote his famous *Toronto of Old*, a reservoir from which Robertson and all succeeding writers have drawn. It would seem like poetic licence to describe the study in the roof, today, as an eyrie, but from his library in the fifties, Dr. Scadding could once gaze on the city that he loved, and, through spires and towers, could see the Island to the south and "Lake Ontario down to Scarborough Bluffs." The library balcony has gone, the glazing bars are missing from the windows, and the view which once extended for miles is now limited to a few feet.

While Toronto has lost most of its historic buildings of undoubted architectural merit, some survive as miracles. In the plans for the vast Eaton development of the Trinity area, it seemed doubtful indeed that Scadding's house would survive. It will, though moved, and the library window and balcony will, we hope, not be neglected.

122

looks on bleak factory walls, and Trinity Square is but a euphemism for truck-filled lanes. Even in his day, the church looked to John Ross Robertson "like some giant entombed" among the skyscrapers that surround it.

Alice Street to the north has gone, but we can still enjoy one side of the approach from Yonge. Near the church is the old rectory, and, closer to Yonge, the home of the late Rev. Dr. Henry Scadding. It is tragic that this house no longer belongs to the church. If history, sentiment, and architectural merit have any meaning, the Scadding house should be preserved as a civic monument.

Today, the church is known for the beauty of its service, and, particularly, for a Christmas play which gives pleasure annually to hundreds. The furnishing of the nave is of a puritanical severity. No cushions take away from the austerity of the pews which are plain boards polished by use and divided by inch-high mouldings into spaces which provide quite generously for the average Anglican worshipper. Unfortunately, this carefully planned module can get out of step when the church is crowded, and the worshipper may sit with something less than rapt attention as he balances on a moulding. Near the small east door facing Yonge Street is a room of considerable interest to students of education in Canada. The story goes back to 1857 when a parochial school was added to the church with a classroom for boys on the ground floor, and one for girls on the second. There were, apparently, fewer girls because the space above was divided into classroom and "winter chapel." Eight years later, the Bishop gave up the struggle in which the issue was church or state in the education of the young of Upper Canada. It was then, or shortly after, that all of the upper floor was devoted to a quite beautiful chapel rarely seen by visitors, with open timber roof and faded decoration over what was once the altar of the winter chapel.

In 1963, we live in an atmosphere in which large-scale planning and redevelopment are not only considered desirable, but also practical. It may, therefore, not be an unrealizable prayer for the Church of the Holy Trinity that a drastic scheme of reconstruction will some day restore order, dignity, and nature back to this "haunt of ancient peace."

There would seem to be no continuous link in the work of the Church of Rome between the Mission at the Rouge, with the Abbé Fénelon and Father d'Urfé, and 1801, when it became the custom for French priests on their way to Detroit to hold services in the houses of citizens of York. Sporadic meetings of this kind continued until 1822 when St. Paul's was built on Power Street, south of the modern St. Paul's (1887) on Queen Street.[9] For some time during the episcopate of Bishop Power, St. Paul's was the cathedral church of the Toronto diocese, and adjacent to it was the first Roman Catholic cemetery.

It is pleasant to record that when a "drive" was made to reduce the debt on St. Paul's in 1829, the collectors were the Solicitor-General, the Honourable W. W. Baldwin, Mr. Simon Washburn and Lt.-Col. James Fitz-Gibbon, all of whom were Anglicans.[10]

And so, we come to St. Michael's Cathedral. One likes to think of cathedrals facing great squares like the Piazza of St. Mark's or St. Peter's, or being surrounded by landscaped grounds that themselves take on a religious atmosphere quite as pervading as that within the sacred precinct itself. Fifty years ago, St. Michael's

123 Oakham House at the corner of Church and Gould streets (1848), Wm. Thomas, architect. Cumberland, Lennox and Thomas are the only architects in the last hundred years and more who have been able to build houses for themselves on anything like the scale of this one. (Lennox's house does not come into the period of this book, but it lies to the west of Casa Loma, as a Roman Catholic institution.) It will always be a puzzle that a man who could design so well in the Greek Revival manner would do his own house (perhaps on the fees from St. Michael's) in a very fake Gothic with heraldic beasts, coats of arms and the two mongrel red dogs at the portal. For some time, the house was a home for boys. The interior has, unfortunately, been changed beyond recognition. The building is now part of the Ryerson Polytechnical Institute.

had such space and trees, but today it is hemmed in by streets to the west, south, and east, and on Bond Street by quite incompatible ecclesiastical buildings to the north.

The Cathedral is supposed to have some kinship architecturally with York Cathedral, but a close examination by this writer has failed to see the connexion unless it be the slight one of a large window over the west door which, in York, is between two towers. Unchallengeable though invisible, however, are the stone fragments from a pier and the piece of oak from the roof of York Cathedral which are contained in a leaden box set in the wall behind the foundation stone.

That exceedingly able William Thomas who designed at least eight Toronto churches[11] was the architect in 1845, and one wonders how his influence could have so waned by 1866 that Messrs. Gundry and Langley were asked to add the tower and spire. Something very strange must have occurred because, in the same year, Mr. Thomas himself prepared a design and made working drawings of a tower and spire, the originals of which are in the Toronto Public Library. At a later date, certainly after 1870, the Gothic dormers were added by the Langley firm. Dormers on a cathedral roof must be exceedingly rare, and the light that is admitted to the nave is negligible.

The interior of St. Michael's is very impressive, columns are light in design and tone and the ceiling is rich with colour, but the visitor who likes to wander down

125 Oakham House, the main entrance, once flanked by crouching dogs.

126 St. Michael's Cathedral, the Bishop's Chair. When Thomas designed this chair, he certainly had in mind a prince of the church at a most exalted level. It is unfortunate that it lost its place in the sanctuary during changes made in this century. Happily, however, it is preserved in a lower, but not undignified region of the cathedral.

127

those byways of history that are recorded in plaques and monuments will be disappointed. There are none.

As early as 1791, Colonel Simcoe had discussed with the President of the Royal Society in England the "desirability of a college of a higher class" in the colony to which he had been appointed. For many years, the most modest proposal would have been impracticable because of the sparseness of the population though Gourlay's scheme (1819) of sending twenty-five students annually to Oxford and Cambridge would have met a very great need. By 1829, we know that Bishop Strachan had engaged Thomas Fowler of London to design a university for York because,

128

127–129 St. Michael's Cathedral, Bond and Shuter streets (1845). Wm. Thomas, who contributed so much to Toronto's 19th century architecture, was the original designer. For some reason he transferred his practice to Montreal, and Henry Langley then became the architect for the tower and spire and the wooden dormers. To the left (**127**) is the façade. The nave (**128**) is the work of Thomas except for changes in the clerestory to the sanctuary. **129** is another view of the interior, looking west to the organ loft; particularly noteworthy here is the refinement of detail in the nave piers and in those supporting the loft. The arches supporting the gallery carry refinement to the point of suggesting wood rather than stone. Further research, for which I am indebted to Father Crummer of St. Michael's, makes the connexion between the cathedral in Toronto and the one in York even closer (see text page 87). Two heads flanking the main doorway are that of Paulinus (died 644) on the left and of King Edwin (585–633) on the right. Paulinus, the first bishop of the Northumbrians and archbishop of York, was consecrated in 625. In 627, he baptized King Edwin who built a wooden church and, later, began one in stone in York.

For note on the stone used in the cathedral see **190**.

129

on March 9th of that year, Fowler sent the Bishop his bill, one would assume on account, for £15. In sending the remittance, His Lordship wrote "we have long been anxious for your plans, etc., as well as the model. . . . I am quite happy to find that you are so much occupied, and have the building of Covent Gardens' Market committed to your care. . . ." To this Fowler, probably greatly disturbed, replied on August 5, 1830, from Gordon Square,

MY DEAR SIR: It is now just twelve months since I forwarded to you that case containing the Model etc., of the proposed university, and I have not yet had any direct intelligence of its safe arrival; but I presume that it was so—If you have not written to me (for I thought it propible [*sic*] that a letter might have miscarried) I attribute it to your being so fully occupied—and to the want of any decision upon the Plans; but if it will not be intruding too much on your time I shall be very glad if you will favor me with some account however brief; for Mr. McGillvray having gone to Mexico, I have no authentic source of intelligence for Canadian affairs. . . . To revert to your University, I shall always feel interested to know the progress you make, being aware that you have many difficulties and much opposition to encounter, but which I doubt not your firmness and good judgment will ultimately surmount. . . .[12]

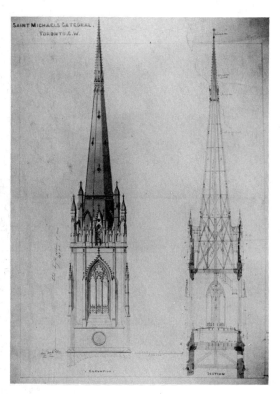

130 Wm. Thomas's rejected design for the tower and spire of St. Michael's Cathedral, sent by him from Montreal. It is a confused piece of work and inferior to that of Langley.

131 Henry Langley's accepted design for the tower and spire of St. Michael's, 1865.

Present research fails to unearth the model and drawings, or to show why the scheme was abandoned. Abandoned, however, it was in favour of a design for a university by Mr. Thomas Young. It was called King's College, and its corner-stone was laid in 1842. The universities of Great Britain are, generally, of two kinds: those ancient seats of learning whose roots go back to the Middle Ages, and those later "red brick" institutions, born in the dirt and smoke of the industrial

133

132

132, 133 Bishop's Palace, Church Street (1845), Wm. Thomas, architect. This is one of the best remaining examples of Victorian Gothic. Built in grey Toronto brick with stone facings, it is a very suitable adjunct to the Cathedral in the same materials. The central gable (**133**) shows Thomas's mastery of Gothic detail. Two heads closer to our time than those of Paulinus and King Edwin (see **127**) are those of the architect and of Bishop Power which appear as corbels to the arch of the doorway (**132**). Thomas's admirers will recall his beautiful St. Thomas's Church in Hamilton.

cities of the late 19th century. The University of Toronto had its birth in neither period, and it is unlikely that any college corner-stone was laid with such colour and such pomp. The event took place on St. George's Day, and Henry Scadding tells us that "a procession such as had never before been seen in these parts" slowly marched up College Avenue to the site of the new University building in Queen's Park, with the soldiers of the 43rd Regiment, bearing arms, lining the route. At a given signal,

The vast procession opened its ranks and his Excellency the Chancellor, with the President, the Lord Bishop of Toronto, on his right, and the Senior Visitor, the Chief Justice, on his left, proceeded on foot through the College Avenue to the University grounds. The countless array moved forward to the sound of military music. The sun shone out with cloudless meridian splendour; one blaze of banners flushed [sic] upon the admiring eye.—The Governor's rich Lord-Lieutenant's dress, the Bishop's sacerdotal robes, the Judicial Ermine of the Chief Justice, the splendid Convocation robes of Dr. McCaul, the gorgeous uniforms of the suite, the accoutrements of the numerous Firemen, . . . the Red Crosses on the breasts of England's congregated sons, the grave habiliments of the Clergy and

134 King's College (1842), Thomas Young, architect. This Athenian building occupied a commanding site at the head of University Avenue where the Legislature now stands.

Lawyers, and the glancing lances and waving plumes of the First Incorporated Dragoons, all formed one moving picture of civic pomp, one glorious spectacle which can never be remembered but with satisfaction by those who had the good fortune to witness it.

Finally, at the site, the Chancellor, Sir Charles Bagot, the Governor-General, accompanied by the officers of the University and his suite, took his place in a pavilion erected for the purpose. "Fronting this was an amphitheatre of seats, . . . densely filled with ladies. . . ." Between the pavilion and the amphitheatre the crowd stood.[13]

The King's College that Young designed was a quite extensive complex of buildings of which only a portion was completed. Even so, its life was short, and the need for a larger university was answered in 1857, not by enlarging King's, but by the building of University College. Like Victoria College in Cobourg at a later date, King's was found to be admirably suited to the primitive 19th century requirements of a mental institution.

135 Osgoode Hall. The principal façade with the earlier wing on the right. Materials, brick (various) and Ohio sandstone.

Architecturally, one feels the cold hand of archaeology in the Greek revival detail of the College, and none of the spirit that made the old Commercial Bank so lively a neighbour for everything new or old on Wellington Street.

Of even greater significance than King's College in the architectural development of Toronto was the building of Osgoode Hall. We know that in the 19th century the Hall went through three stages of construction: in 1829, 1844, and 1857. We have ample documentary proof that Cumberland and Storm were responsible for the last major change in 1857, but for many years the designs of 1829 and 1844 were attributed to Hopkins, Lawford and Nelson of Montreal. It is likely that they would still be given credit, but for recent very painstaking research on the part of Professor John Bland of McGill University, who has cast considerable doubt on their connexion with the Hall at any stage of its development.[14]

In the history of Osgoode Hall, the Montreal firm's name first appears in James Cleland Hamilton's *Osgoode Hall, Reminiscences of the Bench and Bar*, published in

137 A less elaborate cow-gate.

136 Osgoode Hall, cow-gate in the south fence. In an older Toronto, cows had to be kept from the lush grass within the fence, and the device shown in the photograph proved effective. The fixed opening is only twenty inches.

138 Osgoode Hall, plan of ground floor.

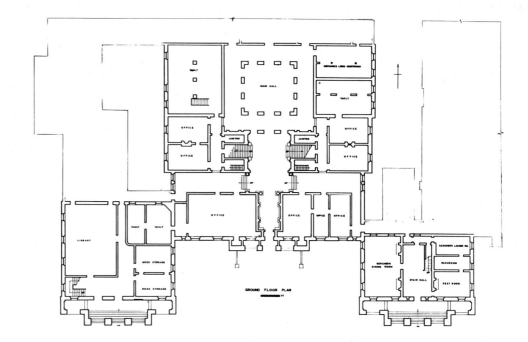

139 Osgoode Hall, plan of first floor.

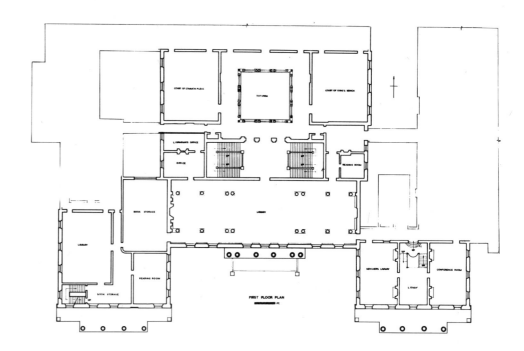

1904. In it, he shows a water colour of the Queen Street façade, signed by Hopkins, Lawford and Nelson, and other writers including myself have assumed from this drawing and Hamilton's acceptance of it that the Montreal architects were responsible for a grand scheme going back to 1844 if not to 1829.[15] In view of the later evidence, we can do so no longer. The senior member of the firm, Mr. J. W. Hopkins, was the first president of the Province of Quebec Association of Architects in 1891. He was born in England on September 9, 1825, and died in Montreal on December 11, 1905. That he was four years old in 1829 and nineteen in 1844, would seem to put him out of the running for building in both those years. We can only conclude with Professor Bland that Hopkins' water colour represented his firm's design for the major reconstruction in 1857 and that it incorporated as much as possible of the old building of 1844.

Other matters are fortunately not open to question. The Law Society had considered building as early as 1820 with a budget not to exceed £500. Nothing was done until 1825 when the government was asked for a grant in aid, and the members were able to pledge £2,000 towards the erection of the building. The first site selected was Russell Square (eventually the site of Upper Canada College), but that was abandoned in favour of the present property which the Society purchased from the Attorney-General, Mr. John Beverley Robinson, for £1,000.

Before discussing the design of the building, it would be comfortable to be able to come to some decision as to what was done at what stage. Unfortunately, the problem is not like the detective story where all possible villains are known to the reader, and only a hint from the author is necessary for him to make up his mind. The east wing, about which there is some confusion as to authorship, was begun in 1829 and finished in 1832. John Ritchie (Ritchey or Richey) was the builder, and

141 The Benchers' dining room.

140 Osgoode Hall, the entrance hall in the old east wing. The door just seen on the left leads to the Benchers' dining room.

John Ewart the superintendent on the job. Historians and others have for long thought of the wing as looking today very much as it did in 1829, except for the mellow patina on stone and the weathered bricks which show a reddish bloom through an ancient coating of grey paint. But, as so many things about the Hall since 1829 are in doubt, we must take seriously John Ross Robertson's statement that the east wing was "a plain square matter-of-fact brick building two and a half stories in height."[16] A more inapt description of the east wing, as we know it, could hardly be imagined, and we can only assume that, if true, the Ionic portico was added at the same time as the west one of 1844, and did not precede it. We know that, two years after the erection of the east block which had included bedrooms in the attic, "twenty-four comfortable bed chambers" were added in a wing to the west under what is now the great library. This may have been a temporary structure, or one structurally sound enough to take another storey.

There would seem to be only two serious contenders for the honour of designing the earliest part of Osgoode Hall, whether a plain brick building or the

142 Osgoode Hall, detail of a window in the Benchers' library. The panels in the reveals are hinged and open as inside shutters. The same excellent craftsmanship persisted right through the century (see the York Club, 349).

143 Landing of the stair (east wing). The dome appears on the upper floor.

scholarly piece of classic architecture that we see today, and they are Chewett and Ewart. Chewett was the architect employed on the "new parliament buildings," and it was he who designed Upper Canada College and occupied the honourable post of Surveyor-General. In addition, he was a member of the building committee of St. James. Professor Bland draws attention to the interesting coincidence that Ritchie, the builder of St. James as well as Osgoode Hall, was a fellow member of the committee along with Mr. D'Arcy Boulton, the Solicitor-General, who, we can assume, would be not uninterested or uninfluential in any proposals for Osgoode Hall.

Even so, our more likely contender is John Ewart. With Dr. Baldwin, he is said to have drawn the plans for the Court House and second jail;[17] and he was the architect for St. Andrew's Church. We may leave Ewart in the rather sound position somewhere between Judge Hamilton's "Mr. John Ritchie was the builder and Mr. John Ewart seems to have superintended the work" and the Law Society's records, 1829–1830, which "confirm that Ewart was regarded as the architect."

145 One of the two fireplaces in the Benchers' Library. The cast-iron fire-back is of the finest design and craftsmanship. The central part is removable. The bust on the mantel is that of John Douglas Armour and the portrait is of the Hon. Edward Blake, who was Treasurer from 1879 to 1893.

144 Osgoode Hall, the dome in the "attic." Once a floor given up to student bedrooms, it is now reserved for storage in book stacks. The curved ceiling, panelled window and neat balustrade all indicate that the "attic" was not neglected in its furnishings.

In fact, at the conclusion of the work, it was recorded that he "has fully justified" the confidence reposed in him by the Society.[18]

We then come to 1844, an important stage in the history of the Hall. Its appearance at that time may be judged from two not dissimilar drawings, an engraving and a water colour. The engraving was published in *Smith's Canadian Gazetteer* and while it is undated it bears the names in the lower left-hand corner of H. B.

146 An engraving of Osgoode Hall, with the names H. B. Lane, Arct.F., and F. C. Lowe, Sc., published in *Smith's Canadian Gazetteer* in 1846. In 1972–1973, Osgoode Hall underwent an overhaul quite as important as those of 1844 and 1854, except that there were no major changes in the exterior, though that has been cleaned to everyone's satisfaction. Internal changes involved an increase in the number of courtrooms from 5 to 10, and in the number of judge's chambers, from 33 to 49. Cost of the work is in the neighbourhood of $7,000,000. Architects, Page and Steele; Eric Arthur, consultant.

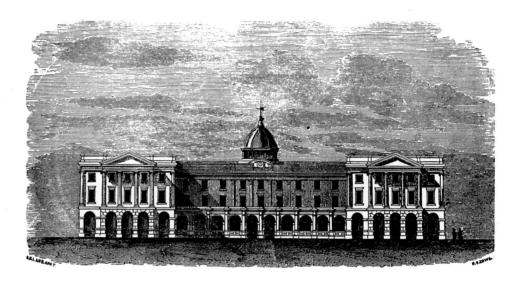

Lane, Arct.F., and in the lower right, F. C. Lowe, Sc. Lane's name is sufficient evidence of date because he was in Toronto between the critical years for the Hall of 1840–1847.

The façade shown in the *Gazetteer* engraving differs in several respects from the water colour. In the former, the building is terminated at the skyline by a high parapet where, in the latter, a hipped roof appears behind a balustraded parapet of modest dimensions. There are differences, too, of detail in the domes. Hopkins' is the more impressive and the more effective as the crowning feature of the whole composition. The octagonal drum, or base of the dome, has attached columns at

147 A water colour drawing of Osgoode Hall signed by Hopkins, Lawford and Nelson, architects, Montreal.

the corners and the "apex" is marked in contrast with the vane on the engraving by the sculptured figure of a woman.

In common with both is an arcaded screen so spaced as to necessitate the placing of a column at its centre. This would be considered a solecism by 18th century purists and, probably, before that by Vitruvius himself, but a good deal of the charm of Osgoode comes from a certain freedom from those classical canons which reduced so much late 18th century architecture to mere academic exercises. In the reconstruction of 1857, the screen was lost, but its location can still be determined by masonry changes in the walls of the two wings.

We can now return to those fascinating, but somehow shadowy figures, the architects who performed on the Toronto stage in the thirties and forties of last century. Undoubtedly, one of them designed Osgoode Hall in something like the manner we see in the water colour or the engraving. Was it H. B. Lane whose name appears on the *Gazetteer* engraving? We have that as evidence of a sort as well as Mr. Kivas Tully's recollection "that Mr. Lane, an English architect then in Toronto was in some way engaged at this time."[19] We know more of Lane than of many of his contemporaries. Colvin's *Biographical Dictionary of English Architects, 1660–1840* mentions a "Lane H. (c. 1787–   ) a pupil of Wm. Inwood," who entered the Royal Academy Schools in 1808 at the age of 21. "He exhib. at the Academy Schools from 1808–1810, and appears to have begun practice in the latter year."

If this Englishman, Henry Bower Lane, was the one who signed the engraving of 1846, we are faced with a quite remarkable individual. At the age of fifty-three (1840), he left a practice built up over thirty years to emigrate to Canada. His subsequent success would indicate that he was a person not without charm or a reputation for ability in his profession because, before he returned to England in 1847, he had designed St. George's on John Street, the graceful Little Trinity on King Street East, the Church of the Holy Trinity, and the City Hall of 1844 on Front Street. Toronto owes much to Henry Bower Lane, but are those Gothic churches and the not too successful essay in classical design which marks the City Hall evidence enough for the critic that Lane was capable of the elegant and, at the same time, scholarly architecture of Osgoode Hall? For this writer they are not, but later research into the origin of the *Gazetteer* engraving may prove him wrong. At the moment, it is the strongest if, also, the most unsatisfactory authority for so honouring his memory.

One other character swaggers across the Osgoode stage. He was that John G. Howard, the drawing master at Upper Canada College, who, as an architect, concerns us now for his well-documented connexion with Osgoode Hall. In his diary for 1837, that momentous year in Toronto's history, he wrote: "made great alterations and additions to the Court of the King's Bench." Everything about the architectural origin of Osgoode Hall is so full of conjecture and surmise, that we can seize with pleasure on the words "alterations and additions," inasmuch as they indicate changes in an already existing room of some importance. It is therefore with pleasure that we learn with certainty of J. G. Howard's connexion with the building at so early a date. His diary is equally explicit, if cryptic, in a sentence in 1843 where he writes: "Laid out the grounds in front of Osgoode Hall."

Neither the published diary (1885), nor recently discovered drawings (1960) show any other connexion between Howard and the Hall. His previous work on the Court of the King's Bench and his commission as a landscape architect in 1843 would seem to put him in an enviable position for the great commission of 1844, but he and history are, alike, silent on the matter. We know of the high regard with which he was held as a citizen, but perhaps less well known was the esteem with which he was regarded by the Law Society of Upper Canada. By 1853, we find the former master at Upper Canada College to be a bencher and a justice of the peace for the united counties of York and Peel who could record with pardonable pride: "I had the honour of sitting on the bench for four years with Chief Justice Robinson, Judge McLean and Judge Richards."[20]

Even in the abridged published version, the diary is extremely valuable, and the entry for June 15, 1842, brings two of our actors briefly together. "W. H. Boulton, Esq., introduced Mr. Lane, architect, wishing me to take him in partnership, but I declined." Perhaps the very absence of reference in the diary to the Hall in 1844 is

148 Osgoode Hall, the Fireplace and the Great Library with portrait of Sir John Beverley Robinson.

sufficient to remove Howard as a contender. He was busy enough in that year with many small jobs as well as the gigantic project which we now know as 999 Queen Street, and he accounted for every hour of the day in his journal.

In 1857, a major reconstruction took place in Osgoode Hall in which the central section was changed beyond all resemblance to the building of 1844. Cumberland and Storm were the architects, and few were more competent. Like their confrères in the rest of the English-speaking world, they were eclectics who could design in Gothic, Greek, or Roman as the mood indicated or the client demanded. Books of classical designs were available to them,[21] and yet the design they produced for the centre has the same faults as its predecessor. It is true the main cornice is continuous, but the band course and the base below ignore the wings, and the new windows are totally unrelated to the old. In short, the new centre is a frontispiece of Caen stone that seems to have been inserted without apology or acknowledgments of any kind to the graceful pavilions of 1829 or 1844.

Of the new front, this writer wrote in 1952 that "the impression one gets of the

149 The Great Library, Osgoode Hall, looking west (1857).

centre part is French, against wings that are as British as St. Paul's Cathedral."[22] Quite recently, Professor Henry Hitchcock confirmed that impression by showing views of Osgoode against the garden front of the palace at Versailles. The similarity of fenestration, the high parapet, and the urns silhouetted against the sky were quite striking.

Behind most of the new façade on the second floor is the Great Library. Thought of only as a room, it is one of the finest in Canada. Cumberland may have read in his *British Architectural Antiquities* of the so-called magic of the double cube room in the Queen's House at Greenwich and at Wilton. He went one better in proportions almost equal to a triple cube. According to Hamilton, the Great Library is 112 feet long by 40 feet wide and 40 feet to the top of the vaulted ceiling. Detail, generally, is classic, but Cumberland's catholic taste permitted him the luxury of a flamboyant fireplace of colossal scale and doubtful historic parentage. Two criticisms may be levelled against the library. As a reading room, it takes the full glare of the sun and as a library, it was not designed to house books. Oak bookcases of the post-Cumberland period cut the great Corinthian pilasters off in their middles or their necks in a way that would horrify the Man of Taste.

Of the same date as the library are the ground floor vestibule, stairs and rotunda, all of which are so competently handled as to give the sense of space one would associate with a much larger building. Scadding was not exaggerating when he likened the interior to a Genoese Renaissance palace.

The traditional hall of the French (and Ottawa) Courts of Justice is the "salle des pas perdus." No footsteps are lost in the halls of Osgoode. A tile is used of unpleasant colour, pattern, texture, and design, and the visitor, awed by the ever present majesty of the law and the classical grandeur that surrounds him, is appalled by the noise he makes. It is rather like the cloppety-clop of the horses in Grofe's Grand Canyon Suite.

With all its faults, Osgoode Hall ranks highest, in the estimation of this writer

152 Spiral cast-iron stair in book storage room.

151 View of a series of halls leading to the grand staircase from the front door which faces Queen Street.

154

153 Osgoode Hall, view from Upper Rotunda.
Scadding was so right when he wrote that this view
reminded him of a Genoese palace. Sunlight from the
roof and the sides adds a radiance to the interior,
and emphasizes the perspective of halls and
staircases leading from it.

154 Court of King's Bench.

155 The great staircase.

155

156 Landing of the main staircase with entrance to the
Library on the left.

among the historic buildings still left to us in Toronto. It cannot be entirely sentiment or a sense of history that draws one to it because strangers have admired it. Is it because Osgoode is something of an anachronism, a relic of a distant past reposing peacefully on its equally ancient lawns? Osgoode is already dominated physically by surrounding colossi, and will shortly have as a neighbour the towering walls of the new City Hall. It will never be dominated spiritually. We are left with the conclusion that Osgoode Hall has a personality sufficiently persuasive and powerful to overcome in the spectator any adverse conclusions he may have reached on solely architectural grounds. To submit to such a conclusion in defiance of aesthetic judgment is in the nature of a confession, especially for an architect, but this writer is prepared to accept it.

157 Osgoode Hall, the west side of the gallery which surrounds the rotunda on the second floor.

158 John Shaw's Hotel (1835) near the Woodbine on the Kingston Road (demolished). Robertson says it was brick, always painted white with green shutters.

160 Kearnsey House, 591 Yonge Street (1848) (demolished). "Kearnsey" was built by Mr. William Proudfoot whose business at King and Frederick was in "wines, groceries and dry goods, wholesale and retail." He had the misfortune to be president of the Bank of Upper Canada at a time when it could be described as "an institution which in the infancy of the country had a mission and fulfilled it, but which grievously betrayed those of the second generation." It failed in 1866.
Even from the photograph one gets the impression of a large house, but it had a drawing room (75′×25′) that has not been approached in size by any house in this century.

157

158

159 Nos. 109, 111 Elizabeth Street. There can have been few cottages in Toronto with the classical pretensions of this one. The walls are a dazzling white, and the well detailed windows and dormers are a bright green. Equally pleasant is the play of light and shade under the eave. Was there always a store below?

160

161 The Jennings Church, southeast corner of Richmond and Bay streets (1848), Wm. Thomas, architect (demolished). The story is told that sometime in 1838 "seven members and twenty-one adherents of the United Succession Church of Scotland, met in a carpenter's shop on Newgate Street" (Adelaide) to talk over the formation of a congregation and the building of a kirk. Their first parson was the Rev. John Jennings and, with him, the congregation led a peripatetic existence, first in a Baptist and then in a Methodist chapel until they found a home in this little Gothic church. A minor miracle was recorded in the early sixties when, in a great wind, a pinnacle fell through the roof dislodging a nail which was impaled in a New Testament at Mark vii: 25, "and the winds blew, and beat upon that house, and it fell not; for it was founded upon a rock."

161

In none of its building periods does Osgoode show evidence of the eclecticism or the romanticism which, it was suggested, were characteristic of the period 1834–1867. In the whole history of architecture, dates of political significance rarely coincide with the beginnings or the ends of movements in architecture, but, in a general way, ours in Toronto do. We are examining the period when a quite shameless eclecticism was the order of the day, and our most successful architects had two or three styles readily on tap. When in doubt, as Cumberland may have been on the Normal School (1851), it was considered evidence of his virtuosity rather than his lack of conviction that he provided a Roman exterior for a Gothic interior. This was an exciting period in 19th century taste with styles ranging all the way from Greek to late Gothic.

162 Store of George Keith and Son, 124 King Street East (*c.* 1850). The store is remarkable now only for the very Greek detail of its doors which can be seen when closed. The threshold still shows the name of the original owner, Thomas D. Harris, ironmonger, whose first store was destroyed in the fire of 1849.

163–165 Normal and Model Schools, Gould Street (1851), F. W. Cumberland and Thomas Ridout, architects (demolished). We will see Cumberland in his Greek mood later (**169,199**); we now see him thumbing through some history of architecture from Roman to Gothic, using both in the Normal School. The old photograph shows a building two storeys high, the fine Roman centrepiece crowned by a cupola in appropriate classical detail. In the remodelling of 1896 (**165**), the heavy attic storey was added, the pediment raised, and the cupola converted into a fearsome thing—half classic, half Gothic. Perhaps to show the architects' virtuosity, the auditorium (**163**) was Gothic (with cast-iron arcading) from the beginning.

163

164 In the fast-moving building program of Ryerson Polytechnical Institute, which took over the Model School and St. James' Park, the beautiful little Gothic auditorium (163) was razed before public opinion could be aroused. A curious decision was to save the centre front with its pediment. It stands today like something in a surrealist painting – a stark façade with bricked-up rear and unglazed windows a focal point on the campus.

165

166

166, 167 House of Mr. William Cawthra at the north-east corner of King and Bay streets (1852). Joseph Sheard, architect (demolished). The foundation of the Cawthra fortune was a frame store at the northwest corner of King and Sherbourne streets. There, in 1806, Mr. Joseph Cawthra advertised the contents of his apothecary's shop which went far beyond the range of the seemingly irrelevant articles in the modern drugstore. He had, he announced, a wide variety of patent medicines "just arrived fron New York," but, in addition, 20,000 Whitechapel needles, forks, scissors, cognac, shoes and hats, and "a few Bed-Ticks." Mr. Cawthra's house was one of the best examples in Toronto of Greek revival architecture. When it was demolished some years ago to provide a site for the Bank of Nova Scotia head office, Mr. Anthony Adamson, a descendant of the original owner, removed sundry fragments of columns and ornaments to provide a "ruin" in his garden at Port Credit. The mantel from the drawing room (shown here) is also in the home of Mr. Adamson. It is unlikely that so finely detailed a mantel in wood, or any other material, could be executed in Toronto in 1852. It was probably imported.

167

168

It was equally exciting politically in ways not always conducive to civic expansion. Toronto bore the brunt of the rebellion of 1837 in Upper Canada, which culminated in the battle of Montgomery's tavern and the expulsion and exile of the city's first mayor, William Lyon Mackenzie. So serious a political upheaval must have caused many prospective builders to wait for better times, and, three years later, another blow was to affect the prestige of the city as the centre of government and to create an atmosphere of uncertainty that was to last for many years.

In both Upper and Lower Canada, there had long been disaffection because of the presence in each of vested interests and the domination of the ruling officialdom —the so-called "Family Compact" in Upper Canada and the "Château Clique" in Lower Canada. In Upper Canada, a principal source of irritation was the assumption by the Executive Council, and by John Strachan in particular, that the Clergy Reserves amounting to one-seventh of the lands granted in every township were the exclusive property of the Church of England. Whatever may have been

168–170 County of York, Magistrates' Court, 57 Adelaide Street (1852), Cumberland and Storm, architects. Cumberland could turn his hand to a variety of historic styles, and this was one of his two attempts at Greek. The front (**169**) is austere, heavy and forbidding, and not helped by the removal of the wings which once supported the central mass. One thinks immediately of the suggested epitaph for Sir John Vanbrugh, the architect of Blenheim Palace –"Lie heavy on him earth, he laid many a heavy load on thee." The rear, on Court Lane (**170**) has a pleasant brick façade.

The delicate and quite un-Greek stair (**168**) leads to the second floor where the Arts and Letters Club of Toronto met from 1910 in the old Assize court room. Certainly strange quarters for such a club, but there the members built the "great fireplace," and there in 1913, they entertained Sir Wilfrid Laurier. J. E. Middleton, R. L. Defries, George Locke, Eden Smith, Sir Edmund Walker, James Mavor, W. A. Langton, Charles Currelly, Sir. Wm. Mulock, the Rt. Hon. Vincent Massey, Dr. Healey Willan and Sir Ernest MacMillan were among the distinguished members who braved the perils of the stair and the "manure heap" on the ill-lit "Police Court Alley." Masonry: Ohio Sandstone.

169

170

171

171 A view of Adelaide Street (south side) looking east from Toronto Street. On the right is the Methodist church (1832) at the corner of Adelaide and Toronto streets. It was the predecessor of the Metropolitan church at Shuter and Church. Adjoining the church is the County of York Magistrates' Court House (1852), showing the wings which have since been removed.

172 Toronto, Canada West, from the top of the jail (c. 1854) by Edwin Whitefield. A nice Georgian town with an esplanade, and its water front as yet undefiled by railways or industry.

173 The Mechanics' Institute, northeast corner of Adelaide and Church streets (1854), Cumberland and Storm, architects. The Institute is better remembered as the first Toronto Public Library (1883). Externally, it was an undistinguished essay on the architects' part in the Renaissance manner. The parapet is fussy, and the juxtaposition of arches of varying diameters on the ground floor was anything but a happy arrangement. A music room on the first floor measured 75'×53'×35'. (Demolished)

the intention of the Act of 1791 which set aside these lands for the "Protestant Clergy," this term could by 1834, indeed long before, be taken to embrace more denominations than the so-called "Established Church," and it was not unnatural that these outsiders should demand a share of so valuable a prize.

Lord Durham was sent by the Government at home to report on conditions in the country and to suggest ways of improvement. The result was the famous Durham Report in which he recommended the union of the two provinces at once, the ultimate union of all British North America and the granting of full self-government in domestic affairs. The union of the two provinces was achieved by the Act of Union (1840), and so it was that in 1841, Upper and Lower Canada became the Province of Canada under a Governor-in-chief (Lord Sydenham).

With tempers still high in both the old capitals, a new centre of government had to be found on neutral ground, reasonably remote from both Toronto and Quebec, and Kingston was the choice. Lord Sydenham wrote "Toronto is too far off, and exposed to many moral inconveniences." But Kingston was found to be small and, consequently, inconvenient for the purposes of government, and, by 1844, we find the capital in Montreal. Montreal was equally central, and could provide all the amenities of a metropolis of 44,000 people. The political climate, however, was such as to make it an uneasy seat for the legislature of the united provinces, and, in a few years, it was to prove untenable as a capital.

In 1849 the Parliament of Canada passed by a large majority what was known as

175 Wadsworth Mills at Weston (1856) (demolished). When Charles and Wm. Rein Wadsworth arrived in Upper Canada in 1828, they were able to purchase the grist mill of James Farr. This they operated until 1856 when they built the splendid mill seen in the photograph (1870). Through several unprecedented floods and ice jams, the original Wadsworth dam and stone wall resisted the Humber in all its tantrums.

174 House of Misses Dorothy and Betty Ashbridge, 1444 Queen Street East (1854; mansard roof 1900). Few Toronto families can look back in a direct line to an 18th century ancestor, and to dwellings on the same site as their present house. Mrs. Sarah Ashbridge and her family came from Pennsylvania to settle in York in 1793. When Mrs. Simcoe called in 1794 she was received in a log cottage on the shore of Ashbridge's Bay. Family records do not tell why Mrs. Ashbridge would prefer so lonely a location to the society and security of York which, in 1795, consisted of 12 families. Miss Ashbridge can remember when the Bay shore was at Eastern Avenue.

This little-known house stands in a property still a city-block wide of lawn, flowering shrubs, and fine trees. It still has a barn to the rear of the house and a well-kept fence encloses the garden. While it is many years later than the log cottage where Mrs. Simcoe was entertained, it is a house and grounds that should rank high in any plans for the preservation of historic buildings in Toronto.

176 Sword's Hotel, later the Queen's, Front Street between Bay and York (1838, 1856, 1892) (demolished). Sword's Hotel has a history going back to 1838 when Captain Dick, a prosperous steamboat man, erected the building as four attached town houses. Six years later Knox College was founded, and College authorities purchased the property and put the houses to academic uses. Their occupancy ended in 1856 when Mr. Sword appears on the scene and the college was converted into a hotel under his management. His reign was only three years, but the building continued to be an hotel right up to its demolition in 1927 for the building of the Royal York. Mr. Sword was succeeded by the same Captain Dick who built the attached town houses, and it was he who gave it the name "Queen's." Many will remember it as the last word in hospitality, for the elegance of its furnishings and the excellence of its cuisine. Its going represented the end of an era.

177, 178 Toronto General Hospital, Gerrard Street (1855–78), Wm. Hay, architect (demolished). From the drawings one would see the old hospital as a gay French castle newly whitewashed, but, actually, it was in grey brick with a heavy coating of ivy in the Toronto manner. The site was chosen against the advice of the *Upper Canada Journal* which drew attention to the awful menace lurking in the "miasmata" of the neighbouring Don. This was offset to some extent by a report on the revolting conditions of the lake shore which would be enough to discourage any thoughts of a downtown site. The top drawing (**177**) shows the north elevation.
The first-floor plans (**178**) are interesting. There was no nurse's station as we know it today, wards were all very large, four bathrooms (two with toilets, but no wash basin) per floor, and, of course, no elevator.

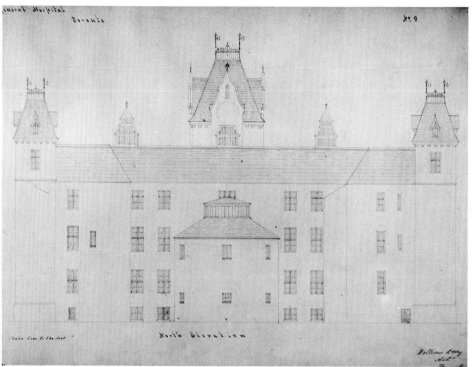

177

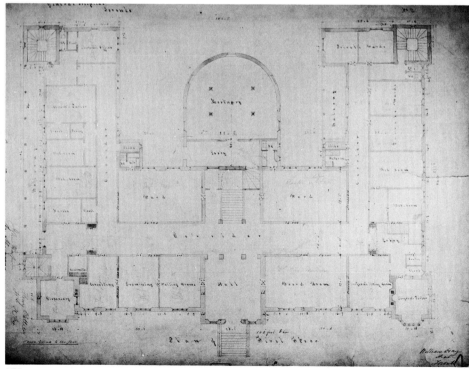

178

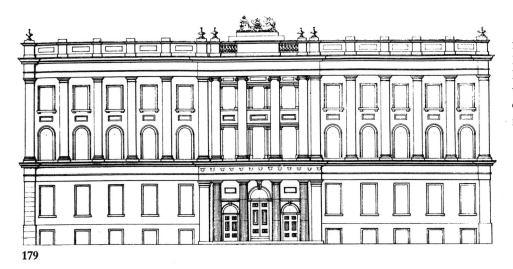

179

179–181 The Toronto Exchange (later Imperial Bank), at the corner of Wellington Street and Leader Lane (1855), James Grand, architect (demolished). This was a fine classical building with an equally distinguished plan. The elevation is shown in **179**, the ground floor in **180**, and finally in **181** the first floor.

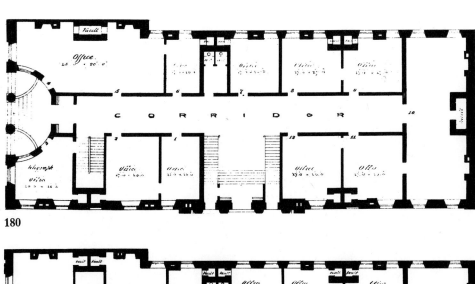

180

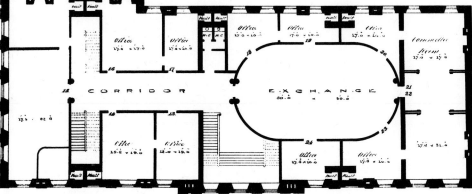

181

182–185 St. Basil's and St. Michael's College, St. Joseph Street (1856), Wm. Hay, architect. Hay was a versatile architect who designed such different buildings as Yorkville Town Hall (**230**) and the old General Hospital (**177**). A comparison of the original plan (**185**), the perspective sketch (**183**) and the photograph of the actual buildings (**182**) shows many points of departure. Since Hay did both church and college, it is difficult to explain or excuse the crudity of the junction between the two. The promise of the original plan with its beautiful cloister and court was not realized. The Bay Street wing (**182**) of the college was demolished in 1971.

Hay's sketch of the seminary and chapel are interesting both for the buildings and the open landscape which we may take to be accurately drawn. The group of buildings surrounding the courtyard look very removed from Ontario. Had they existed in another age, as well they might, one would assume they were built partly for defence. In such a mood, it is not difficult to see riders on the hill beyond with hounds in full cry. It is disillusioning to remember that the street in front is Bay Street and Bloor is not far away. Hay was a romantic character himself who spent his last years restoring St. Giles' Cathedral in Edinburgh. The large photograph (**184**) shows a delicately detailed interior of great beauty.

182

183

184

the "Rebellion Losses Bill," which made broad provisions for compensating citizens of Lower Canada for losses incurred during the rebellion of a decade earlier. A cry was easily raised by the Conservative minority that this was to reward rebellion. An angry mob burned the parliament buildings, and Her Majesty's representative, the Governor-in-chief, Lord Elgin, was actually stoned as he fled in his carriage. His offence in their eyes was that he gave the royal assent to the Bill although he had done so on the ground that in domestic affairs the Canadian Parliament must be supreme. In September of the same year, Montreal ceased to be the capital of the United Provinces.

The union was clearly not a solution to the political problems of the two provinces, but, in so far as the capital was concerned, a modus vivendi was established after 1849 by which the seat of government alternated between Toronto and Quebec.[23]

When one thinks of the sensitivity of the building industry to the faintest of political breezes in the present century, one cannot help but marvel at the courage of Toronto investors between the incorporation of the city and federation in 1867. All our most important buildings were erected in that period, and nothing of comparable significance was built from 1867 to 1900 except the city hall and the legislative buildings. The years that saw the greatest activity in construction were those

186 St. Patrick's Market, 234–240 Queen Street West (1856) (demolished). In 1836, Mr. D'Arcy Boulton presented the city with property on Queen Street, with a depth to a lane of 123 feet on condition that the city build a market and that it be maintained as such forever. The gift was accepted and a frame market erected. It was small, and, apparently, that fact mitigated against both it and its successor (1856) which was falling into ruin when Robertson wrote at the end of the century. For so small a building, it has a powerful Vanbrugh-like scale. The architect is not known.

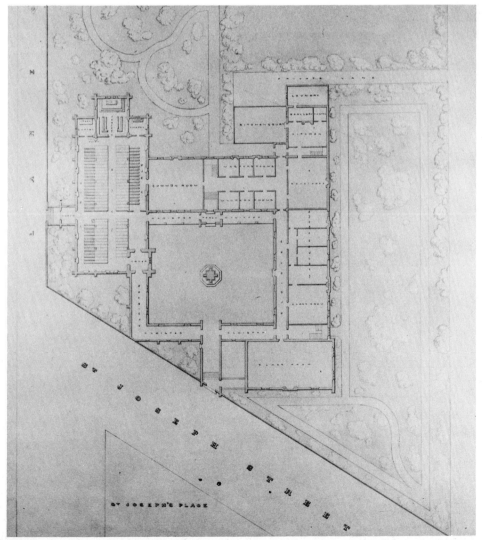

185

187–189 St. Lawrence Hall, King and Jarvis streets (1850), Wm. Thomas, architect. The very old photograph (**187**), shows the Hall before its defacement by signs. A druggist occupied the southwest corner and a tea merchant the southeast. Below left (**188**) is the crowning cupola with its clocks facing north, south, east, and west. The central doorway (**189**) led to the Farmers' Market while the modest one to the right opened on the stairway to the great hall. In 1967, the centennial year, the Hall enjoyed a major restoration paid for by municipal and private funds of nearly two million dollars. The building is still the home of the National Ballet of Canada and the great hall is still a centre for banquets, lectures, political meetings and celebrations just as it was in 1851. The Hall was officially re-opened on October 28, 1967, by the Rt. Hon. Roland Michener, Governor General of Canada.

187

188

189

between 1852 and 1857 when money was "poured out like water upon the building of the Grand Trunk and Great Western Lines." This was "a period of speculative mania which sent governments, municipalities and corporations into a wild rivalry of expenditure and extravagance."[24] In the decade following 1852, railway mileage increased from 12 to 1,974 miles.

Further prosperity came about through a reciprocity treaty which Canada negotiated with the United States in 1854. The treaty gave Canadian natural products free entry into the American market. For both provinces this was a boon which reached its peak during the Civil War of 1861. The treaty was terminated by the United States in 1865, but, during the decade in which it was in force, trade between the two countries was both extensive and profitable for Canada.

The same period saw the rise of our banking institutions and the fall of several.

The competition for business which had previously been waged between the Bank of Upper Canada and the Bank of Montreal as far back as 1822 was intensified by the arrival on the Toronto scene of other banks all anxious to share in the general prosperity. Competition between Toronto and Montreal was never so keen both for business in general and for government business in particular. Before Confederation there were in all eleven banks established with a Toronto head office: the Bank of Upper Canada (1822), the Home District Savings Bank (1830), the Agricultural Bank (1834), the Farmers Bank (1835), the Bank of the People (1835), the Toronto Savings Bank (1854), the Bank of Toronto (1855), the Colonial Bank of Canada (1858), the International Bank (1858), the Royal Canadian Bank (1860) and the Canadian Bank of Commerce (1866). In addition, there were at least nine banks with head offices elsewhere which operated branches in the city in this period.

A feeling of security brought about by unprecedented prosperous conditions in the business community permitted money to go into many civic improvements, and some of our best buildings date from this time. St. Lawrence Hall (1850), the Normal and Model Schools (1851), Trinity College (1851), the seventh Post Office (1853), St. James' Cathedral (1850), the Toronto Exchange (1855), University College (1856), Yorkville Town Hall (1859), and St. Paul's, Bloor Street (1860), all belong to this period, and all but four still stand.

190 St. Lawrence Hall, decorative swags. Theatrical masks alternate with carvings in stone of the Prince of Wales feathers, swords, and bugles.
I am indebted to Mr. Arthur Hibberd (Arthur Hibberd Cut Stone Ltd.) for much valuable information concerning stone used in nineteenth century Toronto buildings. Some of his information comes from a brochure published in 1914 (*Toronto's Building and Ornamental Stones* issued by Toronto Local Stone Cutters), and some from his personal investigations. He has this to say of St. Lawrence Hall, St. James-the-Less, St. Michael's, the Metropolitan Church and the Old Library at the University: "The lack of records and elapsed time make it difficult to determine the source of building stone, but I am convinced that the origin of the original stone was Hallington Quarries near Uttoxeter in Staffordshire, England. The stone was brought here as ballast for ships carrying pottery to the New World, and Lloyds have confirmed that it was feasible to get the stone by water from the St. Lawrence to Lake Ontario in the mid 1800's. Various later stones have been added for additions and restorations." Mr. Hibberd cites as an authority Mr. G. W. Burlington, director of Wandsworth Stonemasonry Works Ltd., in London, and adds that the quarries in question have been in use for over 800 years.

St. Lawrence Hall was an ambitious project combining a hall for public gathering with a frontage on King Street, and a covered market extending for 200 feet to Front Street at the rear. The second market had served its purpose, and had disappeared in the great fire of 1849 which destroyed much of the old town. The new buildings covered the site of the second market as well as the market-place itself with its memories of noisy, busy days going back to 1803 as well as of public floggings and brandings, and of at least one woman in the pillory (1804).

The ravages of this famous fire of 1849 may detain us for a moment. It destroyed from 10 to 15 acres of domestic and commercial building in an old and densely populated section of the city. It started in some frame buildings including stables off George St., and, before it was extinguished by the combined efforts of a poorly equipped fire department and a "smart" shower, had covered an area bounded by George and Church, King and Adelaide. At its height the flames could be seen from St. Catharines. Apart from houses, the following buildings were destroyed: St. James' Cathedral, the Market, the offices of two leading newspapers, the *Toronto Mirror* and the *Patriot*, and several stores, taverns and warehouses. Tin roofs were

191 A ball in St. Lawrence Hall, 1862, in honour of the Governor-General, Lord Monck, and Lady Monck.

192 The auditorium of the Hall, 100′ × 38′6″ with a height of 34′.

common in Toronto at the time, but many had wood shingles, one of which, as a flaming torch, ignited some woodwork on the cathedral tower.[25]

To return to St. Lawrence Hall, a brief list of social events and lectures for which the St. Lawrence Hall was a centre one hundred years ago reads very much like a month in Toronto in 1963. On the musical side, we hear of the Toronto Philharmonic Society, the Toronto Vocal Musical Society, and the Metropolitan Choral Society. In 1857, citizens heard Handel's *Messiah* in Toronto for the first time. Jenny Lind, "the Swedish nightingale," sang before a crowded house (tickets, one price, $3.00) in 1851, and, over the years, the hall echoed to the voices of the great in their generation; Mme Patti came more than once. In his *Recollections and Records*, Mr. W. H. Pearson tells of being actually present at Miss Lind's great concert in 1851. Tickets were sold by Nordheimer's, and the crowd was so great that the store was barricaded and protected by the police. It came as a surprise to him to hear her sing "Coming through the Rye" with a slightly foreign accent. On a number of occasions, anti-slavery meetings were held, and, twice, citizens were able to see "*Uncle Tom's Cabin*—a panorama." Sir John A. Macdonald and the Hon.

195 The south end of the Farmers' Market as it was in 1888. St. James in the distance.

194

193

193 A charming pilaster cap with central lily and, above it, a lyre – part of the detail of the balcony in the auditorium, St. Lawrence Hall.

194 An urn in cast iron from St. Lawrence Hall. This handsome urn, about 6′ high, now graces a lawn on a residential street in Toronto. Family records trace it back to a sale of odds and ends from St. Lawrence Hall half a century ago, but where it stood, or whether it was one of several, is not known.

George Brown could always fill the hall, and, not surprising in a Toronto audience, so could Mr. G. W. Stone on "Electro Biology," or Professor Daniel Wilson who spoke on "Primitive Sources of Historic Truth." The latter was unable to finish, and everyone returned a week later.

Toronto is equally well known for the immediate response of its citizens to charities, especially in emergency. In 1868, a ball was held to raise funds for distressed fishermen in Nova Scotia, and a Christmas dinner, in the same year, was given in the hall to "the boys and girls of the Protestant Home and to the little arabs of the streets." The Dominion of Canada was one year old.

St. Lawrence Hall ranks among the finest of our 19th century buildings. It is today marred and defaced by posters, but the fabric is sound, and its admirers do not despair of its restoration and return to the place of dignity and honour that it once had in the community. Architecturally, it is in the true Renaissance tradition, and would, in Great Britain or the United States, be certain to be classed as an historic monument. The front is stone and the iron balconies, of exquisite design, are cast. Rare, indeed, in Ontario is fine carving on stone which in St. Lawrence Hall is to be seen in Corinthian capitals, swags, and sculptured heads. The auditorium which saw gay balls, was familiar with the voices of Sir John A. Macdonald and Mme Patti and the music of Haydn and Handel has, in our time, been a doss house for the unemployed. But in recent years the great cultural tradition of the hall has been followed by its use as a practice school for the National Ballet of Canada. It is not large—in fact it has something of the gaiety and intimacy of a ballroom for an Esterhazy or some such patron of the arts. The mantle of the noble patron of a former age has fallen on governments, and there are signs in Toronto that the city is not unaware of its responsibility toward its monuments. Of these St. Lawrence Hall is pre-eminently one.

Even the most casual reader of the history of Upper Canada since Governor Simcoe will appreciate the influence of Englishmen (predominantly graduates of Cambridge University) in the social fabric and the government of the province. It was due to their influence in the community that King's College was built, and doubtless their unanimous wish (it was a regulation) that Unitarians and Jews be debarred from membership on the faculty or the governing Council. Bishop Strachan was its president. As the population increased and its character changed, it was inevitable that politicians and citizens should ask why education at its highest level was dominated by one denomination to the exclusion of all other, especially as the institution was maintained by public money.

On May 30, 1849, the end came. By an act of the provincial legislature, in which the university was remodelled under the style, no longer of King's College but of the University of Toronto, it was enacted "that there shall be no Faculty of Divinity in the said university, nor shall there be any professorship, lectureship or teachership in the same. The remodelled university was to be an absolutely secular institution. So it became, and so it has remained ever since." (John Ross Robertson)

Bishop Strachan was in his seventy-second year, and would seem to have met defeat for the first time. "Deprived of the university, what is the church to do? She has now no seminary in which to give a liberal education to her youth." Elsewhere, he referred to the "destruction of the University . . . a calamity not easy to bear."

Nothing daunted, he decided to go to England carrying with him a petition to the Queen praying that Her Majesty would "be graciously pleased to grant a Royal charter for the incorporation of an university, to be established on this clear and unequivocal principle": adherence to the Church of England.[26]

On Wednesday, April 10, 1850, Bishop Strachan left Toronto for England on the steamboat *America* carrying with him a petition with 11,731 signatures. While there, he was given a sympathetic ear by all of those most likely to support him in his mission. Lord Grey, the Secretary for the Colonies, Sir Robert Peel, the Prime Minister, and the Duke of Wellington all promised that his "arguments in favour of a Royal charter would receive every consideration." However, not unaware of the situation in Upper Canada, the Imperial authorities deemed it "impolitic for the time being" to grant the request, although two years later they did so.

In the absence of the Bishop and with confident expectation of the success of his mission, Anglican churchmen from all of Upper Canada gathered in Toronto to raise money for the project, the new university with a faculty of Divinity and a charter containing all that was best in the Anglican tradition of education.

Money was forthcoming in cash, land, and bequests, the largest being a bequest from Dr. Burnside of $24,000. A small competition was held to choose the best designs for a building (the first stage), to cost not more than $32,000. The two contestants were Col. F. W. Cumberland and Mr. Kivas Tully. We have no record of the jury of selection, but they did well to choose Mr. Kivas Tully (in 1851). It must have been no little satisfaction to the jury and the university that the construction tender of Messrs. Metcalfe, Wilson and Forbes was for $31,380! But governing bodies change over the years, and the Council of 1876 seems to have felt under no obligation to Mr. Tully. Mr. Frank Darling was appointed architect to the fabric, and it was under his direction that the Convocation Hall (1876), Chapel (1884) and the west and east wings (1891 and 1894) were added. Long

196 Trinity College (1851), Kivas Tully, architect (demolished). The south front.

197 Trinity College, the entrance gateway on Queen Street.

198 Trinity College. A detailed view of the south front.

199 Trinity College, a design for the chapel proposed by Wm. Hay in 1858 – an engraving made from the original drawing in the possession of Mr. and Mrs. Derrick Leach.

before Darling, in fact in 1858, another architect appears on the scene; let us hope with the best of reasons and on the most ethical grounds! He was Wm. Hay whom we shall later meet as the author of the Yorkville Town Hall. He prepared a sketch of a completed Trinity with particular emphasis on a chapel in a style some centuries earlier than Tully's Gothic. It was not built, but one cannot help feeling sorry for Tully who lived to see his brain child developed by others. He died in 1905. At the same time, the wonder is that Trinity College seemed to be all of a piece, without, as we remember it, a single discordant note.

When the College moved to its present location on Hoskin Avenue, its governing body showed singular lack of imagination in demanding of Darling and Pearson that the new building be a replica of the old, but in stone. Tragic, in a different sense, was the decision of the city to demolish the old building in 1956. The College grounds are still there, but vulnerable for building purposes like all parks in Toronto.

Scadding has little to say of the "University of Trinity College," but much of interest regarding the property. The College grounds occupied the lower part of one of the original park lots which was called Gore Vale in honour of the governor of that name. "Vale denoted the ravine which indented a portion of the lot through whose meadow-land meandered a pleasant little stream. [The University's] brooklet will hereafter be famous in scholastic song. It will be regarded as the Cephissus of a Canadian Academus, the Cherwell of an infant Christ Church."[27] Where the brook crossed Queen Street by a steep mound, a blockhouse once commanded the western approaches to York, and a well-trodden path led to it across the Common from the Garrison. Scadding, in his day, saw many changes, but he would hardly have believed that, in less than a hundred years since he wrote (1873), the College

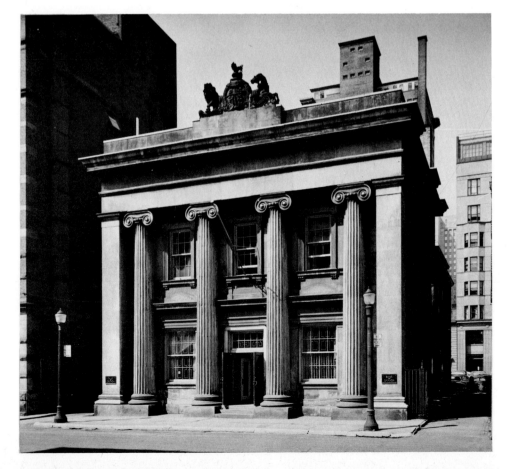

200 The seventh Post Office, Toronto Street (1853), Cumberland and Storm, architects. In this century, the building was occupied for a time by the Bank of Canada, and, more recently, by its present owners, the Argus Corporation, who, probably, saved it from the wreckers. Said in the contemporary press to be modelled after the Temple of Minerva. In 1853 it cost $16,000.

202 The Montgomery Inn, Islington (*c.* 1833). This inn of Thomas Montgomery was a well-known stopping place in its day, and, with its ballroom on the second floor, must have played an important part in the community life of the district in the 19th century. In this century, it had the distinction of serving as a court house with the Sessions' Court in the ballroom. The resemblance to the Post Office is striking – the bar door and the hotel door being the door to the public entrance and the postmaster's apartment in the typical post office.

1973: Plans for restoration have been drawn up and work has begun under the aegis of the Toronto Historical Board.

201 The third Post Office in York (1830) on George Street.

would be razed, the mound made low and the vale exalted. His Cephissus no longer meanders, but runs in a common sewer into Lake Ontario.

One of the most interesting buildings left to us of the 19th century, the seventh Post Office, was built in the exciting decade 1850–1860. It was exactly contemporary with St. James, and was designed by the same architects. By a curious coincidence, the very different functional requirements of the post office, the branch bank, and the inn produced the same façade and a marked similarity of plan. The side door on the main front usually indicated the business entrance to the bank or post office (or the bar in the case of the inn), while the more generous central entrance was reserved for manager, or postmaster and family who lived above. In the seventh Post Office, living quarters above were reached by a side door in the lane to the south, an exception to the usual rule.

This very striking little temple on Toronto Street was designed by Cumberland and Storm in 1853. It was by a happy chance that, in 1959, a group of businessmen who could afford the luxury of lowness in a skyscraper age were able to save it from the wrecker. The interior has been completely changed, but we know something of the old ground floor. "The large public hall, with enriched oak and plate-glass letter-box, had three compartments, intersected by Doric columns, with delivery windows and a separate entrance for ladies. The building, which cost £3,500, reflected credit upon its architects, and also upon the contractors. . . ."[28]

To round out the story of the Post Offices, there was the eighth which once sat so proudly at the top of Toronto Street, by all odds the finest street in Toronto. It had all the charm of a street in some capital city in Europe. People unknowingly sensed its quality—businessmen were unhurried, motor cars hardly exceeded the pace of the carriages of half a century ago, and the buildings on both sides of the street had about them that dignified venerability that commands immediate respect. Today, Toronto Street is the "street that died" and the eighth Post Office has been replaced by a federal building that ignores the axis of the street.

The courage and energy that had been characteristic of the people of St. James in previous catastrophes were again manifest after the total destruction of the Cathedral in 1849. Never, however, had the congregation been so divided as to the form the building should take, or even where it should be placed. Among the various schools of thought were those represented by the dean himself, Dr. Grasett, who would sell off the King Street frontage for commercial purposes, and build the cathedral on Adelaide Street. Another faction was quite happy to augment the insurance money sufficiently to build a parish church and hall on the foundation of the old cathedral.

By June 1850, the Adelaide Street group were sufficiently strong in the Vestry to

203 Toronto Street looking north. This is the street that died, but seen here at its best before the demolition of the eighth Post Office on Adelaide Street. On the left is the seventh Post Office (1853) by Cumberland and Storm (**200**), and, next to it, the Masonic Hall (1857) which later became the Canada Permanent Building (**210**), architect Wm. Kauffman. Closing the vista is the eighth Post Office (1871–73) by Henry Langley, architect (**204**); demolished 1960. In 1973 the only buildings left of note are the seventh Post Office and the Consumers' Gas Company office building on the east side. For the latter see **182**.

204

205

204, 205 The eighth Post Office at the head of Toronto Street on Adelaide (1871–73), Henry Langley, architect. This Second Empire building which sat with such dignity at the head of Toronto Street is no more. It might be thought fussy by some with its picturesque mansard roof and its rows of columns, but the most severe critic would agree that it was in scale with the buildings about it and in front, and that it had a presence that one would associate with the government of Canada.

In 1882, the business of the Post Office was transacted by 52 clerks and 55 letter carriers – 3,135,363 letters were delivered. By comparison, in 1960, there were 1,550 carriers. No figures are available for letters delivered, but revenue for the same year was $39,223,034.24.

The presumably early drawing does not show the pediment and Royal Arms over the front door. The Arms are now preserved on the south side of Lombard Street behind the new Federal Building.

authorize an international competition for a new cathedral. Mr. John G. Howard drew up the conditions which named the jury of award, Messrs. Howard, Johnstone and Young, and offered prizes of £75, £50 and £25. About seven weeks later, the competition was over; Col. Frederick Cumberland was placed first, a Mr. Ortelo second, and Mr. Kivas Tully third.

By that time, it was common knowledge that a majority of the Vestry had voted for the north or Adelaide end of the site, and the leasing of 238 feet on King Street east of Church. The citizens of Toronto became aroused. A meeting of protest was held in the City Hall, and a resolution was passed against leasing the land. There can be few comparable examples of public interference with church government, particularly where a cathedral was involved, and a flurry of vestry meetings followed. Out of it all emerged a resolution rescinding all previous decisions involving the leasing of land, but confirming Cumberland's appointment as architect.

At first, his instructions were to build on the old foundations which were close to Church Street, but these, in turn, were rescinded in favour of a motion putting the cathedral in the centre of the property. This was regarded by some as a cunning scheme to prevent the sale of land at all points of the compass, and gives us an idea of the distrust that still existed of the powerful faction which favoured the Adelaide site.

It was not until July 1, 1850, nearly fifteen months after the fire, that the way was cleared for reconstruction to begin.[29] Only £5,000 remained of the insurance

206 St. James' Cathedral (1850), F. W. Cumberland and Thomas Ridout, architects. A photograph from *Toronto in the Camera* (1868), showing the Cathedral sans pinnacles and spire.

money when all bills had been paid, but £5,000 additional was raised through the sale of pew subscriptions and other sources, and with this sum Cumberland agreed to design a "usable," but not a completed cathedral. Our Gothic churches had one thing in common with the perpendicular medieval churches of England, and that was a picturesque skyline broken whenever possible by pinnacles and finials. In respect of these, St. James was a shorn lamb until 1873–4 when the tower and spire, the transepts, and the pinnacles and finials were all completed. The church clock, the gift of the people of Toronto of all denominations, was installed in 1875, and is still maintained by the City.

207

An old photograph shows the nave before the removal of the triforium or gallery. Such a major change provided many more pews which, in St. James, were a source of revenue even in the first church.[30] Several unusual features will be noticed in the photograph. The pews in the foreground are of a puritanical severity with board seat and a rail at shoulder blade level. Contrary to what one would expect, only the Presbyterians, with their padded pews, showed any regard for comfort in the churches of Upper Canada. An odd sight in the photograph is the central row of pews of chesterfield size with an aisle on each side, an arrangement that must have been peculiar to St. James in the Anglican world. Unusual, also, is the placing of the organ pipes at the main, south entrance to the cathedral instead of the more common location in the chancel above the organist and choir. (In the cathedral of today, some pipes are in the chancel.) The Church of England was

209 An old photograph of St. James, showing the triforium (since removed) and an odd arrangement of pews.

207 St. James' Cathedral, a noble Gothic edifice. In the custom of the time, the cathedral was the subject of an international architectural competition. The winning design was that of Col. Frederick Cumberland, associated with Thomas Ridout. In recent years a broad and greatly used lawn has taken the place of stores on the north side of King Street, and it will eventually extend to Jarvis Street. It would be an act of grace if the city's redevelopment plans for the area permitted the long view, now possible through a parking lot. The clock in the spire was paid for by public subscription, and is maintained by the City. Materials, brick and Ohio sandstone.

208 St. James' Cathedral, the nave.

208

210 Masonic Hall (later Canada Permanent Building) on the west side of Toronto Street (1857), Wm. Kauffman, architect (demolished). A huge building in its day, it dwarfed the seventh Post Office to the south. The design was in a rather hard Gothic, and might lead one to think that the walls were of cast iron. Actually, they were not, but the ground floor was of cast iron as were the window sash and inside shutters. This must represent a very early use of the metal window in North America. Originally, there were four shops on the ground floor.

never so inflexible as the Church of Rome in the matter of orientation, that of placing the church on an east–west axis with the altar at the east end. St. James breaks all the rules by being on the north–south axis with the sanctuary in what Robertson calls "the least ecclesiastical of all points of the compass," a location that in medieval times was considered "the residence of Satan himself." It should be noted that the orientation of St. James was set by the building committee.

For those who like to explore old churches in the manner of Mr. Sacheverell Sitwell, St. James has much to offer. A famous bishop, Dr. John Strachan, and a great dean, Dr. Grasett, are buried in the chancel. Gathered from the graveyard which once adjoined the cathedral are headstones in English and Latin going back many years. In the south porch is one of the best from the point of view of design and beauty of lettering, that of the Hon. Thomas Ridout, the Surveyor-General (1829), and, adjoining, one of the most tragic, that of his son John Ridout who served as a midshipman in the Provincial Navy, and on discharge "commenced with ardour the study of law with the fairest prospects, but a blight came" and he died on the morning of July 12, 1817. The "blight" was a duel with pistols fought near Yonge and Grosvenor between young Ridout and his former friend Samuel P. Jarvis.

Tragic, too, was the end of that William Butcher of Walpole in Sussex whose stone is also in the south porch: "whilst actively engaged in making a scaffold for the spire [he] was precipitated from a height of seventy feet . . . and was taken up dead, October 31st, 1839. Aged 27 years." Mr. Butcher was engaged on that wooden spire on the third St. James which became a torch in the great fire of 1849.

Rather unique among the gravestones of Upper Canada is that of the Such family in Latin and Greek, now in the east porch. The inscription is too long to translate here, but a line like "fuit (o vox lugenda) fuit!" immediately seems to call for the English equivalent. "He was, oh grievous word, he was!" sounds so much less of a lament than the original. And then there was Mary Remington Such, that "Puellula rarissimae formae." The date was MDCCCXXXII. The family of Such came from Rookery Hall, St. Mary Cray, in Kent.

Inside the cathedral, memorial stones and brasses are all of historic interest, and quite a few represent a high standard of design and workmanship. Of these, this writer has known and admired for many years the one erected by the officers of the Toronto Garrison in memory of Col. Sir Casimir Gzowski K.C.M.G., aide-de-camp to the Queen (1818–1898). It is in brass on the east wall of the nave.

St. James' Cathedral is built of Ohio stone and brick—that curious Toronto brick that starts life as a rather bright yellow and enters old age as grey as the most venerable inhabitant. Toronto has just entered on a craze for cleaning historic buildings by sandblasting, and the south porch has not been spared.

One has only to look at any part of University College to say of the architect with Scadding, "here was a man after the heart of Wykeham and Wayneflete." Even a person with a taste so eclectic as was Frederick Cumberland's must have had some architectural manner in which he enjoyed working more than another, and in the entrance hall to University College one feels he was not only enjoying himself, he was revelling in it. From the beginning he had his difficulties, not so much with his client, the Vice-Chancellor, as with the Governor-General, Sir Edmund Head.

As preparation for the building, Cumberland had visited England at a rather momentous time in the history of the Gothic revival. The most important building in England in 1856 was the Oxford museum. The architect was Woodward, but Ruskin became interested and hoped to get the whole pre-Raphaelite brotherhood to work on carving. "I hope to be able to get Millais and Rossetti to design flower

211 Chapel of St. James-the-Less, St. James' Cemetery, Parliament Street (1858), Cumberland and Storm, architects. This is Cumberland at his Gothic best in a setting worthy of the building. The material covering the spire is the only jarring note in an otherwise harmonious composition. The layout of the cemetery grounds was the work of John G. Howard in 1845. The cemetery is of considerable historic interest, and has headstones for such Toronto citizens as Dr. Burnside, Dr. Scadding the author of *Toronto of Old*, Col. Sir Casimir Gzowski (a vault in the style of a minor temple on the Nile), the distinguished architects Wm. Thomas and Col. Frederick Cumberland, and many others of equal eminence. The various stages in the development of architecture in the nineteenth century can be read in the form and the lettering of headstones, which in material range all the way from sandstones to granite; quite a few are cast iron.

212 St. James-the-Less, south façade, a drawing by students in the School of Architecture. For a note on the masonry see **190**.

211

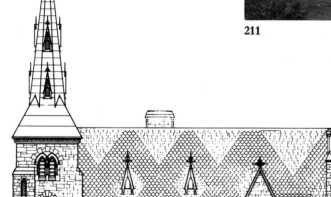

212

and beast borders—crocodiles and various vermin. . . ." Cumberland knew Ruskin, and there is every reason to believe that he was profoundly affected by what he saw and heard at Oxford. The silhouette of the College is markedly similar to the Museum—even to the chemistry department, isolated in a chapter house because of its odours and its intrusion on a building sacred to the humanities.

Having absorbed all that he could from Oxford and burning with a zeal for the architecture of the Middle Ages, second only, we can imagine, to that of Ruskin, the high priest himself, Cumberland prepared a scheme for University College in Toronto. Our knowledge of its fate comes from a letter of the Vice-Chancellor of the University, John Langton (father of W. A. Langton, the architect), who wrote his brother in England:

The site being chosen, Cumberland drew a first sketch of a Gothic building, but the Governor would not hear of Gothic and recommended Italian, shewing us an example of the style, a palazzo at Siena, which if he were not governor-general and had written a book on art, I should have called

213 University College, University of Toronto, a perspective drawing, found among the papers of W. A. Langton, an architect and son of the Vice-Chancellor – quite possibly made in the fifties by, or for, F. W. Cumberland.

The author once presented an old drawing of the building to a friend in the College, and on it in red ink were the "bumps" on the corners of the tower to be seen in 216. A note said that they were "added by Sir Daniel Wilson" (President 1889–92). The drawing has since been lost.

The College will be restored in five stages of which the first, including the circular Croft Chapter House (originally the chemistry department), is complete. Architect, Eric Arthur; Wilson, Newton and Roberts, associates.

214 The Oxford Museum, Oxford, England (1854), Deane and Woodward, architects. Cumberland was undoubtedly influenced by this building when he visited England prior to designing University College.

215 University College, a window in the south wall, photographed by Dean Ellis in 1889.

216 University College (1856), Cumberland and Storm, architects; 1890 restoration after the fire by D. B. Dick, architect. This is the south façade. Masonry, Ohio sandstone.

one of the ugliest buildings I ever saw. However, after a week's absence the Governor came back with a new idea, it was to be Byzantine; and between them they concocted a most hideous elevation. After this the Governor was absent on a tour for several weeks, during which we polished away almost all traces of Byzantine and got a hybrid with some features of Norman, of early English, etc., with faint traces of Byzantium and the Italian palazzo, but altogether a not unsightly building, and on his return His Excellency approved.[31]

Vice-Chancellor Langton took upon himself the responsibility of dealing with the architect and the Governor-General with as little consultation with Dr. Mc-Caul, the Principal, as possible. He did not trust McCaul, and had nobody to back him up "except the professors who from hatred of McCaul stick to me like bricks but without much power. . . ." In a later letter, we find the trusted professors adding to his difficulties: "their demands for space were however outrageous and, at last, it was only by telling them, as the Governor authorized me to do, that if they did not moderate their expectations, he would stop the building altogether, that I succeeded in making a compromise."[32] The Chairman of the Board of

218 University College, the main entrance, photographed by Dean Ellis in 1889: still, it is said, the most photographed piece of architecture in Toronto. The iron gates at the entrance are hardly visible but they, like the ornamental strap hinges on all doors, are of the finest craftsmanship.

217 A Notman view of University College, reflected in a pool in the Taddle.

219 University College, a newel in the east staircase.

220 University College, the atrium.

221

222

Governors of the University of Toronto in 1964 would read of Langton's plight with sympathetic understanding.

But the real enemy was the Governor-General, Sir Edmund Head. Unknown, apparently, to the Vice-Chancellor or to the architect, the Governor-General had assumed that teaching in the College was to be on a purely tutorial basis, and it was with extraordinary perspicacity that he discovered that certain rooms shown on the plans were called "lecture" rooms. This was the last hurdle but one, and was met by Langton through the simple device of "scratching out the words lecture room, and erasing all appearance of seats for the students."

The final hurdle was a serious one, and one that might have had disastrous consequences for a building now regarded with admiration and affection by graduates and undergraduates like. Every possible concession seemed to have been made to the vanity of the Governor-General, and it was, probably, with a lighter heart than he had felt for some months that Langton authorized Cumberland to stake the building on the ground.

But here an unexpected difficulty arose. It seems that His Excellency had all along thought that the south front was to face the east (west?), and nothing would satisfy him but so it must be, and, under his superintendence, we proceeded to measure and stake out; Cumberland's face exhibiting blank despair for it brought his chemical laboratory where no sun would ever shine into it it, his kitchens, etc., into the prettiest part of the grounds, and several other inconveniences which His Excellency said could be easily remedied. However, there stands on the ground an elm tree, a remnant of the old forest, with a long stem as such trees have and a little bush on the top of it, not unlike a broom with its long handle stuck into the ground, and it soon became evident that the tree would fall a sacrifice. This he would not permit and when I hinted that it would certainly be blown down before long, he told me it was the handsomest tree about Toronto (as it certainly is one of the tallest), and politely added "but you Canadians have a prejudice against trees." He then stalked off the ground followed by his ADC. I thought Cumberland would have thrown the whole thing up that day, he was so annoyed, but we took up the stakes and staked it out our way with the south front facing the south, and by a little stuffing and squeezing we got the tree into such a position that it may be saved

221 University College, the cloisters in the quadrangle.

222 "Crocodiles and vermin" carving on University College. The sculptor was a Russian, Ivan Reznikoff, said to be buried in the northeast corner of the quadrangle. His ghost has been seen at regular intervals.

223 University College, detail of the Chapter House wall looking east.

224 University College, a doorway leading from the west lawn to the cloisters and quadrangle.

225 An east doorway, photographed by Dean Ellis in 1889.

226, 227 The City Jail on Gerrard Street East (1858), Wm. Thomas, architect. The Jail was burned before completion in 1858, and was not opened until rebuilt in 1865. It is an impressive building in the manner made famous by Piranesi the etcher, and by Dance the younger who designed Newgate Prison. Compared with the grimness of Newgate, the City Jail is a friendly building in spite of rustications, vermiculated quoins and barred windows. Interesting elements in the design are the flanking ventilators rising out of the roof which might well have come from the hand of the great 18th century English architect, Sir John Vanbrugh.

One might criticize Thomas here for the weakness of the crowning cornice and pediment, and for the complete lack of connexion between the central mass and the flanking wings. The same fault is to be found in the façade of Osgoode Hall, and one wonders, in this case, whether "the hand of the potter slipped" in the rebuilding after the fire.

The large photograph (**227**) shows the main doorway. It is unlikely that convicted law-breakers were introduced by this door, but if they were it would have a sobering effect.

226

but with the almost certainty that, when it is blown down, it will take some of the students' quarters with it. It is some comfort that that will occur before Tom [the writer's eldest son] is old enough to go to college, or I should be uneasy in stormy nights. However I bless that tree and hope its shadow may never be less for it got us out of [the] scrape. When the Governor paid us a visit next day he was quite satisfied and complimentary, and in congratulating us upon the safety of the tree he said to Cumberland with that impertinence which governors-general can so well indulge in, "For I am sure you can never put anything up half as pretty."

It would only be human for the Chancellor of Trinity, the Lord Bishop of Toronto, to smile with contentment as the stories regarding the birth pangs of the "godless" institution reached him in his comfortable medieval quarters on Queen Street.

But the story of University College is not yet fully told. On the night of February 14, 1890, a college servant carrying a tray of lamps stumbled and fell on the stairs in the southeast corner of the building. The kerosene was immediately ablaze; the whole of the east wing was destroyed as well as the library of over thirty thousand volumes, the museum, and the administrative offices of the College; only the west part of the building, including the Croft Chapter House, the residence and the dining hall, remained intact. Professor Keys once told the writer that he appeared before a committee sadly estimating the losses to the library and announced himself as one of the great benefactors of the College: he had seven hundred volumes out in his own name. The fire was a disastrous one, but there

228 St. Stephen's-in-the-Fields, at the corner of College and Bellevue (1858), the first church west of Spadina Avenue. Thomas Fuller, architect; rebuilt 1865, Gundry and Langley, architects. St. Stephen's was the gift, both of site and of structure, of Col. R. B. Denison, the owner of nearby Bellevue. Bishop Strachan laid the foundation stone "with an offering of corn wine and oil." Fuller's church had a brief life of seven years, but the fire which destroyed it left the walls relatively stable. With a break in its history of only one year during which the congregation met in the house of Col. F. W. Cumberland, the restoration was complete in 1866.

A change never thought of by the little band of Anglicans who were its first congregation was the change in the ethnic pattern of the community which now is largely Polish and Italian. Until his death in 1958, the pastor of St. Stephen's was the Rev. Canon James Ward who brought lustre to the church and comfort to many by the sincerity of his preaching over the radio – a field of religious education in which he was a pioneer.

227

229

was never a doubt as to the need for immediate rebuilding. Government and friends came to the rescue and the College was restored in the manner we know it today. The architect was Mr. D. B. Dick.

The decades that followed the building boom of the fifties and sixties were to be far from negligible in the history of architecture in Toronto, but they produced few comparable buildings. Romanticism in its Gothic form was to make sporadic appearances well into the 20th century, and take its final dramatic bow in the reconstruction of the Houses of Parliament in Ottawa, a superb group of buildings by a Toronto architect, Mr. John Pearson. I am aware that there have been Gothic buildings since, but they have lacked the magic that makes St. James' Cathedral, St. James-the-Less, old St. Paul's, Little Trinity, or the Archbishop's Palace on

229, 230 Yorkville Town Hall (St. Paul's Hall), 1859, on the west side of Yonge Street near Davenport Road, Wm. Hay, architect (demolished 1942). "The singular Hotel de Ville . . . has a Flemish look. It might have strayed hither from Ghent" (Scadding).
The Coat of Arms of the Village (**229**) displayed symbols indicating the trades of the first four aldermen – a beer barrel with an S (Mr. John Severn, the brewer); a brick mould with an A (Mr. Thomas Atkinson); an anvil with a W (Mr. James Wallis); a jack plane with a D (Mr. James Dobson), and, centre, an animal's head, being the mark of Mr. Peter Hutty, the butcher.
When Yorkville was incorporated with Toronto in 1883 (St. Paul's ward), the Council chamber was used as a public library, and continued in that capacity until a library was built on Yorkville Avenue in 1907. In its last days the Hall was the armouries of the Yorkville company of the York Rangers (now the Queen's York Rangers, 1st American Regiment).

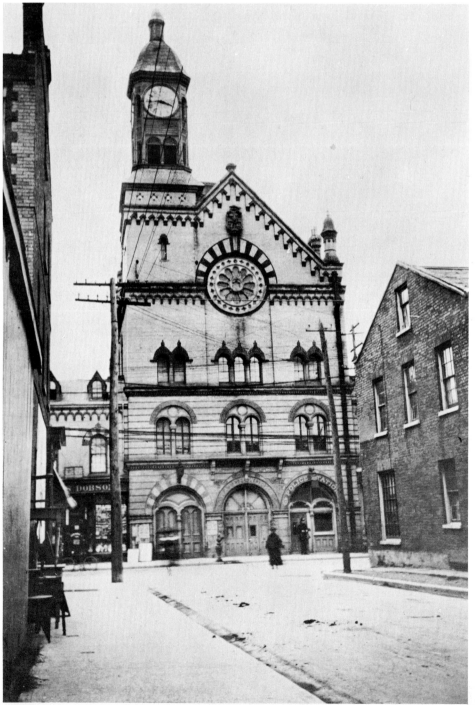

230

231 McLaughlin Flour Mills (*c*. 1860) on Bay and Esplanade (west side), shown in a street view of 1900. (demolished). It is doubtful whether there are craftsmen today who could do such a superb job of brick work as can be seen on this building. The wall itself is well done, but the lower arches and the corbelling above are not inferior to the best in countries like Holland and Germany. The design itself is well worthy of notice and ranks with the best of the industrial buildings of the 19th century – a field we are just beginning to appreciate.

Church Street so unquestionably part of the Toronto scene. Not all the architecture of the period can be described as indigenous, but, where the term can be applied to a building, it is no small tribute to its creator.

One would like to leave the reader who is willing to explore Toronto with a long list of historic buildings ending with the year of Confederation. Nearly all have been demolished, but enough remain to give a romantic glow to many an undistinguished street. The explorer will remember that the buildings he sees were part of a great movement that swept Britain and the United States before we were affected in Canada. He will look at old St. Paul's first of all as a fine piece of architecture wonderfully well built, but he will also remember, with its architect, the village churches and cathedrals of England that inspired it. He may also remember Sir Walter Scott and the influence that he must have had on a movement that was in many ways a literary one. In similar mood, he will admire the old Commercial Bank on Wellington—a truly fine building which cannot help but evoke thoughts of Greece and of Byron, Shelley, Keats and others whose poetry was part of the movement itself in its beginnings. It is appropriate for our interested explorer to dream over what he sees of Old Toronto before Confederation; in the period that follows he must be more alert. Architecture itself was awakening from a long sleep. [*Text continues page 159*]

233 Oaklands (1860), the residence of Senator John Macdonald, Avenue Road Hill. It is regrettable that we have no record of the interior furnishings of this distinguished Victorian house. It is now given up to the classrooms of the De la Salle School. Very unexpected in classrooms are two imported English marble mantels – one very Adam and the other mildly Vanbrugh. Between the ownership of the house by the Senator and the purchase by the school, Oaklands was the property of Miss McCormick, a lady connected with the agricultural implement family of that name in the United States. There were rumours in the writer's early life in Toronto that the lady had a Negro orchestra of her own, a sort of Esterhazy musical pinnacle that no member of the *haut monde* of Toronto society has since equalled, or even approached.

232

233

234

232, 234, 235 House of Col. Sir Casimir Gzowski, facing 396 Bathurst Street (1860). This house is typical in design of the large houses of the sixties and its architect was probably Cumberland whose own house "Pendarvis" of the same date it resembles. The interior is more 1890 than 1860 and represents an accumulation of knick-knacks, family photographs and pictures gathered over half a century. **232** shows the façade with the main entrance, **234** the billiard room-cum-art gallery. **235** is the drawing room in 1896 – a collector's period piece of confusion and clutter including a number of "gifts from royalty."

235

236 The first St. Paul's Church (1841). John G. Howard, architect. Sometimes called Old St. Paul's, the Tollgate Church or Yorkville Church, the building stood on or near the site of a later St. Paul's, now called the Maurice Cody Hall. Scadding describes the raising of the tower and spire in one day under the direction of the architect. This structure, 85′ in height, was built horizontally on the ground and painted. He records that it was raised by an ingenious arrangement of pulleys, and what impressed him most was that, for some reason, the whole operation was conducted in silence with the architect directing the workers by signs. "Like some tall palm, the noiseless fabric sprung." The peregrinations of the little building began before 1861 when the stone St. Paul's was built on the site. Its first resting place was on Bloor Street at the head of North Street (now Bay), where it became a Sunday School and Chapel-of-ease under the name of St. Sepulchre's. Some years later, the Anglican congregation in Yorkville had grown so large that a boundary for St. Paul's parish was set at Yonge Street, and a new one to the west, called the Church of the Redeemer, was formed.

237

237 St. Paul's Church on Bloor Street east of Church Street (1860), G. K. and E. Radford, architects (won in competition). In 1900, nave and aisles were extended to the west roughly at the line of the window seen to the left of the large porch; G. M. Miller, architect. A larger St. Paul's (1913) by E. J. Lennox now overshadows that of 1860, which is known as the Maurice Cody Memorial Hall. Dwarfed though it is, old St. Paul's is a charming little Gothic church that would be a matter of pride in any English village. It has no equal among Toronto churches of the 19th century unless it be St. James-the-Less on Parliament Street by Cumberland.

238 The first Church of the Redeemer at Avenue Road and Bloor Street (*c.* 1871), John G. Howard, architect. This is the first St. Paul's under a new name and on a new site. In addition to this photograph there is a sketch in the Public Library of the church by W. A. Langton, made just before its demolition in 1879.

238

239 Second Church of the Redeemer (1879), Smith and Gemmell, architects, at the corner of Avenue Road and Bloor Street.

240–242 House of Mr. Arthur R. McMaster (1868), of Mr. Hart Massey (1882), and later of Mrs. Massey Treble at the northeast corner of Jarvis and Wellesley Streets. This romantic Gothic Revival house once had grounds to set it off. Turrets, corbels and battlements – all are there, but are less interesting than the Moorish interior. The house is now known as Julie's Restaurant.

The imposing Gothic hall appears in **241**; furniture and fixtures are those of Ryan's Art Galleries and unconnected with 19th century occupants.

The room illustrated in **242** is said to have been done by Mrs. Massey Treble (perhaps about 1894), but was doubtless inspired by her father whose preference for Moorish may be seen in Massey Hall. The rooms are decorated in blue, red and gold, but even a photograph suggests late Victorian soirées where the ladies smoked with long cigarette-holders and the men hookahs while someone read passages from the diary of Lady Hester Stanhope.

240

241

243 Pendarvis, the house of Col. F. W. Cumberland (1860) at the corner of St. George and College streets, F. W. Cumberland, architect. Pendarvis might well be called a mansion by comparison with houses of its period in Ontario. It has no particular style, and might as well be classed as mid-Victorian. Grounds were spacious and the internal arrangements made it admirably suited for entertaining on a large scale. From 1912 till 1915, it was the official residence of the Lieutenant-Governor of Ontario. The house is now the International Student Centre, a property of the University of Toronto, and is known as Cumberland House. It was restored in 1965. Architect, Eric Arthur; Wilson and Newton, associates. The Forestry Building seen next door has since been moved bodily further up St. George Street.

244 House at 32A Gerrard Street (*c.* 1860) (demolished). Like the Mackenzie house on Bond Street (**69**), this one was once part of a terrace. Little imagination is necessary to visualize the kitchen in the basement and the roaring fires and bake oven flue that justified the chimney on the right. Even up to 1870, Toronto's domestic architecture was characterized by many of the elements that go to make up the design of this house – the human scale, the sash window, the grey brick wall and the welcoming doorway.

245 Farm House on York Mills road near the intersection with Don Mills. It is pleasing to the photographer and the historian that so good an example of Victorian elegance and whimsy should be so beautifully maintained. Only the purist in these matters would find fault with the difference in scale between the cusping on the gable and the verandah. Its gaiety is in marked contrast to the lugubriousness of some expensive "ranch homes" a few hundred yards away.

246 House at 112 Gerrard Street East (*c.* 1860). Even in disrepair this is Victorian architecture in its gayest mood. The house faces south and the shadows cast on grey stucco add greatly to the pattern of undulating eave board, the "Gothik" cusping below the bay windows and the protecting roof over the verandah. (demolished in the 1960's)

247 Queen's Wharf Lighthouse (1861). No longer a beacon for ships on the lake, the old lighthouse is one of the few relics of the past that we have had the foresight to preserve. We see it today at peace on a well-kept lawn, but this seemingly frail tower knew snow and rain and the force of equinoctial gales for three-quarters of a century; and its light was never known to fail.

248 Church of Christ or Christian Workers' Church, Denison Avenue (c. 1860), once the Denison Avenue Presbyterian Church (demolished). One would like to know the name of the architect who designed this very attractive church, and to have known the house on the right of which we get only a glimpse.

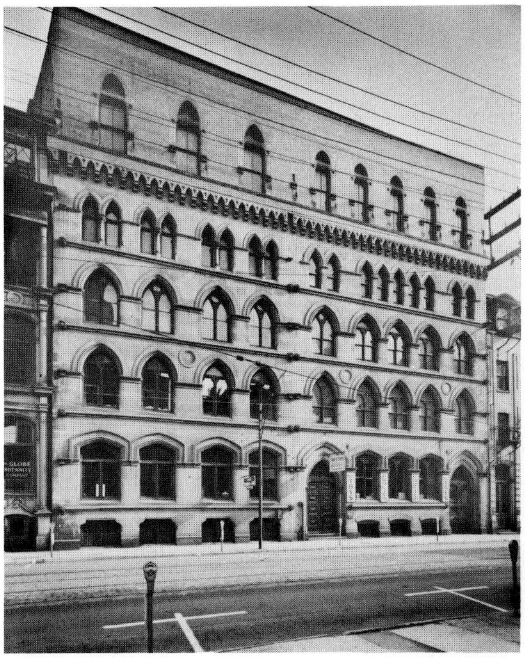

250 Premises of John Macdonald, 21–27 Wellington Street East and on Front Street (1862). Built a decade after the publication of the *Stones of Venice*, numbers 21 and 27 were spoken of as an outstanding dry goods warehouse by all contemporary writers. The original building was a delightful little Venetian palazzo five windows wide, west of the centre line. The very obvious addition above the cornice took the place of a roof with dormers in recent times. (demolished in the 1960's)

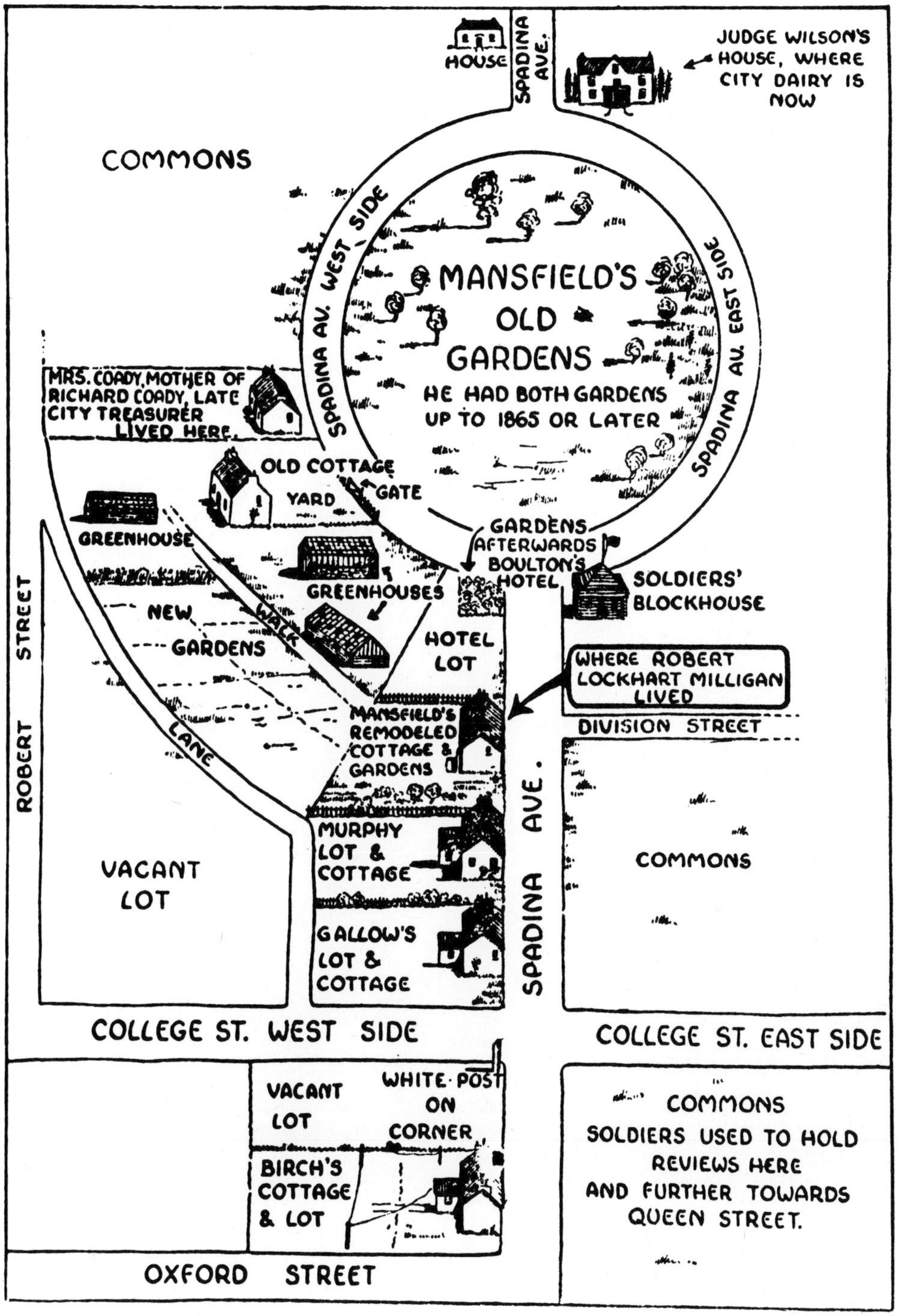
HOUSE
SPADINA AVE.
JUDGE WILSON'S HOUSE, WHERE CITY DAIRY IS NOW
COMMONS
SPADINA AV. WEST SIDE
SPADINA AV. EAST SIDE
MANSFIELD'S OLD GARDENS
HE HAD BOTH GARDENS UP TO 1865 OR LATER
MRS. COADY, MOTHER OF RICHARD COADY, LATE CITY TREASURER LIVED HERE.
OLD COTTAGE
YARD
GATE
GARDENS AFTERWARDS BOULTON'S HOTEL
SOLDIERS' BLOCKHOUSE
GREENHOUSE
GREENHOUSES
NEW GARDENS
WALK
HOTEL LOT
WHERE ROBERT LOCKHART MILLIGAN LIVED
DIVISION STREET
ROBERT STREET
LANE
MANSFIELD'S REMODELED COTTAGE & GARDENS
MURPHY LOT & COTTAGE
VACANT LOT
COMMONS
SPADINA AVE.
GALLOW'S LOT & COTTAGE
COLLEGE ST. WEST SIDE
COLLEGE ST. EAST SIDE
VACANT LOT
WHITE POST ON CORNER
COMMONS
SOLDIERS USED TO HOLD REVIEWS HERE AND FURTHER TOWARDS QUEEN STREET.
BIRCH'S COTTAGE & LOT
OXFORD STREET

249 Spadina Avenue (*c.* 1860), drawn from memory by R. L. Milligan. The circle was for Toronto in 1860, or at any time, a bold piece of planning. It is unfortunate that the idea was not developed with concentric ring streets such as surround the Arc de Triomphe in the centre of the Etoile in Paris. The "lane" was a half-hearted attempt.
It will be remembered that Spadina got its name from Spadina House (1819), the residence of Dr. W. W. Baldwin who laid out Spadina Avenue as early as 1813–18 from Bloor St. to Queen, and made it a gift to York. Spadina is said to mean a sudden rise of ground, and it was at the head of the rise that Spadina House was built. It was destroyed by fire in 1835.

251 A doorway at 397 Grange Place off Dundas near the Art Gallery (*c.* 1865). A very elegant doorway with windows that once knew muntin bars and shutters (see hinges on upper window), now puts on a brave face in a wall of sheet metal, rusticated to imitate masonry. (in 1973 no longer elegant)

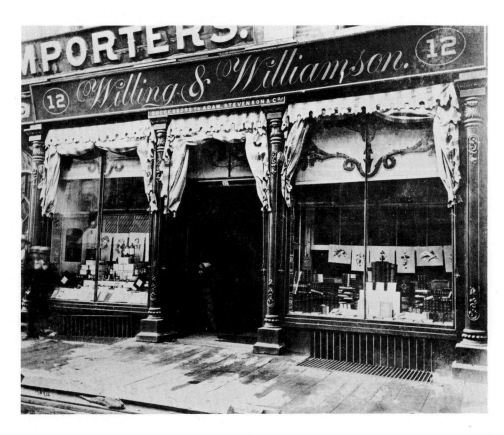

252 The Bank of Toronto (1863), Church and Wellington streets, Wm. Kauffman, architect (demolished). A palazzo type of bank headquarters not quite as rich in detail as the Ontario Bank (Scott and Wellington) a block away (**271**). The photograph was taken by Notman, probably in the seventies when the Georgian cottage leaned against the bank next door. The site is an historic one. Ontario House (**37**) once looked across at the Island from this corner.

253 House at Maitland Street (1865). This attractive little town house (demolished 1971) boasted the only cast iron verandah in Toronto. This served no useful purpose in terms of shade on the north side of the house, but it was beautiful to look at or through, and probably recalled for the owner a visit to New Orleans.

254 Willing and Williamson, 12 King Street East, originally Adam, Stevenson and Co. (*c.* 1860) (demolished). The photograph was taken in 1870. This is the kind of little shop that in London would be "By Appointment" and would have an exclusive business with the gentry. Everything about it is delightful – the lettering might be 1760 instead of 1860; the "strap work" on the inside blinds would, today, be a collector's piece, and the pattern formed by vertical and horizontal rods below the windows is a masterpiece of simplicity. Nothing could be more incongruous than the board sidewalk as a foreground to such sophisticated elegance.

255 The modern "Spadina House" at 258 Spadina Road. In 1866 Mr. James Austin, the founder of the Dominion Bank in 1871 and its president from then until his death in 1897, acquired 80 acres of land stretching from St. Clair Avenue in the north to Davenport on the south with complete protection from development east and west. Consequently, Sir Winston Churchill Park, Casa Loma, the tall apartment houses at St. Clair and Spadina and Ardwold Gate are all on what was once Austin land. Dr. W. W. Baldwin's Spadina was on the property and was demolished to make room for the new Spadina House. All that remains of it is a warm red brick wall in the basement and a handsome eight-panelled door with sidelights under an elliptical arch which was undoubtedly the front door of Dr. Baldwin's house. It is now the back door of the present Spadina, and many of the interior doors were copied from it for the 1866 house.

255

256

257

256–258 This is the Victorian house *par excellence*. Everything is old, in fine condition even to fabrics, and there is none of the clutter seen in contemporary interiors like those on page 145. There is no record of an architect for the house but over the years it has received additions, alterations and an added storey by Mr. Eustace Bird, Col. Vaux Chadwick and Carrere and Hastings (New York) who were also architects for the Bank of Toronto at King and Bay (288), the Royal Bank east of Yonge Street on Bloor and the New York Public Library.

Mrs. Seton Thompson who has the pleasure of owning and living in Spadina House came to it with her parents in 1898, when she was five years old. Mr. James Austin was her grandfather. Her memory of even those early years is remarkable and her son, Mr. Austin Thompson, is now engaged on a history of the house and property. The entrance (255) has a porte-cochère in wrought iron and glass by Carrere and Hastings. The drawing room (256) is large and well proportioned with a mantel in white marble at each end. The billiard room (257) has its art nouveau frieze. The reception room (258) is in red brocade and gold, a beautiful room where guests were received before they passed into the drawing room through a door on the right.

258

259 A view of Yonge Street, east side, looking south
from Colborne Street in 1868. The building at the
corner of Colborne and Yonge (foreground) was
first Ross, Mitchell and Company, then the Bank
of Upper Canada and finally the Bank of Commerce.
The architect was William Thomas.

In the evolution of taste over one hundred years, the last phase, which takes us to the end of the 19th century, might seem to the casual observer in Toronto to be hardly worthy of study. He would be wrong because even a marked deterioration in taste is not uninteresting, and what there was of clutter in the flocked and claustrophobic drawing-rooms of the well-to-do was offset by architectural movements of great significance. A new and virile architecture which was to culminate in the Toronto City Hall (1890) was in the making, and even the seventies showed an awareness of the possibilities of cast iron in the construction of buildings—a technique that was to lead to the sky-scrapers in steel that are now a commonplace in the urban scene. The same seventies saw the arrival on the Canadian artistic scene of the Ontario Society of Artists. Meeting first in 1872 in the house of Mr. J. A. Fraser at 28 Gould Street, the Society is without doubt the oldest society of

5: Romanesque and Cast Iron

260 The Golden Lion, a well-known dry goods store at 35–37 King Street East (demolished), from a photograph taken in 1867. Architecturally, the building is remarkable for the large areas of glass in the lower floors and for the lightness of the mullions that divided it. In 1886, Timperlake commented on the airiness of the façade. The lion on the parapet is every bit as "rampant" as the one that once stood in a similar location on the Duke of Northumberland's house in London.

261 The Golden Griffin, 128, 130 and 132 King Street East (*c.* 1870) (demolished). The date would be not unreasonable in view of the Notman and Fraser photograph of 1873. One would like to have lived to see this splendid emporium (shop seems so inadequate a word), and its even more splendid and defiant golden griffin which presides over the chaos on the board sidewalk below.

its kind in Canada. The seventies also saw an Art School with a provincial grant established over a store at 14 King Street west. By 1912, the school with such humble beginnings became the Ontario College of Art.[1]

For the new architecture that was in the making, we owe a lasting debt to Chicago. In the eighties of the last century, almost all architectural creative activity in North America was concentrated in that city. Where a cold, classic academism had settled on New York and the eastern seaboard, the atmosphere of Chicago was charged with curiosity and experiment in all matters pertaining to building—particularly with cast iron and the seemingly limitless vistas opened up by the electric elevator. From this period, a dozen or more architects have left their mark on the modern movement in architecture, and no work on the history of the movement is complete without a record of the achievements of Jenney, Richardson, Burnham, Root and Sullivan whose pupil was Frank Lloyd Wright.

The architectural excitement that was generated in the midwest was bound to be felt in Toronto. Travel by rail was not difficult, and an entirely new means of communication was available through the architectural magazines which made their appearance in the last quarter of the century. We can be sure that the professional appetite for illustrated architectural literature was as insatiable then as it is today, and that English and American magazines were eagerly sought and thoroughly perused. By 1888, the demand in Toronto was sufficient to warrant the monthly publication of the *Canadian Architect and Builder*, bound copies of which may still be found on the shelves of the older offices.

While there was much poor building in the last quarter of the 19th century, there was much that was good. The poor can hardly be defended, but, to a point, it can be explained. One has to remember, despite the newer currents mentioned,

262 Wellington Street East, north side looking west from 'Change Alley (1868). The building in the right foreground is the Toronto Exchange built in 1855 (**179**). Farther to the left is the corner of Scott and Wellington with Cooper's Arms Hotel on the left and the Ontario Bank on the right (**270**).

the comparative isolation of Toronto in, say, 1875 from such large traditional centres of architectural activity like London, Paris or Berlin—even Chicago was 525 miles away and a severe depression was in the making. Our local architects, like their predecessors, had been brought up in the classic and gothic schools, and, even though they must have been vaguely conscious that the machine was going to affect their ancient craft as it had already affected industry, they could not know whither it would lead, or how.

Such a revelation is not, as a rule, for the anonymous practitioner, but for the genius. Of these, there were several in the 19th century, but the potentialities of the machine through the mass production of building materials and of well-designed everyday things were not revealed to us until architects like Gropius, Le

263 The corner of King and Yonge streets in 1868.

264

264 Wellington Street, south side, looking east, in 1868. From right to left the buildings are: (1) the house of F. C. Capreol, a prominent merchant, financier and railway promoter who lived here from the 1850's to 1874; (2) Edinburgh Life Association; (3) The Commercial Bank (**100**).

265 College Avenue (now University Avenue) from Queen looking north to Queen's Park, photographed *c.* 1868. The street was laid out by the University as an approach to King's College.

266 College Avenue (now College Street) from Yonge looking west, photographed *c.* 1868. The street was laid out by the University as an approach from the east to King's College.

Corbusier and Mies van der Rohe appeared in Europe in the late twenties of this century. In 1964, we cannot excuse the flashy products of the automobile and radio industries on the grounds that we know no better, or that the products of the machine are necessarily ugly. A thousand machine-made objects prove such a statement to be false. Very different was the position of the designer in the groping years of the late 19th century when too often products of the machine, the handicraft industry and building were, alike, ugly. But even if the mediocre dominated,

265

266

163

267 A toll-gate (demolished) Yonge and Marlborough streets, photographed in 1890.

268 Buildings (1870) on Front Street at Wellington.

269 The corner of Bay and Front streets, 1876.

267

268

269

270

270, 271 the Ontario Bank, northeast corner of Scott and Wellington streets (1875), Joseph Sheard and William Irving, architects. This is a very good example of the type of bank that suggested opulence and security, and used the Italian palazzo as a model. Much later in New York, architects like McKim, Mead and White used the same model for banks, clubs and other buildings. The annex to the Royal Bank on King Street is an example of the latter manner. (demolished)

there were fine buildings, large and small, which, even today, we look on with admiration and respect. They were, undoubtedly, inspired by the magazines through which the architect found himself in a new world with ever widening horizons. Without stirring from his office, he could become familiar with the lastest buildings in Europe or the United States, and, compared with his library of ancient monuments, these were alive, of his day, and of immediate concern.

Of the buildings that he would see illustrated, the ones that would strike him most forcibly, would be, as we have said, from Chicago. This Chicago Movement took two forms, both of which were to find an echo in Toronto. The first sprang from the office of an architect named H. H. Richardson, and the second from a realization of the potentialities of cast iron as a building material. Richardson was keenly aware of the humdrum and frequently shoddy building that was going on

271

272-274 These small photographs show a few of the many sculptured key stones on the Ontario Bank.

272

273

274

275–277 House of Mr. T. C. Patteson, founder of the *Mail*, Post Master of Toronto, 399 Sherbourne Street. Later the house of Mr. Samuel Trees whose family in 1960 had occupied it for eighty-five years. The history of this house goes deep into the 19th century with memories of Sir John A. Macdonald who occupied it for two years, and of the first electric lighting in Toronto – a business in which Mr. Trees was associated with Sir Henry Pellatt. The carriages and horses have gone along with the last electric automobile. Mrs. Lucas, a daughter, was certain that, while the house was regularly cleaned, it had never been redecorated.

Mrs. C. S. MacInnes, whose father built 399 Sherbourne, informs me that the bricks came from a house occupied by Capt. Retallack, A.D.C. to Sir Edmund Head, on Government House grounds at the corner of Simcoe and King streets.

The upper picture shows a bedroom, the larger one a drawing room, and the upper one, opposite, a sitting room. (demolished in 1966)

275

276

277

about him, and he sought a substitute. He found it in the Romanesque architecture of northern Italy which, in his hands, became part of the vernacular architecture of the United States. Richardson had a genius for material, and it was part of his genius that he saw an affinity between the rubble walls of northern Italy and the traditional stone walls of his own country. They were rugged, masculine and unaffected, and his Marshall Field store showed his contemporaries that the eternal qualities of proportion, scale and rhythm were attainable even in a purely utilitarian building. When Louis Sullivan saw the Marshall Field store he said "stone and mortar here spring to life and are no more material and sordid things—an elemental urge is there."

Richardson had many admirers both in the United States and in Canada. His architecture, and even that of his imitators, stood out like rocks in the urban sea of insincere and trivial building that characterized his period. In Toronto, nothing for a mile around comes close to the scale of the City Hall, which is a good example of the Richardson manner; and the Legislative Buildings in Queen's Park, a less successful example, reduces almost to insignificance its loftier, younger neighbours.

[*Text continues page 201*]

278 House of Mr. Joseph Gearing, northeast corner of Yonge and Carlton streets (1871) (demolished). Mr. Gearing was a successful builder with Deer Park Church to his credit in 1870. His is likely to have been one of the last of the Georgian houses, and one would hardly believe that eight years later public taste would so change that Police Station 4 (**299**) could be built without public ridicule. There are, of course, signs of uncertainty in the design of the house. The cornice and corbels don't seem right; and the chimneys are small and mean. But these are details that hardly detract from a pleasant group of house and business offices.

280 Gooderham and Worts Distillery on the
Esplanade (1870), David Roberts, architect. This is the
building of 1870 though there is no reason to believe
it was radically different from its predecessor which
burned in 1860. Much has been written recently
of the industrial and commercial buildings of the 19th
century in England. This distillery and the
McLaughlin Flour Mills (**231**) show how high was the
standard of design in Toronto. In this example, we
might criticize the smallness of the windows and the
consequent lighting conditions for workmen
within, but, looking at it just as a building (which, of
course, no good critic would dream of doing), the
masonry is impressive, the gable well proportioned,
and the strong bands tying the window sills give the
building an almost Florentine look – especially if one
could ignore the dormers.

280

279 The arms of England over the entrance to an office
building at Yonge and Wellington streets. It is
generally assumed that the arms come from the Bank
of North America which was once on the same site,
but a magnifying glass on the picture (**108**, above) will
show that the shield on the bank is not round, and,
while the unicorn is facing in the same direction as
the one in the detail, the lion is not. (demolished)

281 Town Houses, 279 and 281 Sherbourne Street. It
was in houses such as these that gentlemen lived
before the move to Rosedale. Well-proportioned
rooms, high ceilings, abundant light and "an address"
were essential requirements.

281

282

282 The Necropolis, Winchester Street, opposite the Zoo (1872), Henry Langley, architect. A very interesting group of buildings as an entrance to an equally interesting old Toronto graveyard. In a study of taste, the gravestones should not be neglected as each phase in the architecture of the 19th century finds an echo in lettering and design in our older cemeteries. For such a study, St. James' Cemetery and the Necropolis provide the best examples.

283 A. R. McMaster and Bro. Dry Goods warehouse, Yonge and Front streets (1871) (demolished). So unlike the very functional warehouses of today in which brick walls enclose a space, nothing less than the Second Empire was good enough for Mr. McMaster. The warehouse resembles the eighth Post Office in the same manner at the head of Toronto Street (**204**).

283

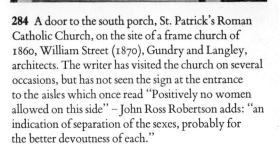

284 A door to the south porch, St. Patrick's Roman Catholic Church, on the site of a frame church of 1860, William Street (1870), Gundry and Langley, architects. The writer has visited the church on several occasions, but has not seen the sign at the entrance to the aisles which once read "Positively no women allowed on this side" – John Ross Robertson adds: "an indication of separation of the sexes, probably for the better devoutness of each."

286 Consumers' Gas Company building, Toronto Street (1873), David Dick, architect. Toronto has never displayed so many contrasts in its architecture as it has in the last decade. The sturdy Renaissance façade of the Gas Company's building dominates completely its loftier and rather naked neighbour. The less important doorway next the glass building has a door worth a visit.

285

285, 287 The new Grand Opera House, south side of Adelaide between Yonge and Bay streets, from the *Canadian Illustrated News* (1874). The "new Grand Opera House" opened in 1874 under the distinguished patronage of the Marquis and Marchioness of Dufferin and Ava. In honour of his Excellency, a descendant of Sheridan, the first play to be seen or heard in the building was *The School for Scandal* with Mrs. Morrison as Lady Teazle. The engraving of the exterior indicates a building of quite frightening scale and proportions. (Demolished)

287

288 Bank of Toronto, King Street (1911), Carrere and Hastings, architects; adjoining building with shops below (1873). The second half of the 19th century produced no finer bank building, or one so rich in rare marbles and brass fittings. Everywhere in the interior and the exterior was evidence of craftsmanship of the highest order. Both buildings were demolished in 1966. Fragments of the marble carving and interior brass have been preserved by Mr. Spencer Clark at the Guild of All Arts. Materials: interior, various rare marbles; exterior, Georgia Pink marble.

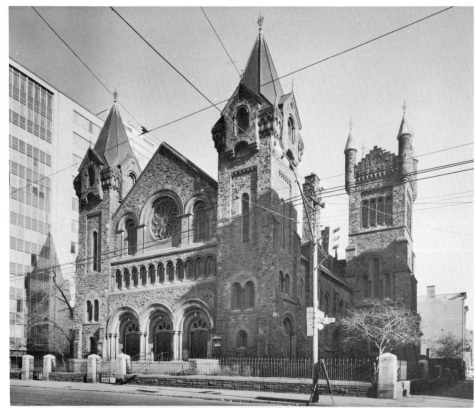

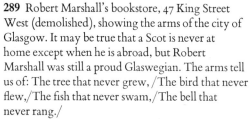

289 Robert Marshall's bookstore, 47 King Street West (demolished), showing the arms of the city of Glasgow. It may be true that a Scot is never at home except when he is abroad, but Robert Marshall was still a proud Glaswegian. The arms tell us of: The tree that never grew, /The bird that never flew, /The fish that never swam, /The bell that never rang./

290 Church of St. Andrew, southeast corner of King and Simcoe streets (1875), William George Storm, architect. Storm's name appears in the architecture of Toronto almost always in conjunction with his partner Cumberland. Here, as with Victoria College (main building), he was on his own. St. Andrew's is a romantic, but powerful design with obvious vernacular influences from the kirk in Scotland. As an example of the "picturesque" it has no equal in Toronto. Masonry, Ohio sandstone.

291, 292 The Customs House at the corner of Front and Yonge streets (1876), R. C. Windeyer, architect (demolished). This building, like the eighth Post Office (**204**), belongs to that period of architecture known as the Second Empire. It was demolished in 1919. Unfortunately, a wrecker sold fragments to a collector who assembled them without rhyme or reason in a façade opposite the City Hall (**291**) (demolished). Rome has many examples of this kind of pilfering, but it was usually better done.

290

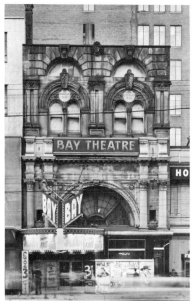

291

292

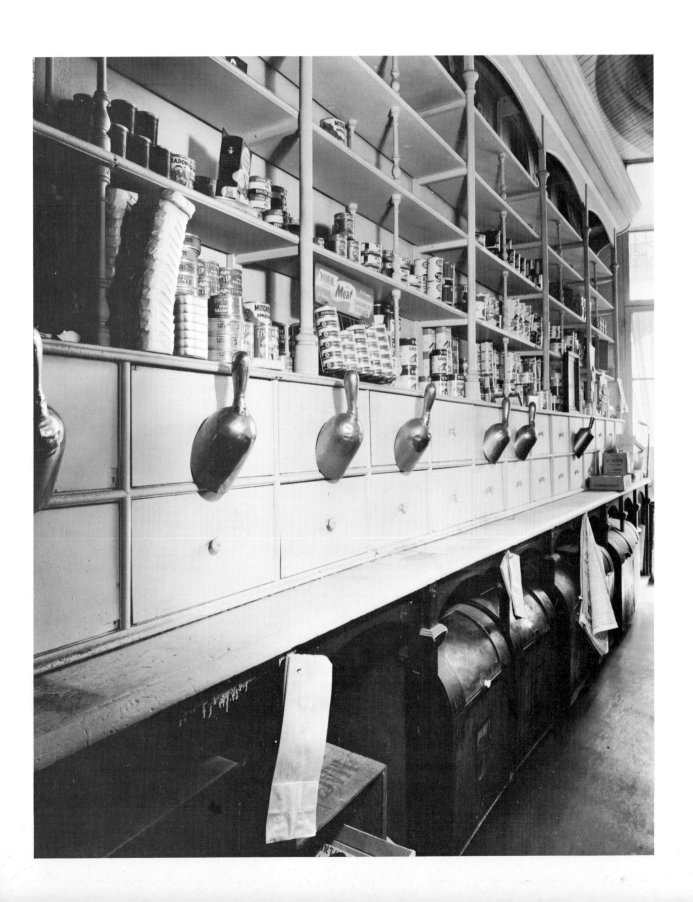

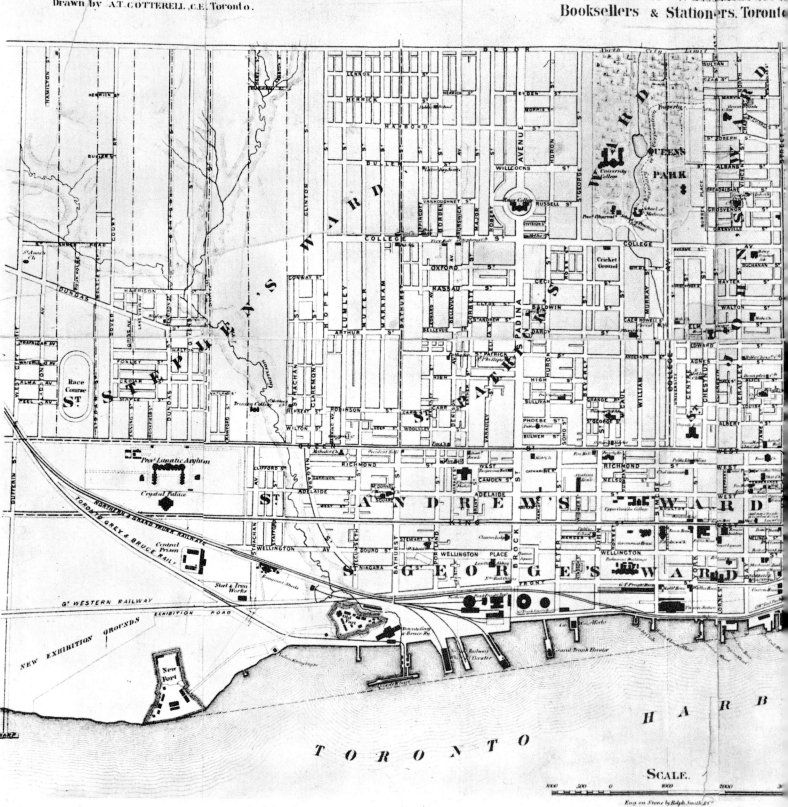

MAP of TORON

Published by
WILLING & WILLIAMSO
Booksellers & Stationers, Toronto

Drawn by A.T. COTTERELL, C.E. Toronto.

SCALE.

1000   500   0   1000   2000   3

Eng on Stone by Ralph Smith & Co

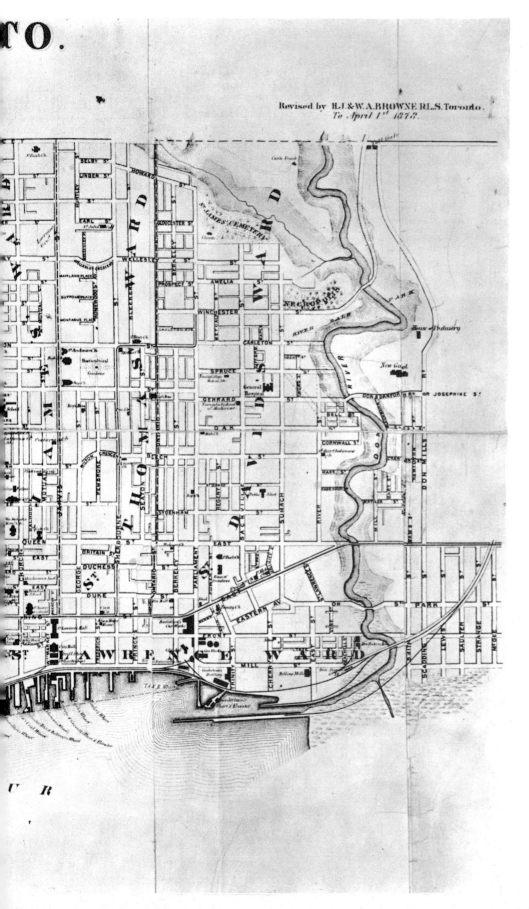

296 Victoria Orange Hall, at the corner of Queen and Berti streets (1886), E. J. Lennox, architect. We are only beginning to appreciate Lennox as an architect. Casa Loma is something hard to live down, but the City Hall and this building are among his best works. The Orange Hall has been neglected by critics, but in the opinion of this writer it is full of charm. Especially in the morning sun, the east side is a symphony formed by the rhythmic play of arches combined with carefully disposed accents in a rising scale of brick piers. It is clear that there were still brick craftsmen in 1886. (demolished 1971)

296

295 A group of houses on Spruce Street (*c.* 1880). Were it not for the dormers one might be looking in the dusk at a stable on a noble estate in provincial France. This is not row housing at its best, but it contributes something to an otherwise uninteresting street.

297 Equity Chambers, at the corner of Adelaide and Victoria streets (1878). This is the building, on the right of the photograph, of which the author of *Toronto Old and New* said: "The building was designed with special reference to giving abundant light and good ventilation, and was the first business block in the city to introduce the elevator for the convenience of its tenants and their clients." A more miserable arrangement of windows for so lofty an ideal could hardly be imagined. (demolished in the late 1960's to provide a parking lot)

297

298 Restaurant of Mr. George S. McConkey, 27, 29 King Street West (1880) (demolished). In 1894, the members of the Ontario Association of Architects moved for their dinner meetings from Webb's to McConkey's. The latter was described as "more elegant" and the resort of *le beau monde*.

299, 300 Police Station and Fire Hall, at the corner of Parliament and Dundas streets (1879). In a study of taste over a century of building, examples that are characteristic of a period cannot be left out. The flower of Toronto architecture is not to be found in Police Station 4. The small garage with the fancy Dutch gable would appear to be older than its brash neighbour to the east. The small photograph shows a keystone.

299

300

301 Terra Cotta panel on a house on Carlton Street opposite Allan Gardens (c. 1880). This is a rather special example of terra cotta in Toronto, but smaller panels were very common in houses of the period. Strangely enough, they seem to have stood the test of time better than the terra cotta of the 20th century which deteriorated badly on buildings like the C.P.R. building and the Toronto General Hospital.

302, 303 T. Eaton store. The first store (1870–1883) was a homely Georgian building, later occupied by Simpson's, at the southwest corner of Queen and Yonge. No adequate photograph remains. In 1883 Mr. Timothy Eaton established himself in the London House at 194 Yonge Street, and, eventually, bought the whole block. The photograph on the right is interesting as showing the genesis of a store that now ranks among the largest on the continent. Eaton's still takes its address on Yonge, no. 190, from the little shop on the left.

Opposite the modern store (left, above) was once Knox Church, and it is an illusion that customers are moving from Eaton's to the Presbyterian Church. Simpson's now occupy the site of old Knox.

304 No. 188 Yonge Street (*c.* 1890). The cavern below is modern, but the top is Victorian in its most whimsical mood. An old Eatonian remembers when the original owner was a Miss Naomi Bilton who sold fish in her store. She left her property to the University of Toronto.

305 The Manning Arcade, King Street West (1884), E. J. Lennox, architect (demolished). A robust piece of design with well-lit offices by the architect of the City Hall. Of interest is the three dimensional effect obtained by placing the bay in a deep sculptured recess in the façade. Something similar can be seen in the old head office of the Bank of Nova Scotia on King St. (**380**). Masonry, Ohio sandstone.

306 Central Prison (1884), Strachan Avenue, south of King Street (demolished). This view of a jail comes from *Picturesque Toronto* (1885), but it is not to be found in the *Landmarks* or in any of the usual sources.

307

307 Canadian Imperial Bank of Commerce, once the Bank of British North America, northeast corner of Yonge and Wellington streets (1885), Henry Langley architect. It is interesting to compare the three banks where the Italian palazzo gave the appearance of opulence and vast resources. The Bank of Toronto (**252**) has gone, but the Ontario Bank (**271**) and the old Bank of North America still more than hold their own against modern neighbouring structures. (The Ontario Bank gave up the struggle and was demolished in 1964.)

308, 309 St. Mary's Roman Catholic Church, west side of Bathurst Street at Adelaide (1885–89), Joseph Connolly, architect; spire by A. W. Holmes, architect. The combination of Connolly and Holmes produced an outstanding church that sits with distinction at the end of the vista of Adelaide Street. It has long been regarded with affection by Roman Catholics in the neighbourhood. The interior is one of the finest in Toronto. It is full of colour and light right up to the splendid timber roof whose ridge is 65′ from the floor. The columns are polished granite with Queenston bases and Ohio sandstone capitals.

308

309

310–312 Bank of Montreal, Front and Yonge streets (1885), Frank Darling and S. G. Curry, architects; Holbrook and Mollington, sculptors. Mr. Frank Darling had his office on Leader Lane, and to it he attracted all the bright young men of his day. Mr. Henry Sproatt, the architect of Hart House, was one of the draftsmen who worked on this building. It is frankly a Beaux Arts design – opulent and impressive in a way still thought necessary in a bank head office. As with the "old lady of Threadneedle Street," one thinks of it as feminine, marvellously well-preserved and still gay in spite of a "modernistic" clock, catchy signs and new unsuitable doors. We can be thankful that, so far, the Bank has not thought it necessary to clean the old lady by sand blasting. That would be the last indignity.

The upper photograph shows the interior at closing time. The large photograph opposite is of the massive and beautiful doorway which was sacrificed in a recent effort to "jazz up" the façade.

Masonry, Ohio sandstone.

310

311

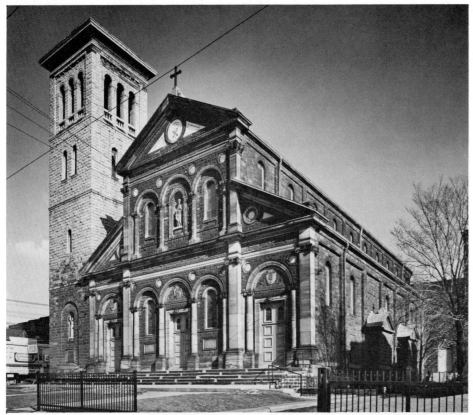

314

315

313–315 St. Paul's Roman Catholic Church, Queen and Power streets (1887), Joseph Connolly, architect. This church was a rather courageous attempt at a design in the Italian Renaissance manner in a city where nearly all churches were Gothic. It is not entirely successful, but it deserves a better setting, which it once had. The interior (opposite) is quite the most beautiful church interior in Toronto and because of it the church should appear in any list of buildings worthy of preservation. The small photograph shows an interior detail, looking toward the pulpit.

316 House of Mr. G. P. Magann, "Thorncrest," on Dowling Avenue, David Roberts, architect (demolished). A large house for Toronto, it once occupied a site overlooking the Humber Bay at the foot of Dowling Avenue. The photograph is not a good one, but it illustrates many features in the building that had their origin in Chicago – the rambling plan that takes advantage of view, sun or breeze, of rugged masonry and outdoor covered space. Frank Lloyd Wright's work in the United States demonstrated the same "hovering planes" over deeply recessed areas, and some of his earliest houses show several of the characteristics of Thorncrest by Roberts.

317 House of Dr. G. R. McDonagh, 329 Church Street (1888), E. J. Lennox, architect. On this very nice town house of a well-to-do doctor the architect for the City Hall lavished a good deal of care. The Richardsonian manner of the City Hall (**351**) shows in the basket weave brickwork, carving and the very handsome dormer.

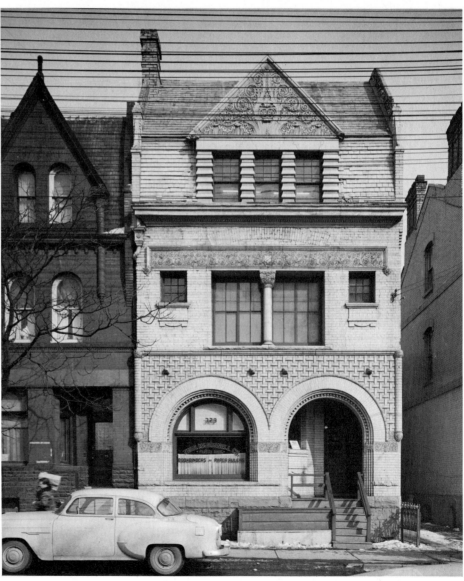

318, 319 The Toronto Club, Wellington and York streets (1897), Frank Darling, architect. The Club was established in 1835, a date that justifies its claim to be second in age only to the Philadelphia Club on this continent. Its continuous minutes go back to 1842 when rooms were secured in the British Coffee House, on the site of the present Toronto Dominion Centre. In 1864, the Club had acquired its own building at 77–79 York Street, where it remained until its present quarters were erected in 1897. It is difficult to give it an architectural label. In a way, it is a history of architecture from Jacobean to Georgian times – all held together by the skill of the architect. Rooms in the Club are spacious with liberal use of wood panelling and broad fireplaces. The small photograph is a view from the hall with the lounge to the south and the reading room to the west.

319

318

321

320

320–322 Benvenuto (1890), Stanford White, architect; on the west side of Avenue Road hill (demolished). This was the residence of Mr. S. H. Janes the successful real estate promoter who laid out the area we know as the Annex, bounded by Avenue Road, Bathurst Street, Dupont and Bloor. The writer remembers the house, which was built of grey rockfaced Kingston stone (still to be seen in a wall on Avenue Road south of Edmund Drive) with very handsome red glazed roof tiles which are now on the house of Mr. R. A. Laidlaw at Roche's Point, Lake Simcoe (H. J. Burden, architect).
The small photograph (320) shows the lodge which, with the gates (322) lasted long after the house had been demolished, the gates in a new position between piers at 40 Burton Road in Toronto. There are no finer examples of wrought iron in Canada. They were made while Mr. Janes and his family were in Italy, and it is quite likely that they made more than one visit to the ironworker at his foundry. For a time the lodge was a tea room, but it and the wall disappeared in the building of the apartment house on the site. 321 shows the south front of the house.

322

323

323 Benvenuto, a bedroom.

324 Benvenuto, the dining room.

324

325 Mr. Janes reading in the gallery of his former home on Jarvis Street.

326 Another view of the gallery. An interesting comparison can be made between the auction room atmosphere of this room and the dining room (**324**) in Benvenuto. While both rooms suggest opulence, one is void of design and the other gives the feeling of order, discrimination and taste. Mr. Janes' architect in this case was Stanford White of the distinguished New York firm of McKim, Mead and White.

328

327 Stables behind 96 Bloor Street West, the residence of Mr. Sandison Pearcy (1890's) (demolished). Mr. Pearcy's house was less striking than the stables which were demolished some years ago. He was a great lover of horses which would account for the extent and picturesqueness of the stable block.

329 House of Mr. John Miller, 33 Murray Street (c. 1890) (demolished). Mr. Miller was a journalist at one time on the staff of the *Mail and Empire*. The house is said to be a copy of one that he admired in Brussels, but it is more likely to have been the result of his extensive travels in the Near East and the Holy Land. The house has gone, but it was always rather tantalizing to pass it. One expected veiled ladies of the household to sun themselves on the upper balcony, or to take a brief walk on Murray Street, as a poor substitute for the casbah in Marrakeech.

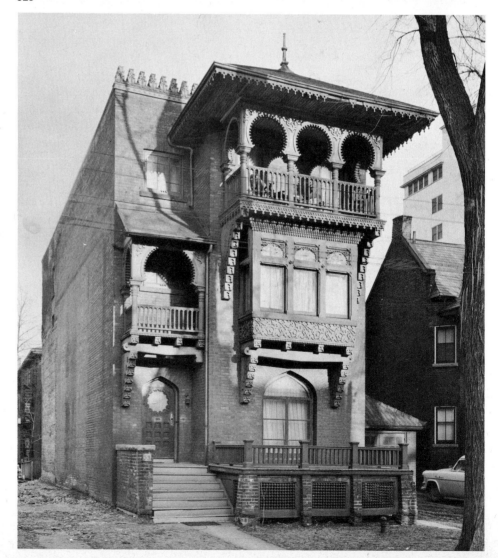

330

328, 330 The University of Toronto Library (1892), David Dick, architect. The west façade (opposite page) shows a rather incoherent design which has not been improved by a recent addition to the north. Faults of the original are made up for in part by the beauty of the dominating tower and the graceful entrance. Some credit for the design of the tower must be given the masons who worked on Kelso Abbey (left) (founded 1128) nearly 800 years before the Library was built. (for stone used see **190**)

331 Notman and Fraser building, 41 King Street East, on the left of the Golden Lion (**260**). China Hall adjoins to the east. The photograph, taken in 1884, shows a sign "Notman and Fraser Photographers to the Queen." Their superb collection of portraits and buildings of the 19th century are now the property of McGill University. The negatives number some 350,000.

331

332 Gooderham Building, Front and Wellington streets (1892), Wm. Kauffman, architect. This well-known building stands on the site of an earlier and blunter flat iron known as the Coffin Block. The old Bank of Toronto, right (**252**), demolished, was built on the site of the famous Ontario House (**37**). The stone employed on the Gooderham building was Kingston limestone from the Black River formation of Ontario. It was also known as Longford.

334 St. John's Church, Portland Street (1893), Eden Smith, architect (demolished). Usually known as the Garrison Church, it saved the troops the fatigue of marching to St. James. Victoria Square nearby is still owned by the Government of Ontario. and is the graveyard of 400 soldiers and early citizens, among them children of Sir John Colborne.
(demolished 1963)

333 House at the corner of Bancroft and Huron streets (*c.* 1890). The house of a reasonably well-to-do citizen in the Romanesque manner characteristic of the Annex. The house is now part of the University of Toronto's health services.

332

334

335

336 The Toronto Hunt Club (1895), Darling and Pearson, architects (this section demolished).

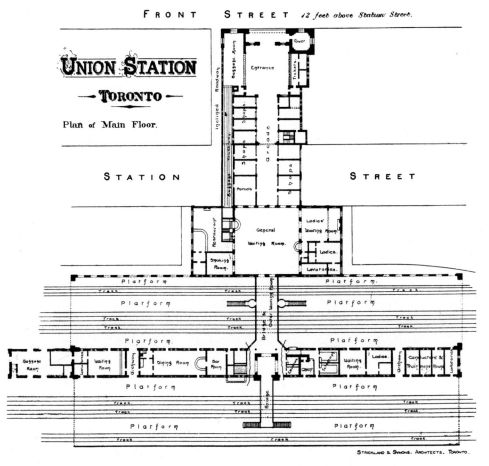

337

335, 337 The Toronto Station (1896), Strickland and Symons, architects. Long after this stage in station planning the customers were in comparatively low, undistinguished waiting-rooms and the trains in lofty glass-vaulted halls. The new, and present station, followed the Pennsylvania Station in New York where the situation was reversed – the passengers were given the lofty halls and the trains were relegated to spaces under low flat roofs. All unwittingly, the Romans had provided North America with the solution in their great thermae of the second century A.D.

339

339, 340 Holy Blossom Temple, Bond Street, now the Greek Orthodox Church (1897), Benjamin Siddall, architect. The picture directly above is of the old building, which now has domes more Christian in character; the Hebraic lettering has been removed from the tympanum. The interior (left, above) has lost nothing in the change of ownership. The brilliant panels of saints in the sanctuary and the winged figures in the pendentives make a striking contrast with the simple whiteness of the walls. Explorers such as Sitwell or church-goers such as Samuel Pepys would find this little bit of Byzantium on Bond Street an interesting and colourful discovery.

338, 341 Loretto Abbey, Wellington Street near Spadina (1897), Beaumont Jarvis, architect (demolished 1961). The Abbey was part of a complex of buildings that included fragments of Vice-Chancellor Jameson's house incorporated in the spacious apartments of the Widder family. The exterior in a red pressed brick was unworthy of the interior which was quite fine. The large photograph opposite shows a detail of the chapel beneath the dome. In its later years the Abbey became a Jesuit Seminary.

341

342, 343 King Edward Hotel, Victoria Room (1903), E. J. Lennox, architect. Modern architecture in Toronto has so far failed to produce a hotel dining room with anything like the flair and the gaiety of this one. The secret of the room's success is the decorative plaster work, which reflects credit on the designer and the craftsmen who executed it. I am indebted to Mrs. H. J. Cody for the distinct recollection of meeting a Mr. Colonna of Montreal, as the designer. Present research would indicate Hynes and Company as the plastering contractors.

342

343

344

345

One can understand public and professional admiration for such "Romanesque" monuments as our City Hall and Trinity Church, Boston, but one would hardly have predicted that the same manner would seize the popular imagination in house building. Yet such was the case in Toronto where many streets in the Annex and much of St. George Street are still silent evidence of a period in the history of taste that led us to northern Italy by way of Chicago. Of the houses inspired by Richardson that are left to us, the York Club is, probably, the most striking. Outside, the walls are a combination of brickwork, ashlar and rockfaced masonry which would be formidable indeed were it not for the free-flowing lines of the carving in appropriate places, and the harmony of colour between stone, red brick and bright green copper.

The Club was originally a Gooderham house, and it is inside that one is conscious of a more human scale, the warmth of natural wood and of well-proportioned rooms. Standing in the hall or the reading room, one does not feel the presence of the original owner and his family so much as of those humble craftsmen who wrought with such skill and apparent delight the woodwork in mantels, stairs and trim in a variety of woods. It is unlikely that, after 1892, there was much call for their talents—the machine had overtaken and displaced them.

This writer is not likely to forget the first of three occasions when he had the pleasure of dining at the York Club with Mr. Frank Lloyd Wright. Students had been invited to meet the great man, and they stood entranced as he touched mouldings with his hand, and recalled as in a dream the days of his youth sixty years before in Chicago. In whatever city we met subsequently, he spoke with affection of the Club at the corner of St. George and Bloor.

The story of the City Hall is a chequered one, but one that in the end produced a really great Toronto building. The story starts with an international competition in 1885 in which fifty architects submitted designs for a court house to cost not

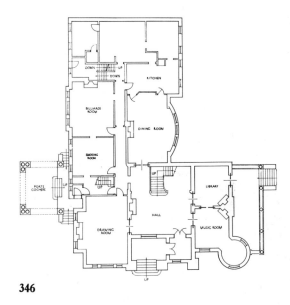

346

344-346 The York Club. South elevation (**344**); the exterior (**345**); first floor plan (**346**). Drawn by students in the School of Architecture.

347

348

349

347-350 The York Club, formerly the residence of Mr. George Gooderham at the corner of St. George and Bloor streets (1890), David Roberts, architect. The Club's motto is "Let's harbour here in York," from *Henry VI*, Part III, Act IV, Scene vii, and is said to have been quoted by Lieutenant-Governor Simcoe in May 1793 as he stepped ashore on his first visit to York.

The main entrance, St. George Street (**347**); the stone carving was done by Holbrook and Mollington. The entrance hall with fireplace (**348**). The reading room, formerly the drawing room (**349**). A staircase detail (**350**). The house is a splendid example of the Romanesque manner made popular in the 1880's by the architect H. H. Richardson whose best-known building is Trinity Church in Boston. A good many of the Annex houses as well as the old City Hall and the Legislative Building might be called Richardsonian Romanesque. Materials, red brick and Portage Brown sandstone.

350

351, 352 The old City Hall and Court House (1890) E. J. Lennox, architect; certainly the best known and probably the best loved of the old buildings in Toronto. Built of red sandstone from the Credit River, it is the best example in Toronto of the manner of building made popular by H. H. Richardson of Chicago in the eighties – especially his Pittsburgh Court House of 1886. The Legislative buildings and much of the Annex show the same influence. Remembering considerably older buildings like Notre Dame in Paris, one wonders why the fine silhouette of the clock tower was spoiled by the removal of the gargoyles a few years ago. Somewhere on the building, E. J. Lennox the architect worked his name into the scroll work of a frieze.
The photograph at the top (**351**) shows the City Hall from Osgoode Hall.

more than $200,000. Nothing came of it because the space requirements were far in excess of the sum of money allowed for building. When, nothing daunted, the City held a new competition the following year, thirteen architects competed. It is here that Mr. E. J. Lennox appears on the scene. His was the winning scheme, and, while he was a long way from building the City Hall, thirteen years in fact, he was not from then on to be diverted from that ultimate goal. It is true there are points of similarity in his scheme with the Pittsburgh Court House of 1884 by Richardson, of which Lennox was no doubt aware, but a comparison of the two would dismiss any suggestion of copying.

The first stumbling block, and it was a real one, was again one of cost. The foundations of the court house were put to tender and came out at $110,000, a financial burden not to be borne in an ultimate building to cost only twice that sum. And so, while the City waited for the next municipal election, the excavation, which should have echoed to the sound of workmen on the foundations, resounded instead to the voices of happy children—the site had become an ice rink.

In the interval, the city fathers decided that what Toronto needed was not a court house only, but a city hall as well and, in 1887, Lennox was asked to prepare drawings for a building to combine both functions. He did so superbly well. That it cost $2,500,000, a figure somewhat in excess of the target of $300,000 set by the City, was explained by Mayor John Shaw on opening day, September 18, 1899:

Why people will spend large sums of money on great buildings opens up a wide field of thought. It may, however, be roughly answered that great buildings symbolize a people's deeds and aspirations. It has been said that, wherever a nation had a conscience and a mind, it recorded the evidence of its being in the highest products of this greatest of all arts. Where no such monuments are to be found, the mental and moral natures of the people have not been above the faculties of the beasts.

After such a statement from the Chief Magistrate, there were few with the temerity to put themselves on the moral level of the beasts, and question the cost of the building.

The City Hall is built in a red sandstone from a quarry near the Forks of the Credit River that provided stone for the Legislative Buildings and much of St.

353 The Old City Hall, decoration in stone with carved heads.

354 The old City Hall, the east doorway on James Street.

355 Romanesque romanticism on James Street looking southeast.

356 The Council Chamber.

357 At the time of writing (March 1973) the old City Hall has been saved from the wrecker, but its use has not been determined. Unfortunately, it has not been seen fit to restore it as a court house. Whatever use is found for the building, it is to be hoped that the extensive court will become a garden and not a parking lot as now. The Hall has been cleaned and a most attractive stone in shades of brown has appeared. Both Sackville and Credit Valley sandstone were used.

358 Legislative Buildings, Queen's Park (1886), R. A. Waite, architect. A Notman photograph. The hipped roofs in the links between the centre and the wings are hardly appropriate in the general massing of the building, but, in the reconstruction after the fire of 1909, the link to the west was changed to a gabled roof with stone dormers. Already there are signs of the fussy Victorian flower-beds which had their origin in the 19th century gardens behind Windsor Castle, and mar the approaches to the Parliament Buildings in the capital cities of every colony and dominion in the Commonwealth. The stone used in the original building was red Credit Valley sandstone from the forks of the Credit River, Ontario. For later additions (north wing) and fire damage repair, the stone was red sandstone from the Sackville freestone quarry at Sackville, N.B.

359 University Avenue looking south from the Legislative Buildings. This Notman photograph shows a heavily wooded city of "dreaming spires." The motor car had not arrived and the citizen could enjoy the city either on foot or in a horse-drawn vehicle. The heavy turreted building on the right is the old Toronto Athletic Club which is now the Police Building. E. J. Lennox was the architect.
Just as Orde Street is closed today so all east-west streets were stopped on the Avenue by a gate or fence. It, and College Street from Yonge to McCaul, were University property, and a twelve-inch strip on College involved legal and financial negotiations before Eaton's College Street store could be built.

George Street. It is a stone that takes a rugged face, and was popular with architects who saw some kinship in it with the masonry of northern Italy. The exterior of the Hall is striking and greatly impressed the international jury that met to judge the designs submitted for the new City Hall in 1958.

On the other hand, it is difficult to enthuse over the interior. The entrance hall

is spacious, but without distinction, and the council chamber is just a room off a corridor. The entrance for the Mayor and distinguished guests is through a passage in which two can walk abreast with difficulty. One can only assume that, even in 1890, the Romanesque did not lend itself to the interiors of rooms for modern use, or that the prototype was much too far from Queen and Bay for serious study.

Obviously, a study of 19th century building in the capital city of Ontario would be incomplete without a reference to its Parliament Buildings. How they came to be as dull as they are is, perhaps, the saddest story ever told when architects meet and the talk is of competitions.

An international competition for the Legislative Buildings in Queen's Park was held in 1880, and thirteen architects competed, seven being Canadian and six American. The jury consisted of the Hon. Alex Mackenzie, W. G. Storm (an architect) and R. A. Waite, an English architect living in Buffalo. As a result of the competition, Gordon and Helliwell were placed first, Darling and Curry second and Smith and Gemmell third. Each indicated a price that was higher than the government estimate of funds available, and an extraordinary decision was reached. The first and second prize-winners were both asked to sharpen their pencils, and prepare working drawings and specifications. This they did at considerable expense with Gordon and Halliwell submitting a price of $542,000 and Darling and Curry $612,000.

Somewhat discouraged by these figures, the Province allowed the work to lapse until 1885, when "the Buffalo individual," as Mr. Waite became known in architectural circles, was asked by the government to decide between the two architectural firms. In the intervening five years, the "unspeakable" Mr. Waite had found favour with the government both as a person and as a poker player, and it did not come as a surprise when, in 1885, he announced that neither design was suitable and that (to quote the *Canadian Architect and Builder*, 1890), "he was the only architect on this continent capable of carrying out such important work." His offer to design the building was accepted and $750,000 was thought to be a realistic price in view of the previous tenders of around $600,000.

Under Mr. Waite's direction, the building cost $1,227,963 and, before he left town for his adopted heath, he designed the head offices of the Canada Life and the Bank of Commerce.

At the same time that Richardson was leaving his mark on the vernacular architecture of the United States, his contemporaries were exploring with equal vigour and greater daring the potentialities of cast iron as a structural material. Cast iron had been used in Great Britain and elsewhere on bridges, railways stations, factories and other structures since the late eighteenth century, but the invention of the electrically driven elevator in 1853 suggested a new use for the material in buildings taller than had been dreamt of up to that time. It was not until the seventies and eighties of the century that intensive reconstruction of the Loop in Chicago saw the incipient skyscraper of ten or twelve storeys with a skeleton, and sometimes a façade, of cast iron. In his book *Space, Time and Architecture* Dr. Sigfried Giedion states that iron had been used for such purposes from 1850 to 1880, and reached what he called its "classic height" in the Paris Exposition of 1889.

An examination of the structural skeleton of downtown Toronto office build-

360 Confederation Life building, northeast corner of Richmond and Yonge streets (1890), Knox, Elliott and Jarvis, architects. When it was built this was considered the last word in office buildings though today we would regard its contemporary, the Temple building (**373**), as superior, largely because it was less flamboyant and more modern in its construction. The walls of the Confederation Life building are of immense thickness and are bearing walls. Materials, brick and Portage Brown sandstone.

ings and warehouses would show quite a number to be in cast iron, and, where alterations are made to existing buildings, columns in that material are still frequently employed. The only example in Toronto, where both the structural system and the façade were of cast iron, was the Royal Canadian Bank building at 27 Wellington Street. It was an unpretentious building passed daily by hundreds without a glance, but, historically, was a landmark in a development that was sociological as well as technological. It was through experiments in iron in simple buildings like this that we arrived at those fantastic towering structures in steel which, in each decade of our century, have risen so high in the sky that Mr. Frank Lloyd Wright's mile-high building seems not outside the bounds of engineering ingenuity. Socially, such monsters are to be condemned for their disastrous effect on traffic and municipal services, and for the sunless, windy canyons which they create in congested urban areas. The lowness of the old Post Office on Toronto

361 Royal Canadian Bank, 27 Wellington Street East (*c.* 1860) (demolished). To the purist there is something quite revolting in a façade of iron simulating stone, but one has to remember the period and its problems. Actually, we are looking at a form of construction that was the precursor of the steel structures of today. The architect was prepared to use a comparatively new material, but he fell back on Renaissance forms. In that respect, he was less courageous than the designer of Oak Hall (**363**).

Street which is now an office building is, unfortunately, something that not every one can afford. Even so, it is an interesting commentary on our time that the first or second floor in a building of 1853 would be considered more desirable than the twenty-second in a new skyscraper.

Like its famous predecessor the Crystal Palace of 1851 in London, the Toronto Exhibition of 1858 was of iron and glass. In view of the rigours of the Toronto climate, it is not surprising that the influence on our architecture of either exhibition was slight, if not negligible. Windows continued to be of normal height and span until we come to 1893, and a quite unusual clothing store called Oak Hall, which once, quite jauntily, faced St. James' Cathedral.

This remarkable building was constructed in 1893 in cast iron and glass, the glass being in the largest sheets to enter Canada at that date. According to the author of *Toronto Illustrated*, the fourteen ladies on their pedestals were cast in bronze while

363 Oak Hall, King Street, opposite St. James' Cathedral (1893) (demolished). In its heyday this was a famous clothing store, but was chiefly remarkable for the lightness of its structure and the breadth of glass at all levels. (See text for comment.)

362

364

362, 364 The First and Second Crystal Palaces. There were few buildings in the world in the 19th century to equal the Crystal Palace of 1851 in Hyde Park, and several exhibition palaces followed in Canada and the United States. Like it, their construction was iron and glass. The First Crystal Palace (1858) was on a site due south of the dome of 999 Queen on King Street (**364**), Fleming and Schreiber, architects. Like the great Crystal Palace of Hyde Park, our first Palace was moved in 1879 to a new site in the present Exhibition Park, just south of the Dufferin Gate, without mishap and with maximum salvage. A ground floor was put under it and a cupola was added (**362**). Sir Sandford Fleming and his partner, Sir Collingwood Schreiber, were alive to see the change, but the design is so inferior one cannot believe them responsible.

the fifteenth, on the topmost pediment, appears to have come to life, Pygmalion-like, and is about to take off. Indeed, in the latter days of Oak Hall, the ladies became more than an embarrassment to the city. When one fell like a lethal bronze missile on King St., her sisters were all removed without even a Potter's Field to mark their resting place.

The building has, also, a serious side. In the evolution of the office building in North America, it might well be considered a landmark. It demonstrates a daringly light structure in cast iron, in which respect it is the forerunner of the steel frame-work of the modern skyscraper. The all-glass façade is a commonplace today, but, in 1893, it would have caused a sensation. The demand for daylight in the office building was recognized in Chicago in the 1880's, but the bay window as a device to direct light still farther into the recesses of the room beyond was not tried in commercial buildings until the Reliance Building of 1894. If Oak Hall were still on the old stand on King St., it would be a place of pilgrimage for architectural historians.

Its proprietor was a Canadian senator, the Hon. W. E. Sanford, who, starting in Hamilton in 1858, eventually owned a chain of Oak Halls in the Province—all dealing in clothing. Only a very modern progressive firm would build such a building, and this is further confirmed by friends now approaching seventy who remember with pleasure that, with every suit of clothes, they received a pea-shooter as a bonus.

The number of buildings with a cast iron skeleton and a façade of the same material designed to simulate stone are rare in North America, but buildings of a certain age which show a façade of brick or stone are, quite frequently, supported internally, by wood or iron columns. An inspection of buildings on the south side of Front Street between Church and Jarvis tells the whole story of construction from the primitive wood post and beam to iron columns of several sections supporting beams in iron or wood. Only the fact that they have been there so long explains their existence in contradiction of modern safety codes for downtown buildings. We shall not see their like again. The wood on the upper floors of 81 Front St. East is as odorous as sandalwood, but its odour comes from nearly a hundred years of contact with rope, caulking and canvas which are the principal stock in trade of Tom Taylor and Co., the ships' chandlers. The old pine floors polished smooth by use, the supporting wooden posts and the elderly employee sitting cross-legged as he binds a sail—all give the impression of a scene long antedating the age of steam. The rear of the store once serviced ships when the waters of the harbour came up to the Esplanade.

Exposed concrete in a building is not something for which Toronto is particularly distinguished. It is true we have grain elevators, but, some years ago, they were so badly cracked or crazed that it became necessary to spray them with a veneer of asphalt embellished with slate chips in several colours. Whether our failure to build in concrete has to do with climate or humidity and the constant freezings and thawings of a Toronto spring is not a proper discussion here, but the fact is that Holy Blossom Temple (1938) on Bathurst St. (Chapman and Oxley, architects) is the only concrete building (without covering of bricks or stone) that we can point to with any pride. On the other hand, our first reinforced concrete

365 No. 60 Front Street West, a loft building just east of the Royal York Hotel (*c.* 1900). This building is said to be the first reinforced concrete structure in Toronto. It was also a very early example of a building with glass from floor to ceiling and column to column. This is a rear view, but the front, except for added storeys in brick, is the same design. (demolished 1973)

building (1900 approximately) still stands, and has recently been exposed on its west flank by the demolition of buildings just east of the Royal York Hotel. It is a warehouse, away ahead of its time in terms of daylight, with windows from floor to ceiling. In that, and its construction, it is unique for its period, but it is not the kind of building about which one would take serious steps toward preservation. Architects and engineers of the future will look at it in a photograph and wonder at its daring. It is, already, sixty-three years old.

The change from a century of cast iron in America to the structural steel skeleton was not heralded in the first building in Toronto by any fanfare of trumpets. At the time, it may have seemed like a natural and inevitable step that made no visible change in the façade of buildings, but neither the builders nor the general public could have foreseen a time when the same construction would have produced a

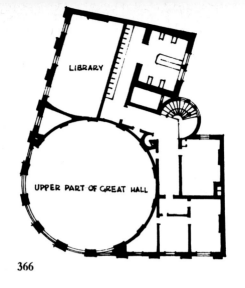

LIBRARY

UPPER PART OF GREAT HALL

366

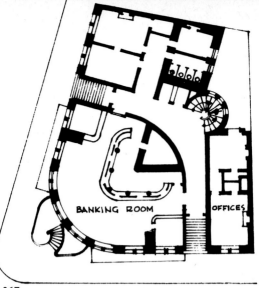

BANKING ROOM

OFFICES

367

368

Bank of Nova Scotia 322 feet high in Toronto, or an Empire State 1,472 feet high in New York.

The building that marked a turning point in Toronto, and opened a new vista with seemingly unlimited possibilities in the field of technology, was the old Board of Trade headquarters at the corner of Yonge and Front streets. The spectator would find it an unusual, but not particularly impressive office building with a curved front and conical roof. He could not know that behind the mask of brick and stone was a structural skeleton of steel. We know it from the records, and, quite recently, we saw the columns and beams laid bare by the wrecker. Like so many Toronto buildings in the 19th century, the Board of Trade was the result of an international competition. Out of a field of seventeen, half of whom were Cana-

366-368 The large photograph (**368**) is a view of Front Street between Bay and Yonge streets, north side, showing a fine office building, the old Bank of Montreal (**311**) and the Board of Trade. Both the office building and the Board of Trade were demolished in the 1960's. The small illustrations show first and second floor plans of the Board of Trade. Masonry, Portage Brown sandstone.

369, 370 Robert Simpson Co. store, southwest corner of Queen and Yonge streets, Burke and Horwood, architects. The land on which it was built was part of an area bounded by Yonge and Bay, Richmond and Queen which was deeded to "the Presbyterians" by a rich landowner and tanner, Jesse Ketchum. In 1894, the church held all that property except for the frontage on Yonge street which it had sold. Knox Church on Spadina Avenue still receives ground rent from a far from negligible piece of land beneath the Robert Simpson store.
The five bays south from Queen on Yonge and the seven bays west from Yonge and Queen date from 1895, the four bays north from Richmond are 1912. The dapple greys and their drivers are ready for the signal to leave with their deliveries – an impressive daily sight until 1928 when horsepower displaced the horses.

369

370

371 Victoria Rink, 277 Huron Street (1887), Norman B. Dick, architect (demolished 1962). When this photograph was taken, the rink was occupied by the University of Toronto, School of Architecture. The rink had a span of 85′ rising in the vault to a height of 55′.

dian architects, Messrs. James and James of New York were declared the winner in April 1889. Professor Ware of New York was the adjudicator. In its latter years it was the head office of the Toronto Transportation Commission.

In a brochure published by the Robert Simpson Company, we read that "the opening of Simpson's handsome new structure designed in the fashionable Romanesque style was an event of 1894." A store had been on the site since 1881 when Mr. Simpson shocked Toronto sensibilities by flagrantly illustrating women's corsets in his newspaper advertisements, and by exposing his first woman clerk to no one knew what perils by employment on the second floor. By 1893, Mr. Simpson had extended his property on both Queen and Yonge, and a new building was begun. Columns and beams were of steel but, one year after the opening in 1894, the store was destroyed by fire. Undaunted, Mr. Simpson proceeded with a new building of steel construction six storeys in height. With very inadequate building by-laws to guide him, but with the lesson learned from the previous fire, columns and beams were encased in concrete and floors were fire-resistant. Of considerable interest to the architectural historian are the dates carved in stone on the pilaster capitals on the Yonge Street side. They show the growth of the store from 1893 (when building started) to 1895 when the floor area was doubled, and on to later years.[2]

A number of other buildings run neck and neck for the honour of being the progenitors of modern construction in steel, but they show no particular use of the material to distinguish them from the earlier Board of Trade or the Robert Simp-

373

372 The Armouries at the corner of University Avenue and Osgoode Street (1891), Thomas Fuller, architect (demolished 1963). This is the work of the architect of St. Stephen's-in-the-Fields (**228**) in Toronto, and, with Chilion Jones, the Parliament Buildings in Ottawa. Like all armouries in North America, it was built in the style of a fortified castle with battlements and dungeon-like windows in the towers. The University armouries were, however, no dead exercise in mediaeval archaeology; they had life and nobility.

373 Temple Building, The Independent Order of Foresters' building, at the corner of Bay and Richmond streets (1895), George W. Gouinlock, architect. The movement started in Chicago by H. H. Richardson produced quite a number of pseudo-Romanesque buildings in Toronto of which this is one of the best. The architect worked with conviction, and his stone carvers were skilled in their craft. The carving below the moose head has a quality and a flourish that might point to the stone carver who later worked on 70 Wellington Street West (**378**) (demolished in 1970). Some of the fine carving on this façade has been preserved at the Guild of All Arts.

son store. Greatly daring for their time in Toronto, however, were the steel roof trusses which spanned the Armouries (1891) on University Avenue (124 feet) and the Manufacturers' Building at the Canadian National Exhibition (108 feet), both now lost to view. The spanning of the Armouries with such a truss was not impressive compared with that of the Galerie des Machines (1891) in Paris where the span was 150 meters, but both were part of an exciting period when the covering of great spaces without intermediate supports stirred the imagination of architects and engineers in Europe and America. These experiments with space would seem, in historical perspective, to have made a greater contribution to modern technology than did the skeletal frame of the incipient skyscraper of the same period.

In spite of the excitement aroused by steel in the construction industry, many Toronto buildings in the nineties continued to be built on the ancient principle of the bearing wall, and one important office building remained faithful to cast iron. The Independent Order of Foresters' building (now called the Temple Building) marks the end as well as the beginning of an era. It was the last tall office building to have a structural frame of cast iron, but its architect, Mr. George Gouinlock, introduced features that were strikingly new in 1895. In the whole history of architecture, few measures had been taken for the protection of human life from fire, and the taller buildings grew, the greater became the hazard and the more urgent the need. In the Temple Building, which would be known as a "prestige" office building in the language of today, cast iron columns and beams were protected by concrete; floors were of fire-resistant tile construction and, earlier than any similar building in Canada as far as I can discover, doors and windows were encased in metal. It is in much the same style as its neighbour the City Hall, and was four years old when the latter was opened in 1899. At the moment of writing we are hoping that, in its seventieth year, it will live to see another City Hall arise to the north on the site of the Manning Chambers and the old Hippodrome.

374 Canadian Bank of Commerce, northwest corner of Yonge and Bloor streets (1897), Darling and Pearson, architects. The design of this bank is not at all in the usual style of Darling and Pearson, but they could hardly escape the Art Nouveau manner that was the vogue in Europe. The exterior presents as fine a bank as any in Toronto. The interior was less interesting, but what evidence there was of Art Nouveau was scraped away (1960) in an attempt at modernization. No organized effort was made to save the bank with the Toronto Ladies Club on the second floor, and it was demolished in 1972 to provide a site for an office tower. Materials, may brick and Ohio sandstone.

375 Coles Restaurant, now a toy shop on the east side of Yonge south of Bloor (c. 1900). The Art Nouveau movement had little effect on Canada, and it is curious that today two of our examples should be near the corner of Bloor and Yonge – Coles and the Bank of Commerce. The movement concerned itself largely with ornament. Florid as these column capitals are, they give the impression of upward movement and strength. Rather disillusioning for the reader is the actual fact that Messrs. Cole were famous for feats of icing on wedding cakes. While the columns are plaster, they do have a disconcerting resemblance to another non-architectural material. (demolished)

In the midst of this period when architects in Toronto were so deeply concerned with the bones of their buildings in cast iron, reinforced concrete and, finally, in steel, there intruded a movement which was largely concerned with decoration. It is perhaps an exaggeration to call the scattered examples of Art Nouveau in Toronto a movement, but they are important to us in a discussion of 19th century taste in that they indicate for the first time an awareness of contemporary art in Europe by architects whose previous concern had been largely with creative activity in the United States.

Earlier than Art Nouveau was the Arts and Crafts movement in England founded by William Morris. For him and his disciples the artist was an indispensable member of society, and the so-called minor arts such as weaving, typography, furniture-making, pottery, and stained glass were as important to the well-being of the community in their civilization as were painting and sculpture.

Against such a background, it is not surprising that the Art Nouveau designers, holding identical views, should all owe a debt to Morris. They, too, were concerned with surface decoration and with the crafts, and while, later, the artist designers turned architect, and became increasingly concerned with architecture and engineering, it is with decoration and the crafts that they are best remembered. The Art Nouveau designers differed fundamentally in outlook from Morris, however, in that, while theirs was an "anti" movement discarding everything that was

376, 377 St Paul's United Church, 121 Avenue Road, the ceiling painted by Gustav Hahn in 1890. Several downtown churches have suffered from the natural tendency of a substantial section of their congregation to move to residential areas further and further north. It has affected St. Paul's, and it is pleasant to learn that a ratepayers group is, at the moment of writing, trying to save the church as a community centre. The plan is for a multi-purpose building combining concert hall, theatre, and kindred cultural facilities. It would all take place in the perfect setting of a unique and very beautiful nave, unique for its art nouveau decoration in Canada if not in North America.

376

historical or traditional in origin and looking to the future, he turned to the Middle Ages for inspiration. He was "anti" only in that he rejected the machine and all its works, and sought a new Jerusalem in industrial Britain where men, once again, would take joy in creative work and the product of their hands.

From the pre-Raphaelites who were contemporary with Morris, the Art Nouveau designers inherited the idea of the human female as the "girl-woman," virginal and frequently emaciated, with flowing hair and an expression more often of melancholy than of any other human emotion. In St. Paul's Church on Avenue Road, Mr. Gustav Hahn shows such figures. Their clothing may conceal either emaciation or a robust female form, but the expression on the face of "Joy" would not indicate that joy was an emotion any more to be desired than Goodness and Temperance which her sister maidens solemnly portray.

Important to Art Nouveau, indeed all important, was the "line," which could be "melodious, agitated, undulating, flowing or flaming," and might appear, for its own sake, as a line, or as the curling tendrils of a plant. In the St. Paul's ceiling, we see the former, in the vertical lines of the drapery and the uplifted lines of the angel's wing. In its broader form are the formal and symmetrical dark ribbon outline of the dress, and the intricate convolutions of the plant tendrils in the adjoining areas of the vault. Peter Selz says of the Art Nouveau designer, "If he used a flower, it was not the ordinary garden or field variety, but rather the languid, exotic hothouse plant whose long stalks and pale blossoms he found exquisite."[3] It was just such a plant that Mr. Hahn used to form a rhythmic pattern of lilies on both sides of the nave. The beauty of the angel figures with their lilies rising into

377

the unadorned area of the vault is given added emphasis and dignity by the juxta-position of the over-all decoration of the tendrils in the triangular spaces. The lily motif itself is so highly conventionalized that, in the gloom of the church, they appear at first sight as candelabra.

It is interesting to be able to record of a ceiling painted in the early 1890's that the artist, Mr. Gustav Hahn, was, at the time of writing, alive and could still talk about his handiwork.[4] When employed on the decoration of the ceiling, Mr. Hahn was the chief designer for a firm of decorators, Elliott & Sons, who specialized in church work and had built up a practice going back a decade or more. The donors of the work at St. Paul's were Mr. E. R. Wood and Mr. W. K. Doherty. The ceiling is not as well known as it might be because of the custom of the church

378, 379 No. 70 Wellington Street West (1905), Wickson and Gregg, architects (demolished). This excellent office building was built at a time when the Art Nouveau movement was sweeping Europe and Great Britain. Characteristic features are to be seen in the detailing of the lower windows, and of the doors in particular. The stone carving is vigorous and obviously the work of a master craftsman of whom there were not a few sixty years ago in Toronto. The weighted strings hanging from the cornice oscillate in a breeze, and seem, effectively, to discourage pigeons from roosting on the ledges of the façade at any level. They are also quite decorative in themselves. On the opposite page (**379**) is a detail of the interior.

378

(along with Methodist and Presbyterian and some Anglican churches in Canada) of keeping the doors locked on week days.

For the professional historian, Victorian architecture covers the sixty-odd years between the accession of Victoria in 1837 and her death in 1901, but to close the century, we are going to look at a more restricted period covering the last years of the old century and the early years of the seventh Edward. In it are those delightful, light-hearted, exuberant buildings that remain to enliven many a street where the architecture of an earlier time has disappeared.

For the most part, our Victorian architecture consists of houses, either single, double or in rows, and nearly always distinguishable by fretwork porches, bay windows and gay gables. In the evolution of architectural design, "ginger-bread"

380 Bank of Nova Scotia, 39 King Street West(1903), drawing by students in the School of Architecture. Covered with a "patina" of soot and guano, the old bank is too difficult to photograph. It is interesting, if only for its sculptured façade in which the wall is deeply recessed behind the Ionic columns. Those were the days (as in the Manning Chambers) when it was not necessary that every foot of floor space should be remunerative. For many years the building was used as a downtown public library. (Darling and Pearson, architects). (demolished, along with the Bank of Quebec at No. 37, in 1969)

379

381

382

383

has little to contribute, but the "ginger-bread" was but a veneer on a basic structure that we are only now beginning to appreciate. In a study of 19th century taste, we can view the decoration as a reflection of the gaiety which is popularly believed to be characteristic of life in the nineties. It may teach us nothing; but may well cause us to wonder to what excesses a later generation may go in a reaction to the curtain wall and the gutless geometry of so much of our modern domestic architecture.

383 Nos. 18–24 Soho Street: an extravaganza involving richness of detail and modelling kept under control by the strong horizontal ridge of the slate roof.

381 No. 295 Sherbourne Street. Toronto was once rich in cast and wrought iron balconies and fences. In wrought iron none was better than this lace-like example near Allan Gardens.

382 Collier Street: sunlight and shadow, the feeling of space and security through enclosure that has disappeared from the modern street. We no longer have residential street architecture – only houses.

385 No. 582 Sherbourne Street.

384 No. 500 Parliament Street. Victorian domestic architecture in its most exuberant mood. Each door once represented the entrance to a house, and it was a house with spacious rooms, high ceilings and abundant light. Perhaps from shortage of cash, the south wing with the mansard roof was not repeated to the north.

225

386 No. 691 Spadina Avenue. A Victorian house with useful bays, charming upper porch and simple railings.

The lesson we can learn from the Victorians as we could from the Georgians is the success with which they created an atmosphere of urban amenity through repetition, a sense of space through enclosure, and a human scale. These qualities in the street architecture of a city were known to the ancients; they provide the charm and the urbanity of so many towns in Britain and on the Continent, and once distinguished the streets and squares of old Toronto. Yet much of the building done in the second half of the century was large-scale speculation, and the architects of the period and their clients could not have been unaware of the attractiveness of the Georgian houses they were destroying in the search for sites.[5] Such houses can be seen in a photograph of 1875 taken from the top of the Metropolitan Church tower. Even at so late a date, Toronto was a Georgian brick town of single, double, row houses and tree-lined squares. The single houses were also united in design, by a common material, brick, a uniform pattern of window, a common cornice line and the distinguishing feature of the framed doorway or porch.

Repetition of a dwelling or a commercial unit on a street of "infinite" length like Yonge Street would be boring to a degree, but the repetition of a single house, even if bizarre in design, on a street of limited length can give pleasure. This is especially true where the vista is terminated by a building, or what is all too rare in modern

387 House at the corner of Spadina Avenue and Bancroft Street (demolished). A striking late Victorian house in black and white.

388 25 Augusta Street, once the house of Mr. Edward Leadlay (1876). In his day, the number and street were 17 Esther. This was a flower that blossomed in the architectural desert of the seventies. It is now cherished by the Felician Sisters who use it as a school.

Toronto, where the ultimate in enclosure is achieved by a square or a cul-de-sac. We still have streets where the Victorian rhythm of bay windows, whimsical porches and fretted gables seen through elms or flowering chestnuts can give real aesthetic enjoyment, an enjoyment that can never be evoked in the dreary lines of strawberry boxes in our newer subdivisions, or in the serried ranks of ranch

389 Toronto from the tower of Metropolitan Church (*c.* 1875). This remarkable photograph of a Georgian town must date from before 1877 because in that year old St. Andrew's Church, on the left, was demolished. Toronto's historical buildings were often needlessly destroyed, but the real loss is seen here. Today on every street individual buildings are in competition with one another; in 1875, we had order and dignity – tree-lined terraces and squares. Any house in the foreground (Queen and Berti) would do credit to Beacon Hill in Boston.

houses in the more salubrious areas developed for the well-to-do.

Space as an emotional experience within a building or formed by a complex of buildings was known to the Victorians, but it is something vital to architecture that we have lost in the meantime. It is recognized as an indispensable principle by all reputable planning authorities, and may yet return as a fundamental truth in civic design. In our haste to turn our backs on everything that was old, we ignored so delightful an element in 18th century planning as the building terminating a vista—a feature, now suspect as "vista mongering," that appears in many places in the Victorian street pattern. Osgoode Hall at the end of York Street or old Knox at the head of Spadina can be compared with the unsatisfactory modern terminations of Toronto Street at Adelaide or Harbord Street at St. George.

Important as were the repetition of a unit to form terraces and the concept of space which produced culs-de-sac and squares, a third quality was necessary to complete the urban picture. That was the human scale that characterized our architecture, both domestic and commercial—Duke Street just as surely as Queen Street.

390 Knox College (1875), Smith and Gemmell, architects. This not undistinguished building stands in the circle at the head of Spadina Avenue, north of College Street. In its day, it has served as college, armouries for the Toronto Regiment and as a penicillin plant for Connaught laboratories. It is rumoured that it may soon rejoin the university family as a student residence. The circle antedates the building, and was once known as Crescent Garden. It was intended as a park under a deed which, on certain conditions, gave the land to the city. The offer was never taken up, and in 1873 the property was sold by a daughter of Robert Baldwin's to the Hon. J. McMurrich, for $10,000. Materials, brick and Indiana limestone.

391, 392 Metropolitan Church (1872), Henry Langley architect. How excellent was the photography of 1880, and how beautiful were the church grounds! The parterre in front has gone, and the park to the north has been sacrificed for Sunday School and church offices. St. Michael's appears without the dormers in the roof which were added some time after the building of the spire in 1866 by Gundry and Langley. The Metropolitan suffered a fire in 1928, and was restored by J. Gibb Morton, architect.

The upper photograph (**391**) shows the cast iron fence of the church, taken down in 1961. It and St. James's fence were scrapped on the offer of the city to maintain the grass in perpetuity, an extraordinarily shortsighted bargain. Enclosure is resented in Toronto and the fight to save the Osgoode fence is perennial. Materials of the church, grey brick and stone (see **190**).

393 The Margaret Eaton School of Literature and Expression (1905), W. R. Mead, architect (demolished). Were it not for the so typical Toronto cottages on each side and the shabby Hydro pole, the central building might be the headquarters, somewhere in Asia Minor, of a mysterious and unrecorded cult. Anything more unlike a school for young girls could hardly be imagined. "Beauty and fitness" is, I am told, a loose translation of the motto on the architrave which must have been a source of bewilderment to taxi-drivers. Except for the Registry Building on Edward Street, this was the swan song of the Greek revival in Toronto.

The amalgam of all three plus walls of brick or stucco and the shade trees for which Toronto is famous are what give so many of our residential streets their restfulness, their sparkle and their charm. When one contrasts the older residential districts in Canadian cities with ours, one feels instinctively that the architects and builders of the past in Toronto have produced something that, in many ways, might be called indigenous. Scores of our old streets, whole neighbourhoods indeed, could exist nowhere but in Toronto, while University Avenue and Bloor Street could be found anywhere in the United States.

An event that had a devastating effect on architecture and town planning in North America was the Chicago Exhibition of 1892, a year, in Toronto, that saw Lennox working on the design of the City Hall, and David Roberts finishing the house for Mr. George Gooderham at the corner of St. George and Bloor. The committee in charge of the Exhibition had on it a group of architects who represented, in almost equal numbers, the virile and creative local school, and the powerful neo-classical school of New York and the eastern seaboard. The vote on which rested the whole character of the exhibition was in favour of the latter, and the result was a White City of Roman buildings on Roman streets about a lake on which American citizens could be ferried on gondolas from one exhibit to another.

No exhibition has ever had more influence on a nation, and Canada was inevit-

394 St. Anne's, Gladstone Avenue (1908), Ford Howland, architect. One of the most colourful church interiors in Toronto, a labour of love on which several of the Group of Seven painters left their mark.

ably affected. The buildings themselves were transitory, but they were the inspiration in Toronto alone for such permanent monuments as the Union Station, the Bank of Toronto at King and Bay, the Royal Bank on King near Yonge, the Princes' Gates, the Registry Building and numerous temple-like branch banks and public libraries. Even the schools of architecture were affected, and the popularity of the Ecole des Beaux Arts in Paris reached an all-time high.

It was not a period in our architectural history either here, in Great Britain, or in the United States, that we can recall with pride. It would be an understatement to say that it lacked the fire of the classical revival of the 19th century. Our forefathers of the eighteen-sixties in Toronto had books illustrating in line the orders of architecture and the great buildings of antiquity, but, when the head office of a bank had to be designed, there were no models from the remote past and few that were contemporary. The situation was very different in the early twentieth century. A flood of illustrated magazines presented the architect with somebody's recent solution to every possible building type, and architecture became rather drearily imitative.

Happily for this writer, the classical revival which followed in the trail of the White City was slow in reaching Toronto, and what it produced, both good and bad, is of the twentieth century—consequently, outside the boundaries of this book.

6: Epilogue

The reader has come on a long and, I hope, not too arduous journey since we looked behind the palisades of the ancient village at the end of the well-trodden Passage de Toronto. We were there in spirit when the Lieutenant-Governor and Mrs. Simcoe sailed into Toronto harbour, and we heard with pride the salute of guns that heralded the founding of York, the capital of Upper Canada. We saw the town prostrate before the guns of the American flotilla in 1813, and we saw it rise again, in two critical decades, as Toronto, the incorporated city.

Toronto never looked back, and it is with reluctance that one leaves the story of its architecture at the threshold of the twentieth century. It has been said more than once in our story that architectural periods cannot be confined by dates, but, socially and politically, the year 1900 seems to suggest the end of an era with more than usual finality, and the century that followed we can leave with confidence to the chronicler who will, almost certainly, write at the turn of the second millennium. It is a sobering thought that he may be one of my own students, at this moment a callow youth in his freshman year. If we have overlapped into his territory, it is because we could do nothing to prevent the Victorian merging with the seventh Edward; Art Nouveau did not expire on the last day of the old century, and architectural practice continued in its gentlemanly, if sometimes pedestrian course, blissfully unaware of the industrial and technological revolution that lay ahead. The young architect of today who is part of a highly organized office will find it difficult to believe that in 1900 A.D. architects wrote their specifications by hand, drawings were laboriously copied and hand coloured because blue-printing was still unknown, and jobs and clients were visited in horse-drawn carriages.

If we found Toronto great where we left it, our future chronicler will write of a greater and more illustrious city, a metropolis known and respected throughout the civilized world. In his day, the "Passage de Toronto" will have become a legend, hardly credible in a provincial capital boasting super highways, underground railways, an airport of international importance, a great university and a harbour to which ships come from the far corners of the earth.

In the march of progress, every vestige of our 19th century "heritage" will have disappeared, and only University College, Osgoode Hall, the old City Hall, St. Lawrence Hall, and a few churches will remain. Even for them, fire is the ever present menace, and it is not inconceivable that by 2000 A.D. all the 19th century buildings dealt with in this book will be one with Nineveh and Tyre.

Much as we may regret the loss of buildings, we have an even greater heritage about which Toronto is peculiarly apathetic. Of the 1,900 acres of ravine we once enjoyed, 840 have been filled for factories, roads and houses. No ravine and no park is absolutely safe from pressures as widely diverse as the Government of Canada and the speculative builder. In an atmosphere always charged with emotion—of wounded soldiers needing beds, or of undergraduates urgently needing desks, we gave Kilgour Park to the federal government for Sunnybrook Hospital, and a botanical garden to York University. In 1962, St. James Square disappeared completely in the enlargement of Ryerson, and the "several acres" that Jesse Ketchum gave as a children's park in Yorkville have dwindled to the dreary pavement of the school that bears his name. Only in the nick of time did the City at last prevent a rash of speculative building in the ravines, and two or three apartments are there now as permanent reminders to posterity of the need for eternal vigilance.

Periodically, there is talk of a school in Howard's High Park. The project will come up again and, almost certainly, will be based on a claim for physically handicapped children. In short, sponsors will be found for a school based on the most laudable and humane principles, and our withers will be most cruelly and unnecessarily wrung.

We show no particular maturity, in either the press or the public, in our stewardship of the natural resources with which we have been endowed. Only in the Metro development of the Island have we seen leadership of the highest order, but, even as I write, the pressure for a bridge, for motor cars, cottages and apartment houses assumes dangerous proportions. A natural, beautiful island would do much to offset our profligate gifts of park land for institutional purposes on the mainland.

Posterity will rightly judge that we were unworthy of University Avenue which, one hundred years ago, was a tree-lined thoroughfare with more dignity than it has today. Twice, in the last few years, the monuments which pepper the avenue have been taken down, but no one has asked in the press why several of them should be put back again. No one has asked why so puerile a piece of sculpture as the stunted Tommy and the dog-like lions should continue to represent the Sons of England, or why the trend should be perpetuated of turning the central strip into a Valhalla for the deceased chief executives of Hydro. Many objections can be raised to design control, but where bad art and politics combine to belittle a great civic avenue, a fine arts committee of unquestionable integrity and authority would seem necessary.

Forty years from now, our chronicler will look with some bewilderment at these pages. Unless we are greatly mistaken, the intervening decades will produce architecture that will have all the attributes of greatness except a human scale. He will look at canyons of office buildings, multi-storey university buildings and skyscraper apartment houses that will be the homes of thousands. By contrast, he will notice that, in spite of unashamed eclecticism and lack of conviction on the part of an earlier generation, we once had an architecture where man was the measure in the greater, as in the humbler, thoroughfares. He will find it difficult to believe that the pursuit of old buildings could be fun and an absorbing hobby. Will he find loveliness in old churches, old houses or even old warehouses, or will age and the patina of age be synonymous with obsolescence? The sand-blasting of the old Bank of Montreal, the porches of St. James' Cathedral, Trinity College and the Metropolitan Church, would indicate that such a point of view is not without its adherents, even in 1963.

Through the ages, many books have been written about great cities, but pride and love for the city of one's birth or adoption have never surpassed Cicero's "civis Romanus sum" or St. Paul's boast that he was "a citizen of no mean city." It is in that spirit that this book has been written, but admiration and affection should not blind us to the all too blatant ugliness of large areas of Toronto. We not only have ugliness in urban and suburban areas, but as a distinguished Canadian once said to me of Danforth Avenue, "I am sometimes convinced that we have even a cult of ugliness in Toronto." The desecration of Toronto Street and the entire absence of design in a civic sense of the filing cabinet façades on both sides of University Avenue would indicate that we are in no position to cast "the first stone" at those who preceded us.

Our worst streets are those Victorian and Edwardian thoroughfares where bad design and poor maintenance give an impression of sordidness and decay. King, Queen, Dundas, and much of Yonge are such streets, and their ugliness is not improved by their stretching, seemingly, to infinity. Where they also presented a grim façade to our worst slums, we have gradually made improvements by subsidizing low rental housing estates, but only the fringe of a vast degenerate area has so far been touched. It is the opinion of this writer that we have farsighted planners with able staffs in both City and Metropolitan Toronto, but without public support, they cannot, themselves, create the kind of political climate that demands the large-scale rehabilitation of blighted urban areas. Boston, Hartford, Baltimore, and San Francisco, to mention only a few American cities, are seeing such citizens' and planners' dreams turn into reality.

Since 1852, when the railways were allowed to ravage the water front and leave on their flanks an unplanned mess of roundhouses, warehouses, factories, and slums, Toronto has turned its back on the lake. We still have an Esplanade, but no longer is it a place for promenade, for seeing ships at anchor or for Easter parades. Today, the pedestrian is rare on the Esplanade. Trucks and trains have taken his place, and the lake front has receded beyond sight. The migration to Parkdale did not escape the railway, but the move to Bloor opened up a new residential area. Then came the Annex, Rosedale, Moore Park, Bayview—always with green fields and singing birds beyond, and the seeds of decay behind.

One would like to think that, with Bayview, we had reached the limit of unplanned escapist growth, and that there were great schemes afoot for the rejuvenation of the old city, not merely for business, but for leisure and urban living. When one thinks of London, Paris or New York, one is conscious only of the *urbs*, the great city. In the judgement of posterity, it may not be to our credit to be remembered only as the city of suburban homes.

The young in every generation are critical of the old, but to understand the architecture of the past sixty years in Toronto one has to remember that fifteen of them were lost in war and the great depression. The modern movement, as we understand it today, did not spring fully born on Toronto soil from the head of Le Corbusier or of Mies van der Rohe. It took root slowly in a field unprepared, and often resistant to it. Most of our older architects who now command the largest commissions were trained under a Beaux Arts system that gave them a familiarity with Georgian and Gothic architecture which they regarded, not so much as history, as a reservoir of design material. The best of these offices gradually saw the light, and their work changed as graduates in their employ were given greater freedom to design. Even in the last decade, younger firms have started practice, and have demonstrated their skill in buildings of great distinction. The possibilities for employment in Toronto have attracted young architects from every province as well as from the United Kingdom and the continent of Europe. At present their influence is slight, but, as their opportunities increase and their confidence grows, we can expect new colour and vitality in the local architectural scene.

The construction of a monumental building like Toronto's new City Hall must be an elevating and exhilarating experience for the community that watches its growth. It must have been so for London and Rome where old men could boast that they saw St. Paul's or St. Peter's rise in all its solemn majesty from the seething human tide at its base to the serenity of the loftiest cross. Such an event is rare in the life of a city or a nation and the whole populace rejoices in its presence.

It is now common knowledge that 520 architects from 44 countries submitted designs for Toronto's new City Hall, and that a Finnish architect, Mr. Viljo Revell, was the successful competitor. In the conditions of competition, there was a statement which must have given all competitors much thought, and doubtless influenced Mr. Revell even before he put pencil to paper. It was this:

In the eighteenth century city, the cathedral and the town hall frequently dominated the urban scene both physically and spiritually. Our present City Hall is largely overshadowed by commercial and financial buildings, but it still dominates by its presence. It differs in that respect from those centres of civic administrations in North America where the "hall" is just another office building. One of the reasons for this competition is to find a building that will proudly express its function as the centre of civic government. How to achieve an atmosphere about a building that suggests government, continuity of democratic traditions and service to the community are problems for the designer of the modern city hall. These were qualities that the architects of other ages endeavoured to embody in the town halls of their times.

They were qualities, too, that Mr. Revell was able to embody to a remarkable degree in his design which will become the very symbol of government at the municipal level.

Where the city hall for Toronto of 1844 lay just outside the shadow of St. James, the present one will dominate the whole city—not that it "vaunteth" itself unnecessarily, but that the ramification of services and the multiplicity of departments of the modern city hall demand a building of truly monumental dimensions. Far reaching in its influence on architecture and momentous in the future history of Toronto, the new City Hall, like a spring in the desert, will give life and beauty to wide areas about it. Another decade will see the rehabilitation of the south side of Queen Street now in all its decrepitude, a renaissance of the whole arid area between Hagerman and Dundas, and a rejuvenation of the ugly warehouses to the east. No city anywhere has, in a century, devoted so generous an amount of urban land for its public square, and the international competition for the building itself focused the attention of the entire world on the corner of Queen and Bay Streets in Toronto.

The City Hall will be unquestionably a landmark in the architecture of the city, but it can also be a beacon in the development of Canadian painting, sculpture and a wide range of skills and handicrafts. In one of the studies prepared for the Royal Commission on the National Development of the Arts, Letters and Sciences of 1951 mention is made of the extent to which artists are employed on government buildings in all European countries. So civilized a custom has not yet reached North America, except in the depression years when painters and sculptors were employed on low rental housing estates in the United States. Many artists got their start on those projects, and were able, through W.P.A., to give pleasure to hundreds of thousands of people.

There is, of course, ample evidence from historic times, the Renaissance in particular, when all public buildings, churches and palaces were enriched by the greatest artists with mural painting and sculpture that, today, are priceless national treasures. Those were the days when the town hall was a symbol of everything that was good and significant in municipal life, and its presence added stature not only to the burgher, but to the city and the nation. Such, once, was the Cloth Hall at Ypres, and such still are the town hall and the guild halls of Brussels, but, happily, one does not have to seek examples only from the distant past. There is at least one modern city where the town hall takes second place to none in the ancient world for the sheer beauty of murals in paint and mosaics, for sculpture, furnishings and landscaping, and that is Stockholm, the capital of Sweden. Won in competition like Toronto's city hall, the design of the town hall in Stockholm has captured the imagination of the Swedish people as no building has in several centuries, and, today, forty years after it was built, it still attracts thousands of tourists annually from many countries. The same is true of Oslo, and the same could be true of Toronto. Only yesterday, I saw that the City Hall had risen high above the surrounding board fence, and, from the seventh floor of a Bay Street office building, the staff could see the great central column and the tremendous sweep of the curved enclosing walls. It will be a supremely great building in terms of function and the monumentality of its public spaces, but one would like to forecast that it will also be an edifice where citizens, for centuries, can see all that was best in art in this generation. It is a challenge for the artists of Canada, but no greater than for the artists of much smaller, less rich and less populated Sweden. This writer is confident that they will meet it.

It was a happy coincidence that as these lines were written so signal an event as the solemn laying of the commemorative plaque by Mayor Phillips had taken place, and that nothing humanly predictable could delay the completion of the City Hall by 1965. Taller buildings will be built before the end of the century here and elsewhere in North America, but there will be no comparable, or no more renowned city hall. One hundred and seventy-two years are as nothing in the life of a city, but, in that brief span, we have seen Toronto grow from the small military establishment which mounted guard on the lives of the Lieutenant-Governor, his family and Council whose only protection for two summers and a hard winter was flimsy coverings of a canvas tent. From that tiny hamlet set precariously on the edge of the wilderness to the proud metropolis of today is a record of achievement hardly to be equalled in history. The new City Hall is the very embodiment of that achievement, and is, at the same time, a portent of greatness to come. Our chronicler of the second millennium will describe a still more illustrious metropolis, but its heart and head will still be at the corner of Queen and Bay.

Notes and
Appendices

1: The Village and the Ancient Trails

1. Confusing for the ordinary reader of the period, and not a little confusing for map-makers of the past was the fact that, until the 18th century, the word Toronto was not used to refer to the mouth of the Humber, but to "le lac Toronto" which was Lake Simcoe.

2. Percy Robinson, *Toronto during the French Régime*, p. 2.

3. *Ibid.*, pp. 2–3.

4. Henry Scadding, *Toronto of Old*, p. 228; Dr. Scadding recalls a time when he himself, in the course of an hour, speared twenty heavy salmon in the Don.

5. *Ibid.*, p. 22. "The poor lake-craft which in 1804 must have accommodated the poet, may have put in at the harbour of York. He certainly alludes to a tranquil evening scene on the waters in that quarter."

6. Robinson, *French Régime*, p. 80.

7. Henry Scadding, *History of the Old French Fort at Toronto and its Monument*, p. 22.

8. Robinson, *French Régime*, p. 147.

9. *Ibid.*, p. 8.

2: As it was in the Beginning

1. Great Britain, Treaties. . . . *Indian Treaties and Surrenders* (Ottawa, 1891), vol. I, p. 34.

2. J. E. Middleton, *The Municipality of Toronto*, vol. I, p. 143. The site is now occupied by London, Ont.

3. *The Diary of Mrs. Simcoe*, edited by J. Ross Robertson, p. 143.

4. *Correspondence of Lieut. Governor John Graves Simcoe*, ed. by E. A. Cruikshank, vol. I, p. 18.

5. Joseph Bouchette, *The British Dominions in North America*, vol. I, p. 89.

6. Mrs. Simcoe is addressing the lady in England to whom her diary record was sent weekly. This extract is given in Edith G. Firth, ed., *The Town of York, 1793–1815*, p. 213; see also Robertson ed., p. 100.

7. Edith Firth, ed., *The Town of York*, p. 213. See also Robertson, ed., *The Diary of Mrs. Simcoe*, p. 179. John Ross Robertson has raised the point that Mrs. Simcoe's statement implies that, as Colonel Simcoe had been to Toronto, he cannot have been on board, but that is quite unthinkable in the story of Toronto.

8. Simcoe's original Executive Council was composed of James Baby, Alexander Grant, William Osgoode, William Robertson (not sworn in, and did not sit) and Peter Russell.
Members of his Legislative Council were James Baby, Richard Cartwright, Alexander Grant, Robert Hamilton, John Munro, William Osgoode, William Robertson (who did not take the oath) and Peter Russell.

9. Edith Firth, ed., *The Town of York, 1793–1815*, p. 10.

10. *Ibid.*, p. xxxvi.

11. *Ibid.*, p. 253.

12. J. E. Middleton, *The Municipality of Toronto*, vol. I, p. 72.

13. *Travels through the United States of North America, the Country of the Iroquois, and Upper Canada* by the Duke de la Rochefoucauld-Liancourt (London, 1799), vol. I, p. 269.

14. Firth, ed., *The Town of York*, p. lxxvi.

15. Scadding, *Toronto of Old*, p. 199.

16. John Ross Robertson, *Landmarks*, Series 1, p. 98.

17. The builder's sketch is in the Russell Papers, Archives of Ontario.
Mention of the painting suggests a note on the topographers whose work sometimes sheds so bright a light on life in early Canada. Many were military men for whom the ability to sketch landscape or features in it would be a valuable accomplishment. Others, like Mrs. Simcoe, Mrs. Jameson and Miss Anne Langton, were talented women with an English education which may well have included drawing in perspective and water colour. The

topographers cannot be said to have contributed much to the development of painting in Canada. Their work was largely documentary and of interest to the student of social history rather than the history of art. For the most part, they all worked in a period prior to the invention of photography, and without them, we could only guess at the appearance of Yonge, King or the water front in York. Quite the most prolific of the topographers was William Henry Bartlett who was commissioned by the London publisher George Virtue to gather material in Canada for a book on Canadian scenery. The book appeared in 1842, and, while many plates deal with scenery, not a few illustrate street scenes and the buildings of the time.

18. "Note on the origin of the name 'Russell Abbey.' " MS in Toronto Public Library.

19. John Ross Robertson, *Landmarks*, Series 1, p. 123.

20. *Ibid.*, p. 352.

21. Public Archives of Ontario, Simcoe Papers, vol. IV, p. 201. See Edith Firth, ed., *The Town of York*, pp. 24–5.

22. Edith Firth, ed., *The Town of York*, pp. 39–40, 46.

23. Public Archives of Canada, Upper Canada Sundries, Estimate of W. Smith, approved by Alexander Grant, Administrator of the province.

24. John McBeath's estimate for repairs approved by Francis Gore, Lieutenant-Governor. Also in P.A.C., Upper Canada Sundries.

25. Richard Cartwright to Isaac Todd, Kingston, Oct. 14, 1793. Edith Firth, ed., *The Town of York*, p. 22.

26. *The Correspondence of the Hon. Peter Russell*, ed. by E. A. Cruikshank, vol. II, p. 128.

27. Edith Firth, ed., *The Town of York*, pp. lx–lxii.

28. *Ibid.*, p. 242.

3: A Late Flowering Georgian

1. Scadding, *Toronto of Old*, p. 116.

2. *Ibid.*, p. 122.

3. John Ross Robertson, *Landmarks*, Series 1, pp. 503, 504.

4. R. S. Jameson, Attorney-General (1833–1837) and Vice-Chancellor (1837–1854) of Upper Canada.

5. Anna Jameson, *Winter Studies and Summer Rambles in Canada* (Toronto, 1923), p. 17.

6. John Ross Robertson, *Landmarks*, Series 1, p. 506.

7. Scadding, *Toronto of Old*, p. 95.

8. *Ibid.*, p. 139.

9. *Ibid.*, p. 184.

10. As a French immigrant, he received a large tract of land in the emigré settlement north of York, now called Oak Ridges. Here a number of royalists had been given contiguous lots by the British Government.

11. John Ross Robertson, *Landmarks*, Series 1, p. 19.

12. Mr. William Willcocks was Dr. Baldwin's father-in-law. This letter is in the W. W. Baldwin Papers, Toronto Public Library.

13. Scadding and Dent, *Toronto, Past and Present*, p. 50.

14. Charles W. Humphries, "The Capture of York," *Ontario History*, volume LI.

15. John Ross Robertson, *Landmarks*, series 1, p. 12.

16. Humphries, "The Capture of York."

17. *Ibid.*

18. *Ibid.*

19. Walter Henry, *Trifles from my Port-folio* (Quebec, 1839), vol. II, p. 112.

4: Prosperity and Eclecticism

1. Anna Jameson, *Winter Studies and Summer Rambles* (Toronto, 1923), pp. 17, 67, 89, 64.

2. John Galt, *Autobiography* (London, 1833) vol. I, p. 334.

3. An English visitor writing to the *Christian Guardian* in 1834 reported that "upwards of two miles of King Street is flagged and paved with stone."

4. Charles Dickens, *American Notes* (Everyman ed., pp. 202–3). Quoted in John Forster's *Life of Charles Dickens* (Household ed.; London, n.d.), p. 123.

5. T. A. Reed, "The Story of Toronto," Ontario Historical Society, *Papers and Records*, 1934, vol. XXX, pp. 205–6.

6. *Ibid.*, p. 206. Accurate statistics for this period are difficult to establish, but in 1832 probably out of a population of 5,502, there were 535 cases of cholera and 205 deaths.

7. Geoffrey Scott, *The Architecture of Humanism* (London: Constable, 1924), p. 39.

8. John Ross Robertson, *Landmarks*, Series 4, p. 16.

9. In 1826, there were only seven Roman Catholic priests in the whole of Upper Canada.

10. John Ross Robertson, *Landmarks*, Series 4, p. 317.

11. F. H. Armstrong, "The Rebuilding of Toronto after the Great Fire of 1849," *Ontario History*, vol. LIII (1961).

12. Strachan Papers, Toronto Public Library.

13. Scadding, *Toronto of Old*, pp. 322–323. The long quotation Scadding took from *Curiae Canadenses*.

14. John Bland, "Osgoode Hall," *R.A.I.C. Journal*, July 1959.

15. C. H. A. Armstrong, *The Honourable Society of Osgoode Hall*, with an essay by E. R. Arthur.

16. John Ross Robertson, *Landmarks*, Series 1, p. 395.

17. Alfred Sylvester, *Sketches of Toronto*.

18. John Bland, *R.A.I.C. Journal*, July 1959.

19. James Cleland Hamilton, *Osgoode Hall: Reminiscences of the Bench and Bar*.

20. *Incidents in the Life of J. G. Howard, Esq. of Colborne Lodge, High Park*.

21. The Osgoode library records show that Cumberland took home the five volumes of *British Architectural Antiquities*.

22. C. H. Armstrong, *The Honourable Society of Osgoode Hall*, with an essay by E. R. Arthur, p. 55.

23. Toronto, Nov. 14, 1849–Sept. 22, 1851; Quebec, Sept. 22, 1851–Oct. 20, 1855; Toronto, Oct. 20, 1855–Sept. 24, 1859; Quebec, Sept. 24, 1859–Oct. 20, 1865; Ottawa, Oct. 20, 1865– .

24. Middleton, *The Municipality of Toronto*, vol. II, pp. 557–8.

25. F. H. Armstrong, "The First Great Fire of Toronto," *Ontario History*, vol. LIII (1961).

26. John Ross Robertson, *Landmarks*, Series 3, p. 7.

27. Scadding, *Toronto of Old*, p. 356.

28. John Ross Robertson, *Landmarks*, Series 1, p. 163.

29. F. H. Armstrong, "The Rebuilding of Toronto after the Great Fire of 1849," *Ontario History*, vol. LIII (1961).

30. When the stone St. James of 1830 was built, the price of pews was set at "twenty-five pounds currency." Pews could be rented but they were also sold by auction.

31. *Early Days in Upper Canada: Letters of John Langton*, edited by W. A. Langton, p. 292.

32. *Ibid.*, p. 284.

5: Romanesque and Cast Iron

1. Of greater significance for Canada, if less for Toronto, was the founding of the Royal Canadian Academy and the National Gallery in 1880. Among the many laudable aims in the Charter of the Academy were "the encouragement of design as applied to painting, sculpture, architecture, engraving and the industrial arts, and the promotion and support of education leading to the production of beautiful and excellent work in manufactures." The Royal Academy's first president was Lucius O'Brien. He was educated at Upper Canada College, and is remembered by a simple brass tablet on the walls of the nave of the little mud brick church at Shanty Bay, the village of his birth on Lake Simcoe.

2. Mr. R. E. Chadwick, past President of the Foundation Co. of Canada, was in Toronto as an engineer in 1906. He has the distinct impression that the columns supporting the Yonge Street wall of the Robert Simpson Co. were "carried on cantilevers; this arrangement being in anticipation of a future subway, and of so arranging things that the subway authorities might be argued into putting a station in the store."

3. Peter Selz, *Art Nouveau* (New York, 1961), p. 16.

4. Mr. Hahn died in September 1962 at the age of 96.

5. At the same time, there were those unscrupulous speculators who left a legacy of congested housing, the deplorable conditions of which were not drawn to public notice until the report of the Lieutenant-Governor's Committee was issued in 1934. The task of eradication and rebuilding as a municipal responsibility has proceeded ever since, but will not be completed in this generation.

The information in this appendix has been gathered from a number of sources, and, while it is as complete as current research can make it, future historians will doubtless fill gaps in our present knowledge. The first architectural magazine, the *Canadian Architect and Builder*, appeared in Toronto in 1888, and from then on it is not too difficult to identify architects with their buildings, or even learn their date of birth and something of their education. Prior to that, one is left with the dry statistics of the city directories and the often uninformative obituaries. Even today the press is singularly remiss in giving credit to an architect, alive or dead, when a building is illustrated, and the amount of news about buildings of the period prior to photography is sparse indeed.

It must be remembered, too, that only in the last hundred years or so has the architect been the professional man we know today in the community. It is true that much earlier there were citizens of the type of Howard, Chewett, Lane, and Hay whose standards and ethics were as high as those of other professional men in this century, but, generally speaking, the architect of a century ago in Canada was only emerging from the building trades. In the society of the time and the limited wealth of the community, it was probably necessary for some to build as well as design to make a living. Earlier than in Canada, the same process was going on in the United States which could boast a Jefferson, but would not overlook Asher Benjamin, Architect and Carpenter, who published the *New System of Architecture* in Boston in 1805.

In many ways the architects mentioned in these lists but without known buildings to their credit are as important in the Toronto architectural story as those greater names with whom one can associate cathedrals and university buildings. They were, in all probability, the people who designed and built Toronto, the anonymous authors of terraced streets and the houses that once adorned our squares. Every old city has such anonymous architecture, and it is our loss that so little of it has survived.

Every age has produced the "prima donna" type of architect who holds himself aloof from his fellows, but, generally, architects are as gregarious as the members of other professions, and delight in each other's company as much as to talk shop. For example, among the papers of Dr. W. W. Baldwin in the Toronto Public Library are his "Notes for a lecture" given in Toronto at a date earlier than 1834. There he said "Much now rests in your hands as embarked in the profession of architects and builders to improve greatly the stile, stability, salubrity and accommodation of our buildings in this city—either by forming an Architectural Society independent of the Mechanics' Institute or as a branch of it—the object of this Society I suggest should be to encourage by honorary notices, either by medals, prizes or public votes of approbation, those architects who may distinguish themselves in the execution of the works they undertake."

We have no clear records of such meetings in Toronto until 1887, although we can be quite sure that education, building codes, town planning, and competitions were discussed whenever architects came together. We know by only a marginal note on a book of 1878 of a "Canadian Institute of Architects," but many attempts must have been made in the interests of professional unity before the first significant step was taken in 1887.

On October 3, 1887, a meeting was held in the office of W. G. Storm at 28 Toronto Street to inaugurate the "Architectural Guild of Toronto." Those present were Edmund Burke, S. G. Curry, Frank Darling, A. R. Denison, N. B. Dick, Grant Helliwell, W. G. Storm, W. R. Strickland, and S. H. Townsend. Members arranged to dine fortnightly or monthly. At the fourth dinner, sixteen architects met in the St. Charles restaurant on Yonge Street, and agreed to discuss subjects of professional interest, to foster friendly criticism of one another's work, to secure better public recognition, and to raise the standards of professional ethics. Any architect in Toronto was eligible if elected by a majority of four to one.

By 1889, the need for an association with a broader base than the Guild was obvious, and, on March 21st of that year the first meeting of the Ontario Association of Architects was held. The Association was later incorporated by act of the legislature on August 13, 1890, and Mr. W. G. Storm, R.C.A., became its first president. There were 154 founder members. As the Association increased in numbers and in influence, the importance of the Guild diminished until, in 1898, its members disbanded in favour of the Toronto Chapter.

It was due to the initiative of members of the Guild that the Government of Ontario was persuaded in 1890 to establish a Department of Architecture in the School of Practical Science. After a year in engineering, Mr. C. E. Langley entered the course in 1890 and became the first graduate of the Department in 1892. His instructors were Mr. C. H. C. Wright (later head of the department and then of the School of Architecture in the University of Toronto) and Mr. Cesare Marani.

It is greatly to the credit of the forefathers of the profession that their clubs and their dinners were all concerned with finer buildings through better education. A club that is well worth recording for posterity was the Architectural 18 Club. It came into existence in 1899 and was composed of eighteen angry young men. It seems that following the examinations for membership in the O.A.A., certain new members were chosen whose marks were lower than those of some who were refused admission. One of the latter entered suit against the Association, and was clearly not satisfied with the defence that he and some others were too young to qualify. It is pleasing to report that several older architects shared the indignation of the younger.

Until 1908, when its differences with the O.A.A. were reconciled, the 18 Club held exhibitions and meetings and ignored, completely, the parent body. Its finest hour was when its members were permitted to appear, along with O.A.A. representatives, before the Senate of the University, with Sir Charles Moss, the Vice-Chancellor, presiding. Their complaint was that the University course in architecture did not fit the student for architecture, and that the University would do the profession a service by conducting external examinations for students in offices. It is recorded that Sir Robert Falconer, the President, "took their representatives very seriously" and organized a series of courses in which "eighteen professors participated." Today, almost all students take the course leading to the degree of Bachelor of Architecture in the School of Architecture. The few who register for the courses offered by the Ontario Association of Architects can do so only after three successful years at a recognized school.

The headquarters of the O.A.A. are that well-known Toronto building at 50 Park Road, a very different affair from the office at 94 King Street West which, for the sum of

$254.41, was furnished in 1900 with Morris chair, a fixed seat, a Japanese rug, a copy of Michelangelo's Moses, and two cuspidors.

395 *Toronto Architectural Guild* at Long Branch in August 1888. R. J. Edwards, Wm. R. Gregg, John Gemmell, H. J. Webster, Edmund Burke, W. A. Langton, Henry Langley, H. B. Gordon, S. G. Curry, N. B. Dick, James Smith, W. G. Storm.

ASHFIELD, JAMES
City of Toronto Engineer, 1877.

BALDWIN, W. W. 1775–1844. M.D. Edin. 1796
Dr. Baldwin settled in York in 1802. A serious shortage of lawyers at the time brought about the creation of several, of whom Baldwin was one. From 1803, he practised law and medicine and, occasionally, architecture. He will be remembered in Toronto for the magnificent gift of Spadina Avenue from Bloor to Front Street which he laid out in 1820 along with a widening of Queen (at Spadina) to 90 feet. Spadina, itself, is 160 feet wide. Spadina is said to mean a sudden rise of ground, and it was on the east of the hill above Davenport east of the present Casa Loma that Dr. Baldwin built his house. Spadina, as it was called, was destroyed by fire in 1835.
PRACTICE
1824 With John Ewart, the Jail and Court House on King St.
1831 With J. G. Chewett, the second market in York on the site of the present St. Lawrence Market.
1837 His own house at Front and Bay.

BECKETT, SAMUEL. d. 1917. B.Arch. Cornell
EDUCATION
School of Architecture, Cornell.
PRACTICE
In the early 90's, he formed a partnership with Col. Vaux Chadwick under the name of Chadwick & Beckett. The practice continued until 1914. (*See* Chadwick, Vaux.)
MILITARY
Col. Beckett served with the Canadian Forces from the outbreak of war and was killed leading the 75th Battalion under a gas attack.

BENNETT, J. H.
City of Toronto Engineer, 1860–1871.

BIRD, EUSTACE. 1870–1950. A.R.I.B.A.
EDUCATION
In 1893, he went to London where he worked in the office of Colcutt & Hamp.
PRACTICE
Returned to Canada in 1894 and formed a partnership with Eden Smith with offices in Toronto and Barrie. Under his own name, he acted as associate architect on the Bank of Toronto at King and Bay streets in 1912, and the Royal Bank on King Street east of Yonge (Carrere & Hastings of New York were the architects).

BOOTH, THOMAS
City of Toronto Engineer, 1857–1858.

BOULTBEE, ALFRED
The third son of Alfred Boultbee who was member of Parliament for East York. Mr. Boultbee Jr. was a character known to his friends as "Pet." His architectural practice was preceded by a rather fruitless year on the Klondike.
PRACTICE
His practice was almost wholly domestic, and, while his education and early architectural activities were 19th century, nothing of that period can be traced. In the 20th century, he was famous for his houses in South Rosedale of which 22 Chestnut Park and 35 Crescent Road with its charming circular swimming pool in Doric order are examples.

BROWN, JOHN FRANCIS. 1866–1942
Born at Levis when his father, Quarter-Master Sergeant J. Brown, R.E., was stationed at the Quebec Citadel. The family returned to England in 1870, and twelve years later J. F. Brown emigrated to Toronto.
EDUCATION
Free School at Plymouth, England. Early architectural training in Toronto offices, including those of Edwards & Webster.
PRACTICE
1888 Resident architect on the Board of Trade Building for the architects James & James of New York.
1891 One of five architects chosen for the second stage of the competition for the Parliament Buildings at Victoria, B.C.
1894 Public School, Burke's Falls.
1895 Rockland Baptist Church.
1899 Public School, Shelbourne.
1900 Town Hall, Gravenhurst.
N.B. The 20th century practice of the firm was extensive, and is now carried on by a son in the firm of Brown, Brisley & Brown.
PROFESSIONAL
Member of the Architectural Draughtsmen's Club 1886–1892; Member of the Eighteen Club 1899–1902; Member of the Ontario Association of Architects 1892.

BRUNEL, ALFRED
City of Toronto Engineer, 1859–1860.

BURKE, EDMUND. 1851–1919
Born in Ireland of parents who emigrated to Toronto.

Upper Canada College, 1863–1865. In 1865 he entered the office of his uncle, Henry Langley, as a student. The firm was then Gundry & Langley.

PRACTICE

Formed a partnership with Henry and Edward Langley in 1873.

1872 Sherbourne Street Methodist Church.
1874 Jarvis Street Baptist Church.
1878 Old St. Andrew's Church, Jarvis and Carlton streets. Horticultural Pavilion, Allan Gardens (burned 1902).
1881 McMaster College, Bloor Street West, with Langley & Langley.
1885 Elm Street Methodist Church, a major alteration, with Henry Langley.
1889 Trinity Methodist Church.
1892 Walmer Road Baptist Church.
1893 Robert Simpson Building (destroyed by fire).
1894 Partnership with J. C. B. Horwood.
1895 Robert Simpson Building, with J. C. B. Horwood.
1900 Castle Memorial Hall.

PROFESSIONAL

Member of the first Council of the O.A.A., 1890. President of the O.A.A., 1894.

CHADWICK, Colonel WILLIAM CRAVEN VAUX. 1868–1941
The son of Edward Marion and Maria Martha Chadwick.

EDUCATION

A preparatory school affiliated with St. George's Church on John Street; Upper Canada College, 1881–1884. Articled to his father in the law firm of Beatty & Chadwick for one year when he forsook the law for architecture. Articled as student to Richard Cunningham Windeyer, a prominent local architect.

PRACTICE

In partnership, briefly, with Mr. Don C. Cassells and, still in the early 1890's, with Mr. Samuel Beckett. Vaux Chadwick's practice was a varied one that included houses, banks, clubs, factories, and churches, nearly all of the 20th century. A permanent memorial to the firm is the district known as Lawrence Park for which it acted as planners.

PROFESSIONAL

Both partners were members of the Eighteen Club.

MILITARY

Commanded the 9th Mississauga Horse and, in 1914, the 4th Canadian Rifles.

CHEWETT, JAMES GRANT. 1793–1862
Son of Wm. Chewett who, in 1791, was Deputy Surveyor-General of Upper Canada.

EDUCATION

Dr. Strachan's School at Cornwall. Apprenticed to his father as surveyor, afterwards received an appointment in the Surveyor-General's office with Thomas Young.

PRACTICE

1829 Legislative Buildings of Upper Canada, Front Street.
1831 Second Market in York and municipal offices on the site of the present St. Lawrence Market.

CONNOLLY, JOSEPH

PRACTICE

1885 St. Mary's Church, Bathurst Street (spire by A. W. Holmes).
1887 St. Paul's Church, Queen and Power streets.

CUMBERLAND, Colonel FREDERICK WILLIAM. 1821–1881
Born in London, England; son of Thomas Cumberland, Secretary to the Viceroy of Ireland at Dublin Castle.

EDUCATION

King's College, Cambridge. Studied in the office of Sir Charles Barry at a time when he was working on the Houses of Parliament at Westminster which he had won in competition.

PRACTICE

In 1847, he emigrated to Canada and settled in Toronto where he was appointed engineer to the County of York. In 1852, he formed a partnership with W. G. Storm which was terminated in 1865.

1850 St. James' Cathedral, with Thomas Ridout. Won in competition.
1851 Engineer-in-Chief, Northern Railway. He completed the road and founded the harbour and town of Collingwood.
Normal and Model School, with Thomas Ridout.
1852 Court House at 57 Adelaide Street.
1853 Seventh Toronto Post Office at 10 Toronto Street.
1854 Mechanics' Institute.
Wall and fence 999 Queen Street West.
1856 University College, with W. G. Storm.
1857 Extensive alterations to Osgoode Hall.
The Observatory.
1858 Chapel of St. James-the-Less.
1860 Residence of Col. Sir Casimir Gzowski, Bathurst St. Pendarvis at St. George and College streets (Cumberland's own house), now known as Baldwin House.

OTHER ACHIEVEMENTS

1853 Elected president of the Mechanics' Institute.
1860 Managing Director, Northern Railway.
1864 Admitted to Osgoode Hall as a student.
1867–1871 Represented Algoma in Ontario Legislature. Member of the Council of Trinity College.
1871–1872 Member, House of Commons, Ottawa.

MILITARY

1861 He organized the 10th Royal Grenadiers of Toronto which he commanded until 1865.

No architect of the 19th century, unless it was J. G. Howard, left so marked an impression on his time as Col. F. W. Cumberland, a great architect whose buildings happily remain while many of those of his contemporaries, and not a few of his successors, have gone. He was also esteemed as a citizen. There are many stories of his generosity, but, probably, none more significant than that he gave the use of his house for a year to the homeless members of St. Stephen's-in-the-Fields after the fire of 1865. (See John Ross Robertson, *Landmarks*, Series 4, p. 27.) Col. Cumberland was buried in St. James' Cemetery.

CURRY, S. G.

PRACTICE

1885 Bank of Montreal, Front and Yonge streets, with Frank Darling.

DARLING, FRANK. 1850–1923. R.C.A., F.R.A.I.C., LL.D.
Son of the Rev. Walter Stewart Darling, Rector of the Church of the Holy Trinity, Trinity Square, Toronto.

EDUCATION

Graduate of Upper Canada College, 1859, and Trinity College. Studied briefly in the office of Henry Langley, and in London, England, in architectural offices, 1868–1871.

PRACTICE

1871 National Life Assurance Building at southeast corner of Toronto and Adelaide streets, with Alan Macdougal.

1876 Convocation Hall of Trinity College, Queen Street.

1879 Home for Incurables (now the Queen Elizabeth Hospital), Dunn Avenue.

1884 Chapel of Trinity College, Queen Street.

1885 Bank of Montreal at Front and Yonge streets, with S. G. Curry.

1888 St. Mary Magdalene Church at Ulster and Manning.

1889 Residential wing, Trinity College.
Interior changes to St. James.

1894 East wing, Trinity College.

1895 Toronto Hunt Club.

1897 Bank of Commerce, Bloor and Yonge streets.
Toronto Club, Wellington and York streets.

1903 Bank of Nova Scotia at 39 King Street West.

An equally long list could be made of work by Darling and Pearson in the 20th century.

DENISON, A. R. d. 1923

Son of Col. Richard Lippincott Denison.

EDUCATION

Upper Canada College 1869-1872 and Royal Military College. Denison studied in the offices of J. G. Howard and Walter Strickland, and later with architects in New York. Like others, he returned to Canada at the time of the fire of 1904.

PRACTICE

St. Andrew's Church on the Island. Large general practice after 1900.

DICK, DAVID

PRACTICE

1873 Consumers' Gas Building, Toronto Street.

1890 Rebuilding of University College after the fire.

1892 University of Toronto Library.

PROFESSIONAL

1893 President of the Ontario Association of Architects.

DICK, NORMAN BETHUNE. 1860-1895

Son of Captain James Dick.

EDUCATION

Studied in the office of Smith & Gemmell, Toronto, and with architectural firms in Cleveland, Kingston, Ont., and Saint John, N.B., before returning to Toronto in 1879.

PRACTICE

1887 Victoria Club, Huron Street.

1889 Granite Club, 511-513 Church Street.
Academy of Music, 165-173 King Street.

1890 Partnership with A. F. Wickson.

PROFESSIONAL

A founder member of the Ontario Association of Architects (1889) and of the Architectural Guild (1887).

ELLIS, JAMES A. b. 1856

Born in Meaford, Ontario

PRACTICE

1891 Disciples' Church, Keele and Annette streets.

1897 Partnership with Henry Simpson.

His work was chiefly in the Toronto Junction and included a number of schools.

EWART, JOHN. 1788-1867

Born in Tranent, East Lothian, Scotland. He is a shadowy figure who appears sporadically between 1824 and 1844. (See text, Osgoode Hall.)

PRACTICE

1824 On April 24 corner-stones were laid for Jail and Court House. J. Ewart and Dr. W. W. Baldwin (1775-1844) were the architects.

1829 Osgoode Hall, east wing (probably, see text).

1830 St. Andrew's Church, Church and Adelaide streets (the spire was added by John G. Howard in 1850).

1833-1834 Ewart's New Wharf, foot of Church Street.

1843-1844 Laid out Strangers' Burial Ground (commonly called Potter's Field), northwest corner of Bloor and Yonge.

OTHER ACHIEVEMENTS

He became a trustee of Potter's Field in 1826 and a director of the Toronto and Lake Huron Railroad in 1846.

FALLOON, JOHN

PRACTICE

1874 All Saints Church, Sherbourne and Dundas streets, with R. C. Windeyer.

1886 The uncompleted St. Alban's Cathedral, with R. C. Windeyer.

FLEMING, Sir SANDFORD. 1827-1915. K.C.M.G.

Born at Kirkcaldy in Fifeshire, he studied surveying and engineering in Scotland. Came to Canada in 1845 when he entered the service of the Northern Railway. Became Engineer-in-Chief of surveys for the C.P.R. He was the designer of the first Canadian postage stamp (1851). He was President of the Royal Society of Canada, and for thirty-five years, Chancellor of Queen's University. He was the promoter of the system of standard time, proposed in 1876 and widely adopted in 1883.

PRACTICE

Like Howard, Tully, Thomas and others of his century Sandford Fleming was engineer and architect.

1858 Crystal Palace, with Sir Collingwood Schreiber.

FULLER, THOMAS. 1823-1898

Born in Bath, England.

EDUCATION

Studied in the offices of architects in Bath and London.

PRACTICE

Before coming to Canada in 1851, he designed Antigua Cathedral and supervised its erection. In 1857, he formed a partnership with Chilion Jones, architect of Toronto.

1858 St. Stephen's-in-the-Fields, College and Bellevue.

1859 Won the competition for the Parliament Buildings, Ottawa, and 2nd Prize for departmental buildings and Government House.

1863 He moved to Ottawa where he was appointed, with Charles Baillargé, joint architect for all government buildings then in course of construction.

1865 He completed work in Ottawa alone. The fire of 1916 which destroyed so much of Fuller's Parliament Buildings fortunately left the circular Parliamentary library, which remains, today, one of the noblest buildings in Canada.

1867 Won the competition for the State Capitol at Albany, New York.

1867-1881 He lived in the United States where he supervised the construction of the State Capitol before moving to San Francisco where he did a number of public buildings.

1891 University Avenue Armouries, Toronto.

GORDON & HELLIWELL
A firm more active in the 20th century.
PRACTICE
1881 Alterations to the interior of Knox Church, Queen Street West.
1890 Church of the Messiah, Avenue Road.
1899 Presbyterian Church, Roxborough and Avenue Road.

GOUINLOCK, GEORGE WALLACE. 1861–1932
Born in Paris, Ontario.
EDUCATION
Paris public and high schools. Apprenticed in Winnipeg to Barber, Bones & Barber, the designers of the Winnipeg City Hall. Came to Toronto in the early 1890's.
PRACTICE
From 1895 dates the Temple Building at the northwest corner of Richmond and Bay streets, a commission won in competition. Until the First World War Gouinlock was architect to the Canadian National Exhibition for which he designed the following buildings: Government, Horticultural, Manufacturers, Transportation, Industrial, Women's, as well as the grandstand and the Gooderham Fountain. Designed by him, too, were the Alexander Apartments and the Library addition on the north side of the Parliament Buildings in Queen's Park.

GOULSTONE, G. T.
No record of building in Toronto as he left early to practise in the United States. He was one of the founder members of the Architectural Draughtsmen's Club (1886), and is remembered with gratitude in the School of Architecture of the University of Toronto as the donor of a scholarship which bears his name.

GRAND, JAMES
PRACTICE
1855 Toronto Exchange, at the corner of Leader Lane and Wellington Street.

GRAY, JAMES WILSON. 1861–1922
Born in Edinburgh, Scotland.
EDUCATION
Liberal arts course at Edinburgh University. Apprenticed to an architect in Edinburgh and spent some years with firms in that city. In 1885 he emigrated to Toronto.
PRACTICE
1887 Partnership with Alan Macdougal.
1900 St. Paul's Presbyterian Church, Bathurst Street and Barton Avenue.
c. 1903 Wm. Apted Printing Establishment, 58 Richmond Street.
1909 Knox Church, Spadina Avenue, where he served as deacon, and later as elder.

GREGG, ALFRED HOLDEN. 1868–1945. F.R.A.I.C.
Born in Toronto, son of the Rev. Professor Wm. Gregg.
EDUCATION
Model School, Toronto Collegiate Institute, Ontario College of Art. His early architectural training was in the office of his brother, Wm. J. Gregg. In 1888, he obtained further experience in architects' offices in Boston.
PRACTICE
In 1904, he formed a partnership with Frank Wickson under the name of Wickson & Gregg. They will best be remembered for Timothy Eaton Church, St. Clair Avenue, Toronto, and 70 Wellington Street, Toronto.

PERSONAL
Mr. Gregg was an early member of the Arts and Letters Club and the Royal Canadian Yacht Club.

GREGG, WM. J.
PRACTICE
1873 Aged Women's Home, Belmont House, Belmont St.
1891 Westminster Presbyterian Church. Rebuilt after fire in 1922 by Sproatt & Rolph.

GUNDRY, THOMAS. d. 1869
Born in England.
PRACTICE
1862 Partnership with Henry Langley. (See Langley, Henry.)

HARRISON, THOMAS H.
City of Toronto Engineer, 1856.

HAY, WILLIAM. 1818–1888
Born in Cruden, Scotland.
EDUCATION
Pupil in the office of John Henderson of Edinburgh, and, later, assistant to Sir Gilbert Scott in London.
PRACTICE
From 1847 to 1852 he was in St. John's, Newfoundland, as clerk of works on the Anglican Cathedral for which Scott was the architect, and, while in St. John's and Halifax, he superintended the erection of government buildings, some of which he designed. In 1852 he settled in Toronto.
1854 House of Providence, Power Street.
1855 Gould Street Presbyterian Church (later Catholic Apostolic). Chancel added in 1900 by Eden Smith. General Hospital, Gerrard Street.
1856 Early part of St. Basil's Church with St. Michael's College, St. Joseph Street.
1857 Alterations including the chapel and two classrooms for the Church of the Holy Trinity.
1858 St. John the Evangelist's Church, Victoria Square West (this church preceded the Garrison Church of Eden Smith).
1860 Yorkville Town Hall, Yonge Street, north of Bloor Street.
1861 Old Parsonage, Trinity Square.
In 1864, Hay left Canada to lead a roving life as architect in many parts of the Empire. However, in 1872, he settled down in Edinburgh where he remained, and built himself a house called "Rabbit Hall" at Portobello on the Firth of Forth. Until his death in 1888, he was engaged on the restoration of St. Giles' Cathedral, a work made possible through the generosity of Mr. William Chambers, the publisher. A bas-relief medallion of Hay may be seen in the vestibule of St. Giles.

HOLLAND, W. J. 1848–1899
PRACTICE
The Cyclorama Building, University and Front.

HOLMES, A. W.
PRACTICE
Spire of St. Mary's Church, Bathurst Street.

HORWOOD, JOHN CHARLES BATSTONE. 1864–1938
Born at Quidi Vidi near St. John's, Newfoundland.
EDUCATION
Ryerson School, Jarvis St. Collegiate Institute, Brooklyn Institute of Arts & Sciences. European travel with a mem-

ber of the staff of the Institute. In 1882 he entered the office of Langley, Langley & Burke. Later went to New York where he gained experience in several offices.

PRACTICE
1889 Church of St. Mary the Virgin, Dovercourt Road.
1894 Entered partnership under the firm name of Burke & Horwood at 28 Toronto Street.
1895 First section of Robert Simpson Store.
1895 Old Globe Building, 64 Yonge Street.
1898 Bible Training College, 110 College Street.
1900 Castle Frank, Bloor Street and Castle Frank Crescent.

PROFESSIONAL
One of the founders of the Eighteen Club and the O.A.A. The practice is now carried on by his son, Mr. Eric Horwood.

HOWARD, JOHN G. 1803–1890. R.C.A.
Born in a village 21 miles from London.

EDUCATION
Boarding School from 9–14 years of age at Hertford, England. When only 15 he went to sea for two years; although, like Nelson, he suffered from continual sea sickness, he acquired a taste for marine surveying and geometry which led him to engineering and architecture. To this end, he entered the office of an uncle, a contractor, and proceeded from this, as a pupil, to Mr. John Grayson, architect in London. His next office was that of Messrs. Cutbushes of Maidstone, and, finally, in 1824, that of Mr. John Ford of Mark Lane in London. In 1827, he married Miss Jemima Frances Meikle, to whom he erected the monument in High Park surrounded by sections of the iron fence which once enclosed part of the grounds of St. Paul's in London. In 1832, he emigrated to York, Upper Canada, on a sea trip that, with many adventures that are described in his published diary, took eleven weeks and three days from London.

PRACTICE
1833 Appointed drawing master at Upper Canada College for three hours a day, four days a week, with permission to carry on his professional work. Sir John Colborne, Mr. James G. Chewett, and Dr. Christopher Widmer were all interested in designs which he produced at this time for real or imaginary situations.
1833 The British Coffee House, King and York streets.
1834 Appointed City Surveyor by Wm. Lyon Mackenzie and held the position for 6 months.
1836 Colborne Lodge, his own house at High Park.
1837 British American Assurance offices, George Street. "Great alterations and additions to the Court of King's Bench."
1840 The third jail.
1841 Spire and aisle on west side of St. Paul's Yorkville, on Bloor Street.
1842 At the request of the Lands Department he prepared a survey and plan for the beautification of the waterfront. The Esplanade was shown as a broad parkway for the enjoyment of citizens.
Layout of St. James' Cemetery.
Two stores, 103–105 King St. "German silver sashes and plate glass."
1843 Certain engineering works at Osgoode Hall.
Layout of Osgoode grounds.
St. John's, York Mills.
1845 Bank of British North America.

1846 Lunatic Asylum, 999 Queen Street West. Won in competition.
1848 House of Industry, Elm Street.
1850 Tower and spire of St. Andrew's, Adelaide and Church streets.

Howard must always rank with the greatest of 19th century Toronto architects for his contribution to its early development. As architect, town planner, and engineer he was in a unique position to do so, and his gift of High Park with its 165 acres and his now historic house, place him in the forefront of the city's benefactors.

HOWLAND, FORD. 1874–1948
Ford Howland gained experience in several New York offices and returned to Canada, as did several of his age, for the building that followed the fire of 1904. As Langley & Howland, the firm had a large practice covering banks, churches, and houses, mostly in the 20th century.

PRACTICE
St. Anne's Church on Gladstone Avenue (1908) is, strictly speaking, outside the period of this book. The interior is one of the most beautiful in Toronto. The decorations of 1923 were by F. Varley, J. E. H. MacDonald, H. S. Palmer, and H. S. Stanfield.

HYNES, J. P. 1868–1953
No buildings in the 19th century and few in the 20th, but a person tireless in the interests of the profession and of education at a critical time in the history of the School of Architecture. Secretary of the O.A.A. 1935–1945.

IRVING, WILLIAM. 1830–1883
Born at Edinburgh, Scotland, son of John Irving, a contractor and stone carver. Wm. Irving married Mary Sheard, daughter of Joseph Sheard, architect, in 1857. E. J. Lennox was his pupil.

EDUCATION
Edinburgh schools and, later, in various architects' offices. Emigrated to Canada and arrived in Toronto in 1852.

PRACTICE
1875 Ontario Bank, Scott and Wellington streets, with Joseph Sheard.

JARVIS, BEAUMONT
PRACTICE
1890 Confederation Life building, with Knox & Elliott.
1897 Chapel, Loretto Abbey (later part of the Jesuit Seminary, Wellington Street West).
c. 1898 House for Mr. Henry Pellatt, 559 Sherbourne Street.

JAMES & JAMES
James & James were a New York firm briefly in Toronto as the successful architects in the Board of Trade Building international competition.
1887 The Board of Trade Building, Yonge and Front (later the T.T.C. headquarters).

JOHNSON, CHARLES W.
City of Toronto Engineer, 1871–1875.

JONES, CHILION
In 1857, with Thomas Fuller, he won the competition for the Parliament Buildings in Ottawa. He came of an architectural family which included Bernal, who was for years with Darling & Pearson, and, latterly, had his own practice in Kitchener; and Hugh G. of Montreal, who designed the Toronto Union Station.

KAUFFMAN, WILLIAM
EDUCATION
Graduate of a German school of architecture and civil engineering.
PRACTICE
1855 Rossin House, King and York streets.
1857 Masonic Hall (Canada Permanent Building on Toronto Street).
1861 Royal Insurance Building, Yonge and Wellington streets.
1863 Bank of Toronto, Church and Wellington streets.
1892 Gooderham Building (the flat iron building at Front and Yonge streets).

KINGSFORD, WILLIAM
City of Toronto Engineer, 1855.

KNOX & ELLIOTT
Architects of Chicago.
PRACTICE
1890 Confederation Life building, with Beaumont Jarvis.

LALOR & MARTIN
PRACTICE
1872 New Grand Opera House, Adelaide between Bay and Yonge streets.

LANE, HENRY BOWER. b. 1787
Born in London, England.
EDUCATION
Student architect in the Royal Academy Schools in London, and later, as a pupil, entered the office of Wm. Inwood in the same city.
PRACTICE
In active practice in London until he emigrated to Toronto in 1840.
1843 Little Trinity Church, 425 King Street East.
1844 City Hall, Front and Jarvis streets.
     Church of St. George the Martyr, John Street.
1846 Church of the Holy Trinity, Trinity Square.
Lane was a most distinguished architect who may have been responsible for the additions to Osgoode Hall in 1844 (*see* text). He returned to England in 1847.

LANGLEY, CHARLES. 1870–1951
Began practice in the 20th century, but he will be remembered as the generous donor of drawings of Toronto public buildings to the Toronto Public Library, and as the first graduate of the School (Department) of Architecture (1892) of the University of Toronto.

LANGLEY, HENRY. 1836–1906
EDUCATION
Toronto Academy (a branch of Knox College). Pupil of Wm. Hay for seven years.
PRACTICE
1862 Formed a partnership with Thomas Gundry formerly of London, England, until the latter's death, 1869.
1863 The Boys' Home, George Street.
     Added lower part of tower of St. James' Cathedral.
1865 St. Peter's Church, Carlton Street.
     Rectory of St. Stephen's-in-the-Fields. Rebuilt the church after the fire.
1866 Northern Railway Station, West Market Street and Esplanade.
     Spire of St. Michael's Cathedral.
1868 Government House, King and Simcoe streets.

1870 St. Patrick's Church, William Street.
1872 Metropolitan Church. Won in competition. (This was burned in 1928 and rebuilt; J. Gibb Morton, architect.)
     Sherbourne Street Methodist Church.
     The Necropolis, Winchester Street.
     The 8th Post Office at the head of Toronto Street.
1874 Spire, east and west porches, and pinnacles of St. James' Cathedral, King Street.
1878 Horticultural Pavilion, Allan Gardens, burned 1902; with Langley & Burke, architects.
     Old St. Andrew's Church, Jarvis and Carlton streets, with Edmund Burke.
1881 McMaster College, Bloor Street West, with Langley & Burke.
1885 Elm Street Methodist Church; Langley & Burke (*see* James Smith, architect).
     Bank of British North America, northeast corner of Yonge and Wellington streets.
1889 College Street Baptist Church; Langley and Burke, architects.
One of the most beautiful small churches in Ontario is the United Church in Parry Sound, a frame building on the main street opposite the post office; Henry Langley, architect.

LANGTON, WILLIAM. 1854–1933
Born at Peterborough, Canada West, the son of John Langton, first Auditor-General of Canada, and Vice-Chancellor of the University of Toronto, 1856–1860.
EDUCATION
Upper Canada College, 1868–1872.
PRACTICE
1889 St. Margaret's, Spadina Avenue.
1906 "A plan for Improvements to Toronto" including "A Solution of the Waterfront, circumambient lines of parkways, and direct lines of travel suitable to a city the size of Toronto." His influence on planning circles in Toronto, especially at the turn of the century, was considerable.
1912 Toronto Golf Club.
PROFESSIONAL
President of the O.A.A., 1902.
OTHER ACHIEVEMENTS
Editor of *Early Days in Upper Canada: Letters of John Langton*. First President of the Arts & Letters Club (1908).

LAW, COMMANDER F. C.
PRACTICE
1884 Our Lady of Lourdes, Sherbourne Street.

LENNOX, EDWARD JAMES. 1855–1933
Born in Toronto of Irish parents.
EDUCATION
Grammar and Model Schools. In 1874 he attended architectural drawing classes at the Mechanics' Institute where he received first prize and diploma. He studied in the office of Wm. Irving for five years. Travelled abroad.
PRACTICE
1877 Founded the firm of Lennox & McGaw. Dissolved in 1882.
1879 Erskine Presbyterian Church, Caer Howell (now Elm Street), facing Simcoe Street.
1879 Bond Street Congregational Church, Dundas and Bond streets.

1884 Bloor Street Baptist Church, Bloor and North (now Bay) streets.
1884 Manning Arcade, King Street West.
1886 Victoria Orange Hall, Queen Street East.
1888 McDonagh house, 329 Church Street.
1890 The City Hall. Won in competition.
1893 Toronto Athletic Club (now Police Bldg.), College Street.

The temptation cannot be resisted to include some 20th century buildings of Lennox such as Casa Loma stables, Casa Loma, Lennox's own house to the west of Casa Loma across Spadina Road, and the King Edward Hotel.

MILLER, G. M.
PRACTICE
1900 Extension to the west of the nave and aisles of old St. Paul's, Bloor Street.

MARANI, CESARE. 1864–1934
Instructor in the course in architecture in the School of Practical Science, 1890. No buildings to his credit, but that deficiency was more than made up by the achievements of his son, Col. F. H. Marani, in the 20th century.

POST, A. A.
PRACTICE
1887 The tower and additions to the nave, St. Basil's Church, St. Joseph Street.

RADFORD, EDWARD and GEORGE
EDUCATION
Pupils of Augustus Welby Pugin, one of the great figures in the Gothic Revival in England. The brothers probably worked on the Houses of Parliament at Westminster. Though Sir Charles Barry was the architect, Pugin was responsible for the design down to the "last ink well." (See Sir Kenneth Clark, *The Gothic Revival*.) The Radfords arrived in Toronto in the late 1850's.
PRACTICE
1860 St. Paul's Church, Bloor Street East, now called Maurice Cody Hall. Won in competition.

RIDOUT, THOMAS. b. 1828
Born in Toronto, the eldest son of Thomas Gibbs Ridout.
PRACTICE
1850 St. James' Cathedral, with F. W. Cumberland.
1851 Normal and Model Schools, with F. W. Cumberland.

ROBERTS, DAVID
PRACTICE
1859 Gooderham & Worts Distillery.
1889 Thorncrest, house of Mr. G. P. Magann, Dowling Ave.
1890 House of Mr. Geo. Gooderham (now the York Club), 135 St. George Street.

SCHREIBER, Sir COLLINGWOOD. 1831–1918. K.C.M.G.
Born in Essex, England, he came to Canada in 1852. In 1873, he was appointed Chief of the Government Railways. In 1880, he succeeded Sir Sandford Fleming as Chief Engineer of the C.P.R.
PRACTICE
1852 Crystal Palace, with Sir Sandford Fleming.

SHANLY, FRANK
City of Toronto Engineer, 1875–1876.

SHEARD, JOSEPH. 1813–1883
Born in Yorkshire, England. Emigrated to York in 1832.

PRACTICE
1852 House of Mr. William Cawthra, northeast corner of King and Bay streets.
Primitive Methodist Church, Alice Street.
Reformed Presbyterian Church, Louisa and James streets.
1856 Romain Building, 44 King Street West.
1875 Ontario Bank, Scott and Wellington streets, with William Irving.
POLITICAL
Alderman at various times for St. Patrick's, St. John's, and St. James' wards. Mayor of Toronto, 1871–1872.

SIDDALL, BENJAMIN
PRACTICE
In 1893 the firm was known as Siddall & Baker.
1897 Holy Blossom Temple (now Greek Orthodox Church), Bond Street.

SIMPSON, HENRY
PRACTICE
1891 Cooke's Church, Queen Street East.
1897 Partnership with J. A. Ellis.

SMITH, EDEN. 1858–1949
Born in England, he emigrated to Canada with his family in 1885.
EDUCATION
Educated in England. Experience in several offices, travel and sketching on the Continent. Family recollections of houses in London, England, but records of their locations are lost. Never liking the business side of architecture, he accompanied a shipmate (a French count and big game hunter) to Manitoba where he built a log cabin, twenty miles from Minnedosa. He farmed there for three years. In 1888, he moved to Toronto and opened an office for the practice of architecture.
PRACTICE
1892 St. John's (Garrison) Church, Portland Street.
St. Thomas' Church, Huron Street.
1900 Chancel of Catholic Apostolic Church, Gould Street.
PROFESSIONAL
President of the Architectural Eighteen Club.
The decision to terminate this history of Toronto building and its architects at 1900 is irrevocable, but Mr. Eden Smith, perhaps more than any other, unless it is Frank Darling, suffers because of it. In the quarter-century prior to his death, he revolutionized house design in Toronto, several branch libraries stand to his credit, and quite a few fine churches and the Toronto Housing Company's terraces on Bain and Sumach streets are still models of their kind. The editor of the English *Architectural Review*, Dr. Nikolaus Pevsner, considered the Studio Building on Severn Street a quite outstanding building for its day (1917) in Toronto.

SMITH, JAMES
PRACTICE
1862 Elm Street Methodist Church. (This was a stuccoed building with a dome, almost totally demolished for the church of 1885 by Henry Langley.)
1867 Northern Congregational Church, Church above Wood Street.

SMITH & GEMMELL
PRACTICE
1871 Berkeley Street Methodist Church.

1872 Armoury and Drill shed, West Market Street.
1875 Knox College, Spadina Crescent.
1878 St. James' Square, Presbyterian Church, Gerrard Street. (Church and square disappeared in 1962.)
1879 Second Church of the Redeemer.
1882 Zion Congregational Church, College and Elizabeth streets.
1887 St. Paul's Methodist Church (now United), Avenue Road and Webster Avenue.
1889 Immanuel Baptist Church, Wellesley and Jarvis streets.

SPROATT, HENRY. 1866–1934. LL.D. (Toronto)

Like others in this list, he was too young to have buildings to his credit in the 19th century. He was a founder member of the Architectural Draughtsmen's Club (1886). With Ernest Rolph, he will be remembered for Hart House at the University of Toronto and the National Club. The practice is now carried on by Mr. Charles Sproatt.

STORM, WILLIAM GEORGE. 1826–1892. R.C.A.

A native of Yorkshire, England, where his father was a builder. The son emigrated to York, Upper Canada, in 1830.

EDUCATION

For some years after his arrival, Storm appears to have gained experience in the building industry as a contractor. Shortly after William Thomas opened an office in Toronto Storm became his pupil. It was during this period (between 1842 and 1849) that he made extensive study trips to Europe.

PRACTICE

1850 In this year he was dissuaded from leaving Toronto for California by the offer of employment in Cumberland's office. The particular attraction was the preparation of drawings for St. James' Cathedral.
1852 He was invited to a partnership with Cumberland under the firm title of Cumberland & Storm. Partnership terminated in 1865.
1852 Court House, 57 Adelaide Street.
1853 Seventh Post Office, 10 Toronto Street.
1854 Mechanics' Institute, northeast corner, Adelaide and Church streets.
1858 Chapel of St. James-the-Less.
1874 Carlton Street Methodist Church near Yonge Street.
1875 New St. Andrew's Presbyterian Church, southeast corner of King and Simcoe streets.
Convocation Hall (Osgoode Hall).
The Law School (Osgoode Hall).
1892 Victoria College, Main Building.
Quarters of the Court of Appeal Judges (Osgoode Hall).

STRICKLAND, W. R.

PRACTICE

See Symons, W. L.

PROFESSIONAL

1887 Founder member of the Architectural Guild.

SYMONS, W. L. *c.* 1870–1934

Born at Stoke Gabriel in Devonshire and educated there. Came to Canada with his parents.

EDUCATION

Early training as pupil with architects in Toronto. Travelled a great deal, especially to England, where his brother was a Member of Parliament.

PRACTICE

Symons appears to have been the designer in the firm which

was early formed with W. R. Strickland.
1888 St. Simon's Church, 40 Howard Street.
St. Matthew's Church, First Avenue.
The old Morgue, Frederick and Esplanade.
The gates and gatehouse of Upper Canada College.
1896 The old Union Station, Front Street.
Goel Tzedek Synagogue, University Avenue.

Symons had a large domestic practice in Rosedale and Forest Hill. As honorary architect to the Canadian Medical Health Commission in the First World War, he designed a chain of hospitals (which he believed to be temporary) including Christie Street and Ste Anne de Bellevue. He was consultant for many years to Queen's University, and consultant to J. Pierpont Morgan in the restoration of Trinity Church, Broadway, N.Y., which had been built in 1839 by R. M. Upjohn.

I am obliged to Dean T. H. B. Symons for much of the above information concerning his grandfather, especially the New York connexion. Apparently, Mr. Symons' association with Morgan induced him to open an office in New York. Certainly the first Canadian architect to do so, and there has been none since, he carried out commissions from New York in Italy, the United States, and England. He had a reputation for not accepting work which did not leave him free to study to the last detail of design. It was typical of his practice that his Jewish clients allowed him three years for the study of ritual and symbolism for the synagogue on University Avenue.

PROFESSIONAL

President of the O.A.A. in 1903.

THOMAS, WILLIAM b. 1800

Born in Stroud in Gloucestershire, England, his training, like that of Kivas Tully and John G. Howard, was such as to produce the architect-engineer, common in their generation. He emigrated to Canada shortly before receiving his first commission.

PRACTICE

1839 Zion Congregational Church, Adelaide and Bay.
1843 Commercial Bank, 15 Wellington Street East, now the offices of Clarkson, Gordon and Co.
1845 St. Michael's Cathedral, Shuter Street.
Bishop's Palace, Church Street.
1848 Oakham House, his own home, Church and Gould streets.
Knox Church, Queen Street West, at the head of James Street.
United Presbyterian Church, Bay and Richmond streets.
1850 St. Lawrence Hall and Farmers' Market.
1852 Louisa Street School.
1853 Appointed City of Toronto Engineer.
1854 Brock's Monument, Queenston Heights.
1857 Bank of Upper Canada, the southeast corner of Yonge and Colborne streets.
St. Paul's in Hamilton.
1858 City jail, Gerrard Street.
1866 Design for a spire for St. Michael's Cathedral.

In 1866, and we don't know for how long before, Thomas was in Montreal. While there he made a design for the spire of the "Catedral"—the drawing is now in the Toronto Public Library. It was not built. (*See* Gundry & Langley.)

William Thomas was buried near the Chapel of St. James-the-Less in St. James' Cemetery in Toronto.

TOWNSEND, SAMUEL HAMILTON. 1856–1940
Born in Brantford, Ontario.
EDUCATION
Model School, Toronto. Pupil of W. G. Storm. Greatly travelled in the United Kingdom and the Continent, much of the time on a "penny farthing" bicycle.
PRACTICE
Largely domestic and included many Rosedale houses of which 1 Cluny Avenue was built around 1899. A great many on Cluny Crescent, Chestnut Park, and elsewhere in South Rosedale were built prior to his retirement in 1913.
PROFESSIONAL
Mr. Townsend was a founder member of the Architectural Guild (1887), the earliest association of architects in Ontario. He was President of the O.A.A. in 1898.
PERSONAL
In addition to his hazardous cycling on the penny farthing in various countries, S. H. Townsend was a keen sailor. He was designer and owner of the *Wah-Wah* which won the Prince of Wales cup in 1897—a cup given to the Royal Canadian Yacht Club by Edward Prince of Wales.

TULLY, KIVAS. 1820–1905
Born in England, he emigrated to Canada in 1844 and settled in Toronto.
EDUCATION
From what one can learn, he was trained, like many in his day on both sides of the Atlantic, as architect and engineer which, in 1867, was his title in the Department of Public Works.
PRACTICE
1845 Bank of Montreal, Yonge and Front streets.
1851 A master plan for Trinity College on Queen Street and the first building programme on the site. Won in a limited competition.
1855 Restoration of St. Andrew's Niagara-on-the-Lake after a severe storm which damaged the church and steeple.
Tully laid out the first sewer system for Toronto, and is remembered in Cobourg for Victoria Hall and, in St. Catharines, for the Town Hall.

WAITE, RICHARD A.
An Englishman practising in Buffalo, N.Y., who came to Toronto for the adjudication of the Ontario Legislative Buildings competition. He remained to do the buildings himself (*see* text).
PRACTICE
1886 Legislative Buildings, Queen's Park.
Canada Life Assurance Company building, King and Bay streets.
1890 Bank of Commerce, King Street.

WALTON, CHARLES
PRACTICE
Yonge Street Arcade.

WHITE, STANFORD. 1853–1906
A member of the well-known New York firm of McKim, Mead & White. He was here, briefly, for the building of Benvenuto. His death at the hand of Harry K. Thaw attracted world attention.
PRACTICE
1890 Benvenuto, for Mr. S. H. Janes, Avenue Road Hill.

WICKSON, A. FRANK. 1861–1936
EDUCATION
Jarvis Collegiate and Upper Canada College (1878). Pupil in the firm of Smith & Gemmell.
PRACTICE
1892 Olivet Congregational Church, Hazelton Avenue, with N. B. Dick.
1904 Partnership with A. H. Gregg. The work of the firm lies outside the period of this study (*see* A. H. Gregg).
PROFESSIONAL
President O.A.A. in 1900. He was a member of the earlier Architectural Guild which met between 1887 and 1898.

WINDEYER, R. C.
Came to Canada from Kent in England in the 1850's and settled for a time in Montreal.
PRACTICE
1874 All Saints Church, Sherbourne and Dundas streets, with John Falloon.
1876 Eighth Customs House, Front and Yonge streets.
1886 Cathedral of St. Alban the Martyr, Howland Avenue, with John Falloon. In 1913, the plans were revised by Ralph Adams Cram, U.S. architect. Nave begun, but never finished.

WOOLNOUGH, J. J.
City Architect, Toronto, 1925–1932
EDUCATION
Passed the examinations of the O.A.A. in 1892.

WRIGHT, C. H. C. 1864–1944
Instructor in the course in architecture in the School of Practical Science, 1890. Professor and head of the School of Architecture, 1901–1934.

YOUNG, THOMAS. d. 1860
Thomas Young came to Toronto in 1835. He was one of the outstanding topographical draftsmen of early Toronto. In 1835–1840, he did a series of views of Toronto, which he dedicated to Sir John Colborne, for Currier & Ives. They are lithographs in black and white and are as follows: (*a*) a general view of the City of Toronto; (*b*) view of the Houses of Parliament and Government offices; (*c*) view of King Street; (*d*) view of Upper Canada College.
PRACTICE
1840 Appointed first City Engineer for Toronto.
1842 King's College, of which only the southeast wing was built (*see* text).

There are other architects listed in city directories from 1850 to 1900 of whom present research has not uncovered buildings or other pertinent information:

Baker, Alfred	King, George
Bousfield, R. W. Gambier	Passmore, F. F.
Cassels, Andrew H.	Paul, Almond E.
Edwards, Robt. J.	Stibbs, William
Ewing, William	Wagner, C. F.
Fowler, Joseph	Webster, Hy. J.
Greenfield, Joseph	

This list has been prepared from Williamson's map of 1878, and the street directories of 1890 and 1900. Only streets of the 18th and 19th century are listed, with 1900 A.D. as a terminal date. Omitted from the following lists are streets whose names are merely descriptive like Lakeshore, geographic like Madeira or where, like Harbord, origins are obscure or unknown.*

Just as the social history of a people may be read in its architecture, the history of a city may be read in the names of its streets. Names like Simcoe, Russell, Baldwin and Osgoode take us back to the very foundation of the city, and others like Brulé, Seneca and Huron recall a remote and pagan past of people who knew well the village at the end of the Passage de Toronto centuries before the settlement at York.

From Simcoe's arrival in 1793, our street names have fallen into many patterns. In the days of York, they indicated quite unmistakably our loyalty to the Crown and the Royal family. The English queens of the 19th century were all there, the royal dukes were not forgotten, and our affection for the Hanoverian sovereigns did not preclude the naming of streets after their ancestral estates in Germany.

This was particularly true of the early days in York, but the British connexion was never lost. Colonial secretaries, British prime ministers, governors-general and lieutenant-governors were recorded with few exceptions along with British heroes like Nelson, Havelock, Gordon, Napier and Wellington and the battles which they fought. So strong was the British element in our street names that it comes as a shock to find that Alderman Steiner had sufficient influence to name one after the Chancellor Bismarck (made more palatable later, it is true, by Asquith), and someone, with a catholic taste in princes, gave us Czar and Sultan streets.

There is no evidence that the ties with Britain ever weakened in Toronto, but as the village became town and the town city, there is less and less indication of colonial dependence. Pride in the city is clearly shown by the numerous streets called after mayors, aldermen, property owners and public-spirited persons whom the city desired to honour, but Sir Wilfrid Laurier, Prime Minister of Canada (1896–1911), stands alone against the almost unbroken chain of colonial secretaries of an earlier time, and only McGee of the Fathers of Confederation is remembered.

Lawyers rank below wives, daughters and aldermen in the number of streets honouring members of their profession, and the medical list is more impressive than lengthy with names like Macaulay, Baldwin and Widmer going back to the 18th century. The church is represented by a Roman Catholic bishop (Power), two Anglican bishops (Strachan Toronto, and Stewart Quebec), and by Church of England parsons, Darling of Holy Trinity, Maynard of Little Trinity who was also a master of Upper Canada College, Charles Winstanley and Addison who was chaplain to the Legislative Assembly. Three Ontario premiers come down to us in streets named after Blake, Mowat and Whitney.

The brewers rate four in Bloor, Doel, Davies and O'Keefe, and universities three, Oxford, Cambridge and Harvard. They are followed by a most exclusive list: architects two (Howard and Langley), cab-drivers two (Paterson and Hazelton), a carpenter (Pears), a biscuit-maker (Christie), a broker (Phipps), a jeweller and watch-maker (Jordan), and a university president (McCaul).

There were street names, long gone, that recall a frontier town with few pretensions to culture. Rabbit-Lane and Fish Lane aptly suggest their proximity to woods and lake, but alleys like Whiskey, Grog and Deadbeat could not have represented the most desirable residential districts.

Research has shown that many streets of 1878 (Williamson's map) disappeared before the city directory of 1890, and some between 1890 and 1900. Still more have been lost in this century. In most cases, one can only regret their absence and deplore the substitution that was made. Ann, it will be remembered, was changed to Granby at the whim of the people on the street, and the name of that Rousseau who acted as pilot when Lieutenant-Governor Simcoe and Mrs. Simcoe made their historic entry into the harbour of Toronto is no longer on the map of the city except, rather obscurely, in St. John's Road. These are but two of many.

Street names which we have been unable to identify are not listed, nor are those where the origin seems at first sight so obvious. It would not be difficult to write "Kintyre, Mull of, Scotland," and it would be tempting to identify "Knox, the Scottish reformer, 1505–1572," but it would be embarrassing if later research proved Kintyre and Knox to be aldermen from wards 2 and 4 respectively. If the writer would seem to show undue timidity in such a decision, he would point to Bellwoods which conjures up a memory of bells heard in a wood. In reality the word is an unromantic combination of the names of two Toronto aldermen, Messrs. Bell and Woods.

This study of street names has been prepared because such a list has appeared only twice, in part, in print: in the *Landmarks of Toronto* (1894) and in the pamphlet by Mary Hoskin Jarvis. It is hoped that it may give citizens, especially school children, a new interest in their city and those who made it what it is; and that by its example of honouring the great and the humble, and those who served it well in politics, the professions and trade, it may set a precedent for the naming of new streets. This is an area in which, today, we show little imagination, or realization of the history, dignity and reputation of Toronto among the cities of the world. When one looks back on the last sixty years of Canadian history, the great events that took place in that time and those who took part in them on our behalf, one wonders how names like Radio Valve Street could find a place on the map of Toronto.

*Sources: John Ross Robertson, *Landmarks of Toronto*, Series 1, p. 516; T. A. Reed's own handwritten and typewritten lists; Mary Hoskin Jarvis, "Streets of Toronto," in *Transaction* 28 of the Women's Canadian Historical Society (1934); also City directories, the Registry office, the City Hall, Osgoode Hall, the Royal Canadian Military Institute and the press of the 19th century.

Appendix B

The Origin of Street Names in Toronto

ABBEY LANE: Russell Abbey, the home of the Hon. Peter Russell, which once stood at the corner of Palace and Princess streets. (*See* Russell.)

ABBS: a market gardener James Abbs in the old village of Parkdale.

ABELL: John Abell, manufacturer of agricultural implements, located in the vicinity.

ABERDEEN: the Earl of Aberdeen, Governor-General of Canada, 1893–1898.

ADDISON: probably the Rev. John Addison, 1755–1829, first incumbent of St. Mark's, Niagara-on-the-Lake, and Chaplain to the Legislative Assembly.

ADELAIDE: the Dowager Queen of William IV. Until 1842–1843 Adelaide Street was called after Newgate St. in London.

ADMIRAL: Admiral Augustus W. Baldwin, 1776–1866, a member of the same family as Hon. W. W. Baldwin. (*See* Baldwin.)

AFTON: probably the "Sweet Afton" of Robert Burns.

AGNES: probably a friend or member of the Macaulay family. (*See* Macaulay.)

ALBANY: the Duke of Albany, youngest son of Queen Victoria.

ALBERT: Albert, Prince Consort, husband of Queen Victoria. Albert Street was previously Macaulay Lane.

ALEXANDER: Alexander Wood who purchased 25 acres lying north of Carlton Street from Mrs. Mary Elmsley in 1826. This area was for many years known as Molly Wood's bush. (*See* Wood.)

ALICE: probably a friend or member of the Macaulay family. (*See* Macaulay.)

ALLEN: Thomas Allen, Alderman, 1877–1879, 1883–1886, 1890–1891, 1895–1897.

ALMA: the battle of the Alma in the Crimean War, 1854; part of a sub-division of military names.

AMELIA: the wife of John Scadding who bought 200 acres in this area from the Simcoe Estate of Castle Frank. (*See* Scadding.)

ANCROFT: Anthony Croft, owner of property on Maple Avenue, in the same vicinity.

ANDERSON: a property owner in the district. Anderson Street and Anderson Lane are now Dundas and McCaul streets.

ANN: Ann, widow of Andrew McGill, who later married Rt. Rev. Dr. John Strachan. In 1834, Dr. Strachan purchased 25 acres north of Gerrard Street of which he and his wife deeded certain portions to the city in the same year. The name superseded the original St. Anne Street in 1843. Now Granby. (*See* McGill, Strachan.)

ANNE: Anne, daughter of Dr. James Macaulay, who married Dr. Peter Diehl in 1829. Unfortunately for the memory of Anne, the street was later re-named Alice and, finally, Teraulay. (*See* Macaulay.)

ARGYLE: the Duke of Argyle, father of the Marquis of Lorne, Governor-General of Canada, 1878–1883. (*See* Lorne.)

ARMSTRONG: James Armstrong, property owner in the district.

ARTHUR: Arthur, Duke of Connaught (1850–1942), 3rd son of Queen Victoria, a visitor to Toronto in 1870.

AUGUSTA: a female member of the Denison family (*see* Denison) *or* Charlotte Augusta, only daughter of George IV (*see* Charlotte).

AUSTIN: James Austin, who came to Canada from Ireland in 1828 and, as a youth, was employed by William Lyon Mackenzie in the printing business. Later, with the Hon. John Ross, he founded the Dominion Bank of which he became the first president, 1871–1879. In 1865, Austin purchased considerable land on Davenport Road from the Baldwin Estate and built his own home there.

BADGEROW: George Washington Badgerow, the County Attorney, *circa* 1890, admitted as a student at Osgoode Hall in 1866, called to the Bar in 1871.

BAIN: the family of that name, residents in the district.

BALDWIN: Dr. William Warren Baldwin, owner of the country house on the hill called "Spadina." (*See* Admiral, Heyden, Phoebe, Robert, St. George, Spadina, Sullivan, Walmer, Willcocks.)

BALMORAL: the Royal residence in Scotland.

BALMUTO: a friend of Arthur R. Boswell, K.C., Mayor of Toronto 1883–1884. (*See* Boswell.)

BARTLETT: a property owner of that name in the district.

BARTON: Edward W. Barton, broom manufacturer and Alderman, old St. Stephen's Ward, 1884–1888.

BATHURST: Henry, third Earl Bathurst, Secretary for War and the Colonies, 1812–1827. This name applied to the present street south of Queen (then Lot) when given in 1820. The northern section was known as Crookshank's Lane, after the Hon. George Crookshank who owned a large estate there. (*See* Crookshank.)

BATTYE: a property owner of that name.

BAXTER: John Baxter, resident of York in 1830. Alderman and Councilman for St. Patrick's Ward intermittently between 1860 and 1890.

BAY: from the legend of the bear chased into the bay. Bay is a corruption of the original Bear Street—the western boundary of the town of York.

BEACHELL: William Beachell who was connected with the Grand Trunk Railway.

BEACONSFIELD: Benjamin Disraeli, Lord Beaconsfield, Prime Minister of Great Britain, 1868–1874.

BEAR: *see* Bay.

BEATRICE: a daughter of E. O. Bickford of Gore Vale. (*See* Gore Vale.)

BEATY: James Beaty, K.C., Mayor of Toronto, 1879–1880.

BEDFORD: the Duke of Bedford, the head of the Irish branch of the family of Hon. Peter Russell who received an original grant of land in this vicinity. (*See* Russell.)

BELL: John Foli Bell, admitted as a student to Osgoode Hall in 1864, a solicitor.

BELLAIR: Walter Bellairs, nephew of Walter McKenzie of Castle Frank. His house was on the north side of Yorkville, west of Yonge and nearly opposite Bellair. Mr. Bellairs was a well-known man about town.

BELLEVUE: the home of George Taylor Denison who owned 150 acres as early as 1817. Bellevue Avenue was one of the roads to the family homestead at Denison Square. (*See* Denison.)

BELLWOODS: William Bell, Alderman, St. Stephen's Ward 1881–1883, 1888–1891; Ward 5, 1892–1893; and collector, St. Stephen's Ward, 1884–1886. John Woods, Alderman, St. Stephen's Ward, 1882; St. Mark's Ward 1885–1886. Bellwoods Avenue was formerly Strachan Street. Its name was changed in 1882.

BELMONT: Belmont, England, the birthplace of John Sheppard, a property owner in the vicinity.

BERKELEY: John Small's home, Berkeley House. John Small was first clerk of the Executive Council of Upper Canada 1793–1831. He was born in Berkeley, Gloucestershire, in 1746. His house stood at the southwest corner of Berkeley and King Streets from 1796 to 1926. Berkeley Street was formerly Parliament Street. The name was transferred when the road from the Parliament Buildings to Castle Frank was opened up. (*See* Coxwell.)

BERNARD: Bernard Saunders, Alderman, St. Paul's Ward 1883–1900 with few interruptions; executor of the Noah L. Piper Estate, through which the street ran from Avenue Road to near Bedford Park.

BERCZY: Charles Albert Berczy (1794–1858), born at Newark (Upper Canada), Postmaster of Toronto.

BERRYMAN: Dr. Charles Berryman, a well-known practitioner in Yorkville, who was instrumental in getting the village incorporated and succeeded James Severn, the first reeve.

BEVERLEY: Beverley House, home of Sir John Beverley Robinson, 1791–1863, the Attorney-General, built on the southeast corner of Queen and John streets. (*See* Robinson.)

BINSCARTH: after the family of William Bain Scarth, born 1837 in Scotland. His father, James Scarth, was a descendant of the family of the Scarths of Binscarth, Orkney Islands. (*See* Scarth.)

BISHOP: Dr. John Strachan, 1778–1867, first Bishop of Toronto, 1839–1867. (*See* Strachan.)

BISMARCK: the German Chancellor's name was given by Alderman John Steiner (1880–1881, 1883–1886, 1899), to the former Jarvis Street, Yorkville. Changed to Asquith Avenue during First World War. (*See* Steiner.)

BLAKE: Probably the Hon. Edward Blake (1833–1912), Premier of Ontario 1871–1874.

BLEECKER: Charlotte Bleecker Powell, daughter of Grant Powell of Albany, N.Y. who married John Ridout, Registrar of Deeds, 1855–1894. (*See* Sherbourne.)

BLEVINS: John B. Blevins, City Clerk, 1885–1900 and Alderman for St. David's Ward 1864–1884.

BLONG: Henry Blong, a butcher in the district. The name appears in the Directory of 1866.

BLOOR: Joseph Bloor, 1788–1862, a brewer who lived at 100 Bloor Street. Mr. Bloor and Sheriff Jarvis laid out the village plots for the town of Yorkville, just north of Bloor. For many years Bloor was the northern limit of the city proper. It was formerly known as St. Paul's Road, Sydenham Road, and Toll-Gate Road, the latter after the toll-gate which stood at the corner of Yonge Street.

BOND: Thomas Bond, who appears in the Directory of 1837 as "Thos. Bond, brick maker, Lot Street." J. G. Howard's Diary for 1845 mentions the drawing of plans and specifications for sewers on Church and several short streets contracted for by Thomas Bond in 1845–1848.

BOOTH: George S. Booth, Alderman 1889–1890, who was a coppersmith.

BORDEN: Esther Borden Lippincott, daughter of Captain Richard Lippincott, an officer in the Revolutionary War and early settler in York. She married George Taylor Denison. (*See* Denison.)

BOSWELL: Arthur R. Boswell, K.C., Mayor of Toronto 1883–1884. (*See* Balmuto.)

BOULTBEE: Alfred Boultbee, who practised law in Newmarket for 25 years before moving to Toronto, member of Parliament for North York in 1871, for East York in 1878.

BOULTON: probably W. H. Boulton, Mayor 1845–1846, 1847, 1858. (*See* D'Arcy, Emily, Grange, Henry.)

BOUSTEAD: James B. Boustead, Councilman, St. David's Ward 1865 and St. James' Ward 1866; Alderman, St. James' Ward intermittently from 1869 to 1891; Ward 3, 1896.

BOWDEN: John B. Bowden, a contractor.

BRACONDALE: the suburban village of Bracondale, northwest of Bathurst and Dupont which took its name from the estate of Robert John Turner, a solicitor from Yarmouth, England, who settled here, practised law and became Accountant-General of the Court of Chancery. He died in 1872. (*See* Turner.)

BRANT: Joseph Brant, born 1742 on the Ohio River, a chief of the Mohawk tribe who settled in this province, and, in 1786, visited England to raise funds to build the first Episcopal church in Upper Canada. He died in 1807.

BREADALBANE: probably John Campbell, 2nd Marquis of Breadalbane, 1796–1862.

BRIGHT: John Bright, son of James Bright, a resident of the east end, whose father, also a resident of York, fought under Brock at Queenston Heights.

BROCK: General Sir Isaac Brock (1769–1812), Administrator of Upper Canada, who fell at Queenston Heights. Now part of Spadina Avenue south of Queen. Brock Street was formerly Broadway Place.

BROOKFIELD: Brookfield House, the home of Sophia Denison, widow of Captain John Denison. (*See* Denison.)

BROWN: the Hon. George Brown (1818–1880), journalist and statesman, editor of the *Globe*. Elected to the Legislative Assembly 1851, appointed to the Senate 1871.

BRUNSWICK: Caroline of Brunswick-Wolfenbüttel (1768–1821), wife of George IV. (*See* Caroline.)

BUCHANAN: Sir James Buchanan Macaulay (1793–1859), born at Newark (Niagara) Upper Canada, son of Dr. James Macaulay. (*See* Macaulay.)

BULLER: Charles Buller, 1806–1848, an Englishman who was secretary to Lord Durham in 1838.

BULWER: probably the English statesman and author, Edward George, Earl Lytton, Secretary for the colonies 1858–1859 and author under the name Bulwer-Lytton of many popular novels from 1827 to 1873. (*See* Lytton.)

CAER HOWELL: Caer Howell in Montgomeryshire, Wales, the family seat of Hon. William Dummer Powell, Chief Justice of Upper Canada 1815–1825. Later incorporated in Elm Street which was always distinguished for its horse chestnuts and a solitary elm. (*See* Elm Street.)

CAMBRIDGE: the English university of that name; next to it is Oxford Street.

CAMERON: John Hillyard Cameron, lawyer and M.P. (1817–1876). Educated Upper Canada College; 1860 Treasurer of the Law Society of Upper Canada. One of the founders of Trinity College of which he was Chancellor in 1864.

CAMPBELL: probably William Campbell who purchased a large section of land in this district, the western section of Davenport Road. (*See* Edwin, Royce.)

CARLAW: Major John A. Carlaw (b. 1840), cashier of the Grand Trunk Railway in Toronto, and property owner in the district.

CARLTON: Guy Carleton Wood, son of Dr. G. Wood, United Empire Loyalist of Cornwall. Named by his sister Ann McGill, wife of Rev. Dr. John Strachan. The present spelling is "Carlton." (*See* Ann.)

CARLING: Hon. John Carling (1828–1911), brewer and politician. Federal Minister of Agriculture 1867–1871. Entered his father's business and succeeded him as President of Carling's Breweries.

CARLYLE: William Carlyle, Alderman for St. Thomas's Ward 1879–1890.

CAROLINE: named by Gov. Simcoe after Caroline, Princess of Wales, later Queen of George IV. At present, part of Sherbourne Street, south of Queen. (*See* Brunswick.)

CARR: probably John Carr, City Councillor, Alderman, Clerk and Commissioner, 1847–1873. Carr Street was originally Elizabeth Street, part of Bellevue Estate owned by Colonel George Denison. The name was changed in 1870. Mr. John Carr resided at 21 Denison Avenue in 1873.

CARROLL: Dr. John A. Carroll, Alderman for St. Matthew's Ward, 1884.

CASIMIR: Col. Sir Casimir Gzowski (1813–1898), the street being in the vicinity of his home "The Hall," now Alexandra Park, Bathurst and Dundas Streets.

CATHARINE: Catharine, Mrs. Stephen Howard, the street named by her father, Hon. George Crookshank. (*See* Crookshank.)

CAWTHRA: William Cawthra (1801–1880) who, in 1847, purchased a block on Jarvis Street from S. F. Jarvis.

CECIL: first after Colonel Givins' daughter Cecilia, and later re-named Halton Street after one of his sons. Colonel Givins had accompanied Gov. Simcoe to Canada and for many years was Superintendent of Indian Affairs. (*See* Givens.)

CEDAR: a cedar swamp on the west side of Dundas, north of Queen.

CENTRE: obscure; it was located on the property of the Rev. Thomas Raddish who was the nominee for the Rectorship of York. When he returned to England after a few months he conveyed his large lot to Chief Justice Elmsley who, in turn, sold it to Alexander Wood and John Beverley Robinson.

CHAPEL: the Roman Catholic Chapel, afterwards St. Paul's Church, Power Street, to which the street led.

CHARLES: James Charles or, perhaps, the Rev. Charles Winstanley, both property owners in the 1840's.

CHARLOTTE: Charlotte Augusta (1796–1817) only daughter of George IV and Queen Caroline, who married Leopold of Saxe-Coburg in 1816. She died in childbirth in 1817. (*See* Augusta, Claremont, Leopold.)

CHRISTIE: William Christie (1829–1900), a baker of that district. His bakery was moved later to Yonge Street.

CHRISTOPHER: Christopher Robinson (1837–1923), son of Chief Justice Robinson, born at Thorah, Upper Canada, editor and publisher. (*See* Robinson.)

CHURCH: from the fact that since 1807, a St. James' Church (now the Cathedral) had been there.

CHURCHILL: the "Church on the Hill" built by Richard Lippincott Denison of Dovercourt. (*See* Denison.)

CIBOLA: probably after the legendary "seven cities of Cibola" in Mexico. A boat called Cibola once plied regularly between Niagara-on-the-Lake and Toronto.

CLANDEBOYE: the County Seat in Ireland of the Marquis of Dufferin and Ava, Governor-General of Canada 1872–1879. (*See* Dufferin.)

CLAREMONT: Claremont House, near Esher, England, built for Lord Clive, afterwards the home of Princess Charlotte, daughter of George IV. (*See* Charlotte.)

CLARENCE: named after Albert Victor, Duke of Clarence 1864–1892, elder son of Edward VII, when the title was revived in 1890.

CLARKE: Edward F. Clarke, Mayor of Toronto 1888–1891.

CLINTON: probably Henry Clinton (1811–1864), Secretary for the Colonies 1852–1854. He visited Canada in 1860.

CLOSE: P. G. Close, Alderman 1873–1878 and 1880.

COATSWORTH: Emerson C. Coatsworth, City Commissioner of Toronto from 1873 to 1903 when the office was abolished. (*See* Virgin.)

COLBORNE: Sir John Colborne (1778–1863), first Baron Seaton, Lt.-Gov. of Upper Canada 1828–1836. Formerly Market Lane. (*See* Seaton.)

COLLACHIE: Angus MacDonell (d. 1804), son of Allan MacDonell of Collachie. Treasurer of the Law Society of Upper Canada, 1801–1804. He was drowned in the loss of the *Speedy* on Lake Ontario. (*See* Macdonell.)

COLLEGE: its original use (1829) was as a private avenue of approach to King's College, but it was leased by the University of Toronto, along with the University Avenue, as public streets (*circa* 1888). College Avenue is now College Street. (*See* University.)

COLLIER: an official in the Canada Company, *or* Frank Collier Draper (1837–1894), Chief of Police and son of Chief Justice Draper. F. C. Draper reorganized the police force about 1870. (*See* Draper.)

CONDUIT: probably a street of that name running between Regent Street and Bond Street in London.

CONSTANCE: the daughter of Colonel Walter O'Hara who was captain in the 47th Regiment during the Peninsular War. (*See* O'Hara.)

COOLMINE: from the Kirkpatrick family, originating with Alexander Kirkpatrick of Coolmine Co. Dublin (1749–1818). His grandson, George B. Kirkpatrick, born 1835, was Director of Surveys of the Province of Ontario.

COOPER: George Cooper, a property owner in the district.

COXWELL: Charles Coxwell Small (1746–1831), son of Mayor John Small of Berkeley House, and Clerk of Common Pleas 1825–1864. (*See* Berkeley.)

CRAWFORD: Joshua Crawford, who filed a plan in 1856. In 1887 this name was changed to Elliot Street. The present Crawford Street was named after Hon. Thomas Crawford, Speaker of the Legislative Assembly.

CROCKER: James Crocker, Alderman 1875–1889.

CROOKSHANK: Hon. George Crookshank (1773–1859), Deputy Commissary General from 1796 until the end of the war of 1812, and a member of the Legislative Council of Upper Canada. (*See* Bathurst, Wilton.)

CUMBERLAND: the birth place of James Wallace, one of the early Councillors of Yorkville.

CURZON: the street in London of the same name.

CUTTLE: Thomas Cuttle, printer in this district and a resident of 49 Trinity Square in 1873.

CZAR: the Russian ruler, named at a time when that country was held in high esteem. Czar Street is now Charles Street West. (*See* Sultan.)

DALE: the residence of Dr. John Hoskin, K.C. (1836–1921). (*See* Hoskin.)

DALHOUSIE: the Marquis of Dalhousie, Governor-General of Canada 1820–1828.

DANFORTH: Asa Danforth, contractor for the construction of this road between York and the Bay of Quinte in 1799.

D'ARCY: D'Arcy Boulton (1785–1846), owner of the Grange, now part of the Art Gallery of Toronto. (*See* Boulton.)

DARLING: Rev. W. S. Darling (1818–1886), Rector of the Church of the Holy Trinity. Father of Frank Darling, architect.

DARTNELL: Georgina Dartnell, wife of Col. Frederick Wells (1822–1877), son of Hon. J. Wells and veteran of the Crimean War. (*See* Wells.)

DAVENPORT: residence of Col. the Hon. Joseph Wells (1773–1853) on the hill to which it led. Originally, the "new road to Niagara." In 1844 and 1852 called "Plank Road." (*See* Wells.)

DAVIES: Thomas Davies, brewer, Alderman 1873–1874, 1881–1884, 1889, 1893, 1895–1896, 1898–1899.

DEAN: Harriet Dean, daughter of Joseph K. Dean (1810–1871) and wife of George Gooderham. (*See* Matilda, Mill.)

DEFOE: D. M. Defoe, Alderman 1884.

DEFRIES: Robert Defries, brewer, and other members of the well-known family of that name, long resident in the east end of the city.

DE GRASSI: Alfio De Grassi, merchant, insurance agent and prominent Mason in the 1870's.

DENISON: the street was one of the roads to the Denison house at Denison Square owned by George Taylor Denison, and, after his decease, by his son Lt.-Col. Robert Brittain Denison (1821–1900). (*See* Augusta, Bedford, Bellevue, Borden, Brookfield, Churchill, Dewson, Dovercourt, Esther, Lippincott, Major, Ossington, Robert, Rolyat, Rusholme.)

DERBY: Probably the earls of Derby in Lancashire.

DEVONSHIRE PLACE: the birthplace of Dr. John Hoskin, member of the Board of Trustees of University of Toronto in 1889, when the street was laid out. (*See* Hoskin.)

DEWSON: Mary Ann Dewson, wife of George Taylor Denison II (1816–1873). (*See* Denison.)

DOEL: W. H. Doel of Broadview Avenue, son of John Doel (1790–1871), brewer at northwest corner of Adelaide and Bay streets.

DON MILLS: because of its proximity to the river Don. There were several mills in the vicinity.

DORSET: Dorset House, Wellington Street, home of George Ridout (1791–1871), second son of Hon. Thomas Ridout. (*See* Sherbourne.)

DOURO: probably after one of the Duke of Wellington's titles. Now part of Wellington Street. (*See* Wellington.)

DOVERCOURT: "Dovercourt" was the name of the estate owned by Richard Lippincott Denison. Its name is derived from Dovercourt, near Harwich in the County of Essex, the home of Sophia Taylor his mother. (*See* Denison.)

DOWLING: Col. Dowling, who married the sister of Col. A. R. Dunn, V.C. (*See* Dunn.)

DRAPER: William Henry Draper (1801–1877), politician and jurist. Chief Justice of Upper Canada 1863–1869. (*See* Collier.)

DRUMSNAB: the home of Frank Cayley (1807–1890) at 5 Castle Frank Crescent.

DUBLIN: original name of Township of York.

DUCHESS: the Duchess of York, daughter-in-law of George III and eldest daughter of the King of Prussia. The first Duchess Street was laid out by Gov. Simcoe in 1793. It later became Duke Street, and a second Duchess, the one we know today, was laid out in 1797 one block north.

DUFFERIN: the Marquis of Dufferin and Ava, Governor-General of Canada 1872–1878. (*See* Clandeboye.)

DUKE: the Duke of York, son of George III, one of the streets in the Town of York laid out by Gov. Simcoe in 1793, being the northern boundary. Duke is now King Street. (*See* Frederick.)

DUNDAS: Sir Henry Dundas, first Viscount Melville, Home Secretary 1791–1794. Dundas Street East was Wilton Avenue and before that Crookshank Street—with Yonge Street it was one of the first streets laid out by Gov. Simcoe.

DUNEDIN: the Gaelic name of Edinburgh.

DUNN: John Henry Dunn (d. 1854), Receiver-General of Canada, father of Col. A. R. Dunn, V.C., who fought at Balaclava. (*See* Dowling.)

DUPONT: George Dupont Wells (1814–1854), son of Col. the Hon. J. Wells of Davenport, County York. (*See* Wells.)

DURHAM: John George Lambton, first Earl of Durham 1792–1840, Governor-General of Canada 1838. Durham Street is now Shanly Street. (*See* Lambton.)

EAST: after its location, north to Eastern Avenue just east of the Don River. Changed to Water Street in 1876.

EASTERN: formerly South Park Street since it was part of an area set aside for a park.

EDGAR: Edgar John Jarvis of Rosedale (born 1835), nephew of the original owner. (*See* Jarvis.)

EDWARD: probably after a friend or member of the Macaulay family. (*See* Macaulay.)

EDWIN: a member of the family of William Campbell, a large landowner in the Davenport district. (*See* Campbell.)

ELGIN: the Earl of Elgin, Governor-General of Canada 1847–1854.

ELIZABETH: Elizabeth Hayter, wife of Dr. James Macaulay, Surgeon of the Queen's Rangers and Deputy Inspector-General of Hospitals, 1813–1822. This street was the southern part of a large property owned by him in 1799, and, later, laid out in building streets and lots as a remote suburban district for working people and known as Macaulay Town. (*See* Macaulay.)

ELLIOT: Thomas E. Elliot, Alderman of St. Matthew's Ward, 1884–1886.

ELLIS: John Ellis, J.P., a landowner in the district.

ELM AVE.: an avenue in Rosedale named by Edgar Jarvis and planted with elm trees. (*See* Jarvis.)

ELM ST.: after a legendary ancient landmark, a solitary elm tree that once stood near the corner of Yonge and Elm streets.

ELMSLEY: Hon. John Elmsley (1801–1863), son of Chief Justice John Elmsley. (*See* St. Alban, Surrey.)

EMILY: Emily, wife of D'Arcy Boulton, 1785–1846, whose residence, the Grange, is now part of the Art Gallery of Toronto. Emily Street is now Wyndham Street. (*See* Boulton.)

ERNEST: Ernest Albert MacDonald, Alderman for St. Matthew's Ward 1886–1887, 1889, 1890, 1896, and Mayor 1900.

ESPLANADE: after the road skirting the harbour front behind the stores on Front Street, first appearing in 1864.

ESTHER: Esther Borden Lippincott who became the wife of George Taylor Denison I. Esther Street is now Augusta Avenue. (*See* Denison.)

EUCLID: the Greek mathematician.

EVANS: George M. Evans, Alderman of St. Patrick's Ward, 1879–1883.

FARLEY: William Farley, Alderman of St. Andrew's Ward, 1874.

FARQUHAR: the family of that name who were contractors in the district.

FEE'S: probably Joseph Fee, groceryman and large property owner in the district.

FENNINGS: John Fennings Taylor (1817–1882), author, appointed chief clerk of the Legislative Assembly of Upper Canada in 1836. 1867, Senate of Canada. (*See* Rolyat.)

FERMANAGH: the birthplace in Ireland of Col. Walter O'Hara. (*See* O'Hara.)

FORT ROUILLÉ: the Dufferin St. Fort Rouillé, built 1750–1751.

FOSTER: Joseph Foster who owned property on Elizabeth Street, *circa* 1861.

FOXLEY: Foxley Grove, the home of Judge Samuel Bealey Harrison (1802–1867), and eminent legal authority. His gardens and orchards were the admiration of the community. (*See* Harrison.)

FRANKLAND: Henry Robert Frankland, butcher and cattle exporter, Alderman for Ward I, 1895, 1898–1899; later Collector of Inland Revenue for the Toronto Division; County Police Magistrate and Director of the Canadian National Exhibition.

FRANKISH: Charles Frankish, a property owner in the district.

FRANKLIN: probably Sir John Franklin, the Arctic explorer, 1786–1847.

FRASER: the Hon. C. F. Fraser, born 1839 in Brockville, member of the Ontario Cabinet, 1890. He was one of the originators of the Ontario Catholic League.

FREDERICK: Frederick, Duke of York, son of King George III. One of the streets laid out by Gov. Simcoe in 1793. (*See* Duke.)

FRIZZELL: Rev. William Frizzell, Minister of Queen Street East Presbyterian Church, who died in 1910.

FRONT: probably because it was the first and foremost street facing the lake, or "fronting" it when York was laid out in 1793 by Gov. Simcoe. It was thus the southern boundary. East of the market, Front Street was originally called Palace Street since it led to the Parliament Buildings and the reserve where the Governor's residence was to be erected.

FULLER: Valancy England Fuller, son of Thomas Brock Fuller (1810–1884), first Bishop of Niagara, who purchased four acres in the vicinity in 1878.

FUNSTON: J. J. Funston, a large property owner in the district.

GALLEY: Edward Galley, builder and Alderman for St. Thomas' Ward, 1885–1887.

GALT: John Galt (1779–1830), the Secretary of the Canada Company, *or* his son, Sir A. T. Galt (1817–1893), one of the Fathers of Confederation.

GARNET: Col. Garnet Joseph Wolseley (1833–1913), later Lord Wolseley, Assistant Quartermaster-General in Canada in 1861. In 1895 Commander in Chief of the British Army. (*See* Wolseley.)

GARRISON: after its proximity to the old army garrison where the troops of York were billeted. Garrison Street was changed to Mitchell Avenue, 1882–1883.

GEOFFREY: the son of Col. Walter O'Hara. (*See* O'Hara.)

GEORGE: George, Prince of Wales, son of George III. The boundaries of the town laid out by Gov. Simcoe in 1793 were George, Duke, Parliament and Front.

GERRARD: a friend of Captain John McGill, Receiver-General, 1813–1822.

GILEAD: probably biblical. "Is there no balm in Gilead? . . ." (Jeremiah 8:22).

GIVENS: James Givins (1759?–1846), who accompanied Governor Simcoe to Upper Canada, attained the rank of colonel and for many years was Superintendent of Indian Affairs. His log house, built about 1800, stood at the head of Givens Street until the 1890's. The original spelling was Givins. (*See* Cecil, Halton.)

GLADSTONE: the Prime Minister of Great Britain, the Hon. William Ewart Gladstone, 1809–1898.

GORDON: Charles George Gordon (Chinese Gordon) (1833–1885). Governor-General of the Soudan and hero of Khartoum, *or* the family name of the Marquesses of Huntly (*see* Huntley).

GORE VALE: from Duncan Cameron's house, built *circa* 1820, and named after Sir Francis Gore, Lieutenant-Governor of Upper Canada 1806–1817. Duncan Cameron was a member of the Executive Council of Upper Canada and warden of St. James', 1811–1812. A later owner of the property was E. O. Bickford. (*See* Beatrice, Grace.)

GOULD: Nathaniel Gould, a director of the British American Land Co. and a Montreal friend of Captain John McGill.

GOULDING: William Goulding, carpenter, who resided at No. 1 in 1890. Goulding Street was formerly Renforth Place.

GRACE: the daughter of E. O. Bickford of Gore Vale. (*See* Gore Vale.)

GRAHAM: Alderman Graham, St. Stephen's Ward 1887–1891; Ward 5, 1892, 1895, 1899; elected to Board of Control (by fellow-Aldermen) 1897.

GRAND OPERA HOUSE: the Opera House on the corner, which was built in 1874, burned 1879. This is a lane on the south side of Adelaide between Bay and Yonge.

GRANGE: "The Grange," residence of Mr. D'Arcy Boulton, son of Mr. Justice Boulton. (*See* Boulton.)

GREENWOOD: a gardener of that name in the district.

GRENVILLE: probably the English statesman, Richard Temple Grenville, first Duke of Buckingham, 1776–1839.

GROSVENOR: probably the English Whig, Robert Grosvenor, first Marquis of Westminster, who laid out Belgravia in London in 1826.

GROVE: Foxley Grove, the home of Hon. S. B. Harrison, of which it and Foxley Street were a part. (*See* Harrison.)

GUELPH: after the British Royal family.

GWYNNE: Doctor William Gwynne (1806–1875), who owned 200 acres west side of Dufferin Street, south of Queen. (*See* Huxley, Spencer, Springhurst, Tyndall.)

HAGERMAN: Christopher Alexander Hagerman (1792–1847), born in Adolphustown, Upper Canada, the son-in-law of Dr. James Macaulay. Attorney-General; Judge of the Court of Queen's Bench 1840. Regarded as one of the pillars of the Family Compact.

HALLAM: probably John Hallam (1833–1900) born in Chorley, Lancashire, who resided at Linden Villa, Isabella Street, and was Chairman of Parks and Gardens. He was Alderman for St. Lawrence Ward 1870–1872, 1876–1883, 1888–1891 and for Ward 2, 1892–1899. In 1882 Mr. Hallam secured the passage of the Public Library Act. (*See* Linden.)

HALTON: Halton, the fifth son of Col. Givins. The original name was Cecil Street after Col. Givins' daughter Cecilia. (*See* Givens.)

HAMILTON: probably William Hamilton, Jr., City Councilman, 1865 and Alderman 1870–1875.

HAMMERSMITH: the western metropolitan borough of London, near the birthplace of Joseph Williams, a farmer who named several streets in Toronto on land formerly owned by him. (*See* Kew.)

HANLAN'S: Edward Hanlan (1850–1908), champion sculler of Canada, United States and England, 1879.

HARBOUR: after its location near the harbour.

HARMAN: Samuel Bickerton Harman (1819–1892), City Treasurer 1874–1888; Assessment Commissioner 1874–1875; Mayor 1869–1870; Chairman, Board of Evaluators, 1873.

HARRISON: the Hon. Samuel Bealey Harrison (1802–1867), of Foxley Grove, Judge of County Court. (*See* Foxley, Grove.)

HARVARD: probably the university of that name.

HASTINGS: Thomas Hastings, Alderman 1883–1886.

HAVELOCK: General Sir Henry Havelock, 1795–1857.

HAYDEN: William Hayden, a carpenter of Yorkville on Yonge Street, south of Bloor, who bought 6 acres from Mrs. Mary Elmsley in 1829. He was the contractor for the Jail and Court House in 1824.

HAYTER: Elizabeth Hayter, wife of Dr. James Macaulay. (*See* Macaulay.)

HAZELTON: Joseph Hazelton, cab-driver of Yorkville, and later owner of an extensive livery business, *or* George Hazelton White, a landowner whose mother was a Miss Hazelton.

HECTOR: a christian name in the family of Frank Turner, C.E. (*See* Turner.)

HENRY: William Henry Boulton (1812–1874) of the Grange. From 1844 to 1853 he represented Toronto in the Legislative Assembly of Canada. (*See* Boulton.)

HEPBOURNE: Susan Maria Hepbourne, wife of Richard Lippincott Denison. (*See* Denison.)

HERRICK: Dr. George Herrick, born in Ireland in 1789 who emigrated to York in 1838, and opened an office at 42 Lot Street. He remained a bachelor and an eccentric all his life, but was well liked as a teacher and highly respected as a specialist in the diseases of women and children.

HEWITT: William Hewitt, hardware merchant, Adelaide and Yonge streets.

HEYDEN: Lawrence Heyden (1804–1868), a well-known Toronto barrister and a relative of the Baldwins. He was Clerk to the Court of Common Pleas and later Clerk in the High Court. (*See* Baldwin.) The later spelling was Hayden, and the street is now called Sussex Avenue.

HOGARTH: George Hogarth, who resided at No. 66 and owned considerable property in the vicinity.

HOMEWOOD: "The Homewood," residence of Benjamin Homer Dixon (b. 1819), Consul-General for the Netherlands. "The Homewood" stood in the centre of a beautiful wood, the present site of Wellesley Hospital.

HOSKIN: Dr. John Hoskin, 1836–1921, Chairman of the Board of Trustees of the University of Toronto 1904–1905, and in 1906 Chairman of Board of Governors. (*See* Dale; Devonshire.)

HOWARD: Allen Maclean Howard, clerk of the Division Court. Howard Street was originally East Street.

HOWARD PARK: John George Howard (1803–1890), architect, who donated High Park in the same district to the city of Toronto. (*See* Sunnyside.)

HOWLAND: Sir William Pierce Howland (1811–1907), Lt.-Gov. of Ontario, 1868–1873; in the plan of 1857, Howland Avenue is called Pierce Street, second name of Sir William. *Or*: W. H. Howland, Mayor of Toronto, 1886–1887; the Howland Syndicate owned the block Bloor to Dupont, and Howland to Bathurst.

HUNTER: Thomas Hunter, Alderman for St. John's Ward, 1884–1887, and one of the promoters of the Baseball Stadium south of Queen Street East, near Broadview Avenue.

HUNTLEY: the Moss Farm or Mossfield near Huntly in Aberdeenshire, Scotland, birthplace of Colonel William Allan, second postmaster and collector of customs in York. Colonel Allan was one of the signatories to the surrender of York to the Americans in April 1813. Formerly Bridge Street. (*See* Gordon, Moss Park.)

HUXLEY: Thomas Henry Huxley (1825–1895) English biologist. President of the Royal Society 1883–1885. So named by Dr. Wm. Gwynne. (*See* Gwynne.)

INDIAN: after the old Indian trail which ran close to the Humber River, and was laid out by J. G. Howard.

INGHAM: Joshua Ingham, Alderman 1887.

INKERMAN: the Crimean battle of 1854.

IRWIN: John Irwin, born in Ireland, 1824, emigrated to Toronto in 1850. He was proprietor of the General Wolfe Hotel at Church and King and an alderman for St. John's Ward. He was reputed to be the last man to hitch a horse to a steam fire-engine.

ISABELLA: Mrs. Isabella Roaf, daughter of Dr. James Richardson, or perhaps Isabella Charles, sister of James Charles.

JAMES: Dr. James Macaulay, Surgeon of the Queen's Rangers. (*See* Macaulay.)

JAMESON: Robert Sympson Jameson (d. 1854), Attorney-General 1833, Vice-Chancellor of Upper Canada, 1837–1854, who owned property there. He was the husband of Anna Brownell Jameson, noted woman of letters (*Winter Studies and Summer Rambles in Canada; Characteristics of Women*, etc.), who resided in York in 1836–1837. (*See* Maynard.)

JARVIS: Samuel Peters Jarvis (1792–1857), who opened up and named Jarvis Street from Queen to Bloor. His father, William Jarvis, was appointed Registrar of Upper Canada in 1792. The lower part of Jarvis Street was originally New Street (1797), and afterwards, Nelson Street. (*See* Edgar, Elm Ave., Meredith, Mutual, Nanton, Orde, Rosedale.)

JEFFERSON: probably Thomas Jefferson (1743–1826), third President of the United States, 1801–1809.

JOHN: Lt.-Col. John Graves Simcoe (1752–1806), first Lt.-Gov. of Upper Canada, 1791–1796. (*See* Simcoe.)

JOHNSON: a carter who owned a row of houses on the street.

JONES: John Jones, Alderman, 1884–1888.

JORDAN: Jordan Post, jeweller, who owned land between Yonge and Bay streets in 1802. (*See* Melinda.)

KEELE: William Keele, solicitor, who owned property in Toronto Junction.

KENILWORTH: the Scottish castle made famous by the novel of that name by Sir Walter Scott.

KENT: Edward Augustus, Duke of Kent (1767–1820), fourth son of George III, and father of Queen Victoria. Kent Street was formerly Surrey Street.

KETCHUM: Jesse Ketchum (1782–1867), an American philanthropist who came to Canada in 1799. He amassed a great fortune from leather, particularly through sales to the Canadian Government. His generosity extended to the various religious denominations in Toronto and to the gift of the land for the Jesse Ketchum School, Jesse Ketchum Park in Yorkville, and Knox Church which once occupied a site bounded by James, Yonge, Richmond and Queen. (*See* Rose, Temperance.)

KEW: Kew Gardens in England, the street being named by Joseph Williams who was born there, emigrated to Canada in 1853, and owned a large farm in the eastern section of Toronto which he sold later for building purposes. (*See* Hammersmith.)

KING: after the sovereign, George III; one of the streets laid out by Governor Simcoe in 1793. This King Street was changed to Palace as early as 1797. The present King Street was formerly Duke.

LAMBTON: John George Lambton, first Earl of Durham. (*See* Durham.)

LAMPORT: Henry Lamport whose parents came to Canada from France in 1800. Mr. Henry Lamport prospered as a merchant in Vittoria, Norfolk County, but moved to Toronto where he became the owner of considerable farm property in what is now Rosedale. His house was on Jarvis Street at the corner of Earl Street on the site of the present Highways Building of the provincial government. Mr. Lamport was the grandfather of former Mayor (now Controller) Allan Lamport.

LANGLEY: Henry Langley (b. 1836), architect.

LANSDOWNE: the Marquis of Lansdowne, Governor-General of Canada, 1883–1888.

LAURIER: Sir Wilfrid Laurier (1841–1919), Prime Minister of Canada, 1896–1911.

LEADER: *The Leader*, Tory paper from 1852 to 1878. Originally, Leader Lane ran from Colborne Street to King Street. The southern part of Leader Lane to Wellington Street was originally Berczy Street and later, on the completion of the Toronto Exchange in 1855, 'Change Alley.

LENNOX: Joseph Lennox, a property owner in the district.

LEOPOLD: Leopold of Saxe-Coburg who married Charlotte Augusta, only daughter of George IV, in 1816. (*See* Charlotte.)

LESLIE: the Leslie family of Leslieville, an eastern suburb of Toronto.

LEWIS: Catherine Lewis, wife of John Saulter, who owned a farm here (*see* Saulter), *or* after Lewis Bright, who settled in York in 1802 and whose descendants lived in the vicinity.

LINDEN: "Linden Villa," residence of John Hallam, Alderman and merchant of Toronto. (*See* Hallam.)

LINDSEY: Charles Lindsey, city registrar and son-in-law of William Lyon Mackenzie. He was editor of the *Leader* and purchaser of the Foxley Estate. (*See* Mackenzie.)

LIPPINCOTT: Esther Borden Lippincott, wife of George Taylor Denison and daughter of Captain Richard Lippincott. (*See* Denison.)

LISGAR: Sir John Young (1807–1876), Baron Lisgar, Governor-General of Canada, 1869–1872.

LITTLE ARTHUR: Prince Arthur, Duke of Connaught (1850–1942), seventh child of Queen Victoria. The name was changed to Hickson in 1890. (*See* Prince Arthur.)

LOBB: James Lobb, who was Alderman in 1880, 1881, 1884.

LOGAN: the Logan family, in the 1850's market gardeners in the district.

LOGIE: probably James Logie, born in Elgin, Scotland, 1863, who emigrated to Toronto in 1889. Mr. Logie was connected with the E. B. Eddy Company for 20 years.

LOMBARD: after the celebrated financial street in London. Lombard Street was originally March Street after the Earl of March, second title of the Duke of Richmond, and, later, Stanley Street, after George Stanley, 14th Earl of Derby, Colonial Minister, 1841–1845.

LORNE: the Marquis of Lorne, 1845–1914, afterwards 9th Duke of Argyll, Governor-General of Canada 1878–1883, who was received here on his first visit to Toronto in September, 1879. This was a short street between Bay and York, now the site of the Union Station. (*See* Argyle.)

LOUISA: probably a friend or member of the Macaulay family. Was formerly Macaulay Lane. (*See* Macaulay.)

LOVATT: Thomas Lovatt, a large property owner in the district now part of South Regent Park.

LUMLEY: M. Lumley, wholesale clothier, now Euclid Avenue.

LYND: Dr. Adam Lynd, a resident of the village of Parkdale and Mayor of Parkdale, 1887–1888.

LYTTON: Edward George, Baron Lytton (1803–1873). (*See* Bulwer.)

MACAULAY: Dr. James Macaulay (1759–1822), born in Scotland, an early medical practitioner and large landowner in York. He was also Surgeon with the Queen's Rangers under Lt.-Col. Simcoe until the regiment disbanded. The district between Queen and Yonge and Bay and College streets was known as "Macaulay Town" and the original residence Teraulay Cottage stood on the site of Holy Trinity Church. (*See* Agnes, Alice, Anne, Buchanan, Edward, Elizabeth, Hagerman, Hayter, James, Louisa, Teraulay, Vanauley.)

MACDONELL: Angus Macdonell (d. 1804), a lawyer, eldest son of Allan Macdonell who fought at Culloden in 1745 under Bonnie Prince Charlie. (*See* Collachie.)

MACKENZIE CRES.: William Lyon Mackenzie (1795–1861), Mayor 1834, named by his son-in-law, Charles Lindsey, who purchased the old Foxley property. (*See* Lindsey.)

MACPHERSON: Senator Sir David L. Macpherson (1818–1896) of Chestnut Park. In 1880 he was appointed Speaker of the Senate; associate in railway construction with Casimir Gzowski.

McCAUL: Dr. John McCaul (1807–1886), first president of the University of Toronto (1853–1880).

McFARREN'S: Andrew McFarren, grocer, wine, flour and feed merchant in the district in 1873.

McGEE: Thomas D'Arcy McGee (1825–1868), one of the Fathers of Confederation. McGee Street was formerly D'Arcy Street.

McGILL: Ann McGill, wife of Rev. Dr. John Strachan. (Not to be confused with McGill Square. The residence of Captain John McGill, Receiver-General 1813–1822, stood in McGill Square on a grant of land received in 1799, on the present site of the Metropolitan Church.) (*See* Ann, Gerrard, Gould, Mutual, Shuter, Strachan.)

McMASTER: Senator, the Hon. William J. McMaster (1811–1887) born at Rathnally, Ireland. Settled in York, Upper Canada, 1833. First President of the Bank of Commerce. The bulk of his estate went to McMaster University. (*See* Rathnally.)

McMURRICH: William B. McMurrich, Mayor of Toronto 1881–1882.

MADISON: James Madison (1751–1836), fourth President of the United States 1809–1817, the street being named by S. H. Janes, who laid out the district.

MAITLAND: Sir Peregrine Maitland (1777–1854), Lieutenant-Governor of Upper Canada 1818–1828. (*See* Richmond.)

MAJOR: Major Robert Brittain Denison (1821–1900). (*See* Denison.)

MANNING: Alexander Manning, Mayor of Toronto, 1873 and 1885.

MARIA: Maria Willcocks, who was left property here in 1822 by her cousin, Elizabeth Russell, stepsister of the Hon. Peter Russell. Maria Street is now Soho Street. (*See* Russell, Willcocks.)

MARK: Mark Defries, son of Richard Defries, gardener, Kingston Road.

MARKET: after the market to which it led. Market Street is now Wellington Street.

MARKHAM: probably a Captain Markham of the 32nd Regiment.

MARION: Probably the grandmother of John F. McCrae, Marion Munro, wife of David McCrae who in the 90's developed this district (*see* Marmaduke), *or* Marion, the wife of Col. Walter O'Hara who was a Captain in the 47th Regiment during the Peninsular War (*see* O'Hara).

MARLBOROUGH: the 7th Duke of Marlborough, John Winston Spencer Churchill (1822–1883), Lord-Lieutenant of Ireland 1876–1880.

MARMADUKE: Marmaduke McCrae, the street being named by his great-grandson John F. McCrae, real estate agent and owner of considerable property in the vicinity. (*See* Marion.)

MASSEY: Hart A. Massey (1823–1896), founder of the Massey Harris Company, philanthropist. (*See* Vincent.)

MATILDA: probably after a member of the Gooderham family. (*See* Dean.)

MAYNARD: Rev. George Maynard, a master of Upper Canada College 1836–1856 who received property in this vicinity under the will of Vice-Chancellor R. S. Jameson. (*See* Jameson.)

MELBOURNE: probably William Lamb, second Viscount Melbourne (1779–1848), and a favourite of Queen Victoria.

MELADY: P. Melady, dry goods merchant.

MELINDA: Melinda, the wife of Jordan Post (1767–1845), York's leading clock-maker and jeweller who owned property there. (*See* Jordan.)

MELITA: a christian name in the family of Frank Turner, C.E. (*See* Turner.)

MERCER: Andrew Mercer (1778–1871) who owned property in this street. He came to York, Upper Canada, in the year 1800 and amassed a great fortune. He died intestate, and out of the funds taken over by the Crown, the Mercer Reformatory was built. His house stood at Bay and Wellington.

MEREDITH: E. A. Meredith, LL.D. (1817–1898), Principal, McGill University 1846–1853, Under-Secretary of State for Canada 1878, and husband of Fanny Jarvis, daughter of Sheriff Jarvis. The street was named by the Jarvis family. (*See* Jarvis.)

METCALFE: probably Sir Charles, 1st Baron Metcalfe (1785–1846), Governor of Canada 1843–1845.

MILL: after the old Gooderham and Worts windmill which stood on the Bay shore just east of Parliament Street, and was for many years a famous landmark. (*See* Dean, Trinity.)

MILLICENT: the daughter of Elmes Henderson, who opened this street through property he owned there.

MINCING LANE: after the ancient street of that name in London, England.

MINTO: the Earl of Minto, Governor-General of Canada, 1898–1904.

MITCHELL: Alderman John E. Mitchell, 1880–1881, 1884–1885.

MONCK: Lord Monck (1819–1894), Governor-General of Canada 1861–1868.

MORRIS: James H. Morris, Alderman, St. Andrew's Ward, 1880.

MORRISON: Angus Morrison, Mayor of Toronto 1876–78.

MORSE: George D. Morse, a cattle dealer who drowned in the Don River.

MOSS PARK: Moss Park was the estate of William Allan and the Hon. G. W. Allan. It received its name from the birthplace of William Allan near Huntly in Aberdeenshire in Scotland. (*See* Huntley.)

MOUNTSTEPHEN: George Stephen (1829–1921), born in Banffshire, Scotland; later Baron Mount Stephen, financier. He was president of the C.P.R. from 1881 to 1891.

MOWAT: Hon. Oliver Mowat, Premier of Ontario, 1872–1896.

MULOCK: Sir William Mulock, K.C.M.G. (1844–1944), born at Bond Head, Chief Justice of Ontario, Chancellor of the University of Toronto 1924–1944.

MUNN: George Munn, a carter in the vicinity. Munn Lane was changed to Mincing Lane.

MUNRO: George Monro, Mayor of Toronto, 1841. Present spelling is Munro.

MURRAY: maiden name of Mrs. William Powell, wife of Hon. William Powell, Chief Justice of Upper Canada, 1815–1825. (See Powell.)

MUTER: Lt.-Col. Robert Muter of the Royal Canadian Regiment. Muter Street is now Palmerston Avenue.

MUTRAY: Col. Mutray (or Moutray), born in Ireland, who served with the 7th Regiment of Fusiliers on the Peninsula and who lived for some time on the street bearing his name.

MUTUAL: probably from the fact that it was once a "mutual" road surveyed between the park lots owned by the Jarvis and McGill families. (See Jarvis, McGill.)

NANTON: Augustus Nanton, barrister, admitted as a student to Osgoode Hall in 1846, called to the Bar in 1852, who married a daughter of Sheriff W. B. Jarvis. (See Jarvis.)

NAPIER: Sir Charles Napier (1782–1853), the hero of Sind, *or* after the three brothers known as "The Wellington Colonels" of which he was one.

NASSAU: one of the four districts of Upper Canada, 1788–1792. These districts were doubtless given German names with the intention of honouring the Royal family. They were as follows: (1) Luneburg—the former principality of Brunswick-Luneburg, part of the Kingdom of Hanover; (2) Mecklenburg—George III's Queen was Charlotte Sophie of Mecklenburg-Strelitz; (3) Nassau—the Countess of Nassau was an ancestress of George III; and (4) Hesse—the Duchess of Hesse was an ancestress of George III.

NELSON: Horatio, Viscount Nelson (1758–1805). Nelson Street is now that part of Jarvis Street south of Queen.

NEW FORT: after Stanley Barracks (1840). (See Stanley.)

NIAGARA: after the original path along the east bank of the old Garrison Creek made by the troops from old Fort York on their journey around the head of the Lake to Niagara.

NINA: the daughter of Col. Frederick Wells, wife of the Rev. Adam Uriah de Pencier, Bishop of New Westminster. (See Wells.)

NORTH: that part of Bay Street between St. Mary's and Bloor which ran north to what was then the northern city limits, Bloor Street.

NORTHCOTE: Sir Stafford Henry Northcote (1818–1887), British statesman.

NORTHERN: after its location, running north from the Northern Railroad.

NORTHUMBERLAND: probably the Dukes of Northumberland. (See Percy.)

O'HARA: Colonel Walter O'Hara (1784–1874), Captain 47th Regiment, Peninsular War, who came to Canada in 1831 and became Adjutant-General of forces in Upper Canada. In 1840, he purchased 420 acres. (See Constance, Fermanagh, Geoffrey, Marion, Roncesvalles, Ruth, Sorauren, West Lodge.)

O'KEEFE: Eugene O'Keefe (1827–1913), founder of O'Keefe Breweries. Came to Upper Canada from Bandon, County Cork, in 1832. In 1909 appointed Papal Chamberlain of the Roman Catholic Church.

OLIVE: Olive Grove, the home of William Campbell, the proprietor of the Ontario House, and later of J. S. Howard, Postmaster of York, Treasurer of the Counties of York and Peel. Now Balmoral Avenue at Yonge.

ONTARIO: "so called from the end of the old trail to the Carrying Place to Lake Ontario" (T. A. Reed). Ontario Street was the eastern limit of the town in 1797.

ORDE: Lewis Orde, a government official who in 1860 owned property on the street. He married Sarah, the daughter of W. B. Jarvis and Mary Powell. (See Jarvis, Powell.)

ORFORD: a family of that name, resident in the district.

OSBORNE: the Rev. A. Osborne, Rector of St. Saviour's Church, East Toronto, 1903–1909.

OSGOODE: the Hon. William Osgoode (1754–1824), first Chief Justice of Upper Canada, 1792–1794.

OSLER: after a member of the Osler family, probably E. B. Osler, who was M.P. for West Toronto in 1896.

OSSINGTON: Ossington House, near Newark in Nottinghamshire, England, was the family seat of the Denison family. (See Denison.)

OXFORD: after the English university. Next to it is Cambridge Street. Oxford Street was originally Augustus Street.

PALMERSTON: Lord Palmerston, Prime Minister of England, 1855–1858.

PAPE: after the family of Albert Pape or John Pape, market gardeners for three generations in that vicinity.

PARDEE: Hon. T. B. Pardee, Minister of Crown Lands, Province of Ontario, 1873–1888.

PARK: after the area which was originally the Government Park or Reserve for public buildings.

PARLIAMENT: after the first Parliament buildings on Front Street between Berkeley and Parliament streets.

PATERSON: George Paterson, a cab-driver of the district known as Cabbagetown.

PEARS: Leonard Pears, brick-maker of Yorkville.

PEARSON: Pearson Brothers, real estate brokers, who opened up this district.

PEEL: Sir Robert Peel, the English statesman (1788–1850), Under-Secretary for the Colonies under Lord Liverpool

1810–1812, and Prime Minister 1841–1845.

PELHAM: Probably George Pelham (1766–1827) bishop successively of Bristol, Exeter and Lincoln, *or* John Thomas Pelham (1811–1894) bishop of Norwich.

PERCY: probably after the Dukes of Northumberland whose family name is Percy. (*See* Northumberland.)

PETER: the Hon. Peter Russell, President and Administrator of the Province 1796–1799 and owner of the farm, Petersfield, to which the road led. (*See* Russell.)

PHIPPS: a broker of that name.

PHOEBE: Phoebe Willcocks, cousin of Hon. Peter Russell, who became the wife of Dr. William Warren Baldwin in 1803. (*See* Baldwin, Willcocks.)

PIPER: Noah Piper, a hardware merchant, and Harry Piper, Alderman and zoo proprietor. Originally Murray Street.

POPLAR PLAINS: from the fact that the table land above the present winding street was formerly called Poplar Plains.

PORTLAND: the 3rd Duke of Portland (1738–1809), Prime Minister of England 1807.

POUCHER: John Poucher, builder and landowner in the district and valuator for the City of Toronto.

POULETT: Charles Poulett Thomson, 1st Baron Sydenham of Kent and Toronto. Governor-General of Canada 1839–1841, and a one-time resident of Toronto. (*See* Sydenham.)

POWELL: after the Powell family (originally Ap Howell), connected with the Jarvis family who laid out Rosedale. Mary Powell, granddaughter of Chief Justice William Dummer Powell, married Sheriff William B. Jarvis and lived in Rosedale. (*See* Caer Howell, Jarvis, Murray, Rosedale, St. Patrick, William.)

POWER: Bishop Michael Power, first Roman Catholic Bishop of Toronto 1842–1847.

PRICE: after the property of Miss Sarah Price of Thornwood (near the corner of Price and Yonge), so called because her father, Joseph Price, an official of the Dominion Bank from Thornwood in Essex, willed 10 acres to his daughter in 1846. (*See* Thornwood.)

PRINCESS: originally Princes, after the various princes who were members of George III's family. Princes Street was the second most easterly of the streets running north and south as laid out by Governor Simcoe in 1793.

PRINCE ARTHUR: Arthur, Duke of Connaught (1850–1942), who first visited Canada in 1870 and became Governor-General of Canada 1911–1916. (*See* Little Arthur.)

QUEEN: Queen Victoria (1819–1901). So named about 1843. Queen Street was formerly Lot Street because of the "park lots" abutting it and extending north to Bloor Street. Lot became the northern limit of the town in 1797 as it grew beyond the original boundary of Duke.

QUEEN'S PARK: after Queen Victoria and dedicated by Albert Edward, Prince of Wales (later Edward VII) in 1860, during his visit to Toronto in the name of his mother, "for the recreation of the citizens." Formerly University Park.

RADENHURST: John Radenhurst (1795–1853) who for many years was Chief Clerk in the Surveyor-General's office.

RAINS: Rains was a christian name in the family of Frank Turner, C.E. (*See* Turner.)

RATHNALLY: from the estate of W. J. McMaster whose birthplace was Rathnally in Ireland. (*See* McMaster.)

REBECCA: after the Rebeccaites, of South Wales, who, in 1843, destroyed the toll-gates and bars. Rebecca was so called because it was originally a lane to avoid the toll-gate at Ossington and Queen streets. "Rebecca . . . let thy seed possess the gate" (Gen. 24:60).

REGENT: the street of that name in London, England, *or* the Prince Regent who became George IV.

REID: John Reid, a painter and councilman.

REYNOLDS: William Reynolds, born 1818, who was a baker in the vicinity of Yonge and Bloor streets, *circa* 1843, and a member of a well-known Yorkville family.

RICHMOND: the Duke of Richmond, Governor-General of Canada 1818–1819, and father-in-law of Sir Peregrine Maitland, Lt.-Gov. of Upper Canada 1818–1828. Richmond Street was formerly (until about 1840) Hospital Street because of a site for a hospital on the street. (*See* Maitland.)

RITCHIE: John Ritchie, Ritchey or Richey, the builder in 1829 of the east (first) wing of Osgoode Hall.

RIVER: after the Don River which it parallels.

RIVERDALE: after the Don River which flows through it.

ROBERT: Hon. Robert Baldwin (*see* Baldwin), *or* Col. Robert Denison (*see* Denison).

ROBINSON: Sir John Beverley Robinson (1791–1863), first Chancellor of Trinity College 1853, near which the street was situated. (*See* Beverley, Christopher, Sayre.)

RODEN: Ephraim P. Roden, Public School Trustee 1874–1897, and employee of the City Engineer's Department 1883.

ROLYAT: from John Fennings Taylor the elder (1801–1876), son-in-law of John Denison. Rolyat is Taylor reversed. Appointed Assistant Clerk of the Legislative Council by Gov. Sydenham 1841; Master of Chancery 1843; Clerk, by Lord Elgin, 1850; and Lt.-Col., by Lord Elgin, 1853. (*See* Fennings.)

RONCESVALLES: after the battle in Spain in 1813, the street so named by Col. Walter O'Hara who fought there. (*See* O'Hara.)

ROSE: Sir John Rose (1820–1888), Minister of Finance in the first Dominion Cabinet 1867, *or* Anna, daughter of Jesse Ketchum (1782–1867), who married Walter Rose, a private banker (*see* Ketchum).

ROSEBERRY: the Marquis of Rosebery, Prime Minister of Great Britain 1894–1896; British Foreign Secretary 1886 and 1892–1894.

ROSEDALE: the residence of William Botsford Jarvis, Sheriff from 1827 to 1856, who purchased this land in 1824 from J. E. Small, builder of the original house there in 1821.

Reputedly received its name in 1827 from Mary Powell when she came as the bride of Sheriff Jarvis to discover the hillsides covered with wild roses. (*See* Jarvis, Powell.)

ROSS: Hon. John Ross, Q.C. (1818-1871), born in county Antrim, Ireland, educated in the district school Brockville. He was a member of the Legislative Council of Canada 1852-1862, a Senator, and in 1869 Speaker of the Senate. Married Augusta, daughter of the Hon. Robert Baldwin. (*See* Baldwin.)

ROWANWOOD: the residence of James Grant Macdonald, situated north of Sir David Macpherson's Chestnut Park.

ROYCE: the Royce family whose farm adjoined Davenport. William Campbell, who purchased large sections of land in the district, married a Royce. (*See* Campbell.)

RUNNYMEDE: the name given by John Scarlett to his house on Dundas Street in 1838.

RUSH: the town on the Irish Sea, fifteen miles from Dublin, *or* Frank Rush, a grocer on Queen Street.

RUSHOLME: the estate "Rusholme," owned by Col. George Taylor Denison II (1816-1873), adjoined the "Dovercourt" estate of his brother Richard Lippincott Denison. (*See* Denison.)

RUSKIN: John Ruskin (1819-1900), art critic and writer.

RUSSELL: probably Hon. Peter Russell (1733-1808), President and Administrator of the Province 1796-1799. (*See* Abbey Lane, Bedford, Maria, Peter, Russell Hill.)

RUSSELL HILL: the Hon. Peter Russell. (*See* Russell.)

RUTH: probably after a member of the O'Hara family. Ruth Street is now Fern. (*See* O'Hara.)

ST. ALBAN: an expression of the religious zeal of the Hon. John Elmsley who, in the 1830's, became a convert to the Roman Catholic Church. (*See* St. Joseph, St. Mary, St. Thomas, St. Nicholas and St. Charles'.) St. Alban Street is now Wellesley Street West. (*See* Elmsley.)

ST. ANDREW'S: after the patron saint of Scotland.

ST. ANNE'S: from its proximity to St. Anne's Anglican Church.

ST. CHARLES': (*See* St. Alban.)

ST. DAVID: after its location in old St. David's Ward.

ST. GEORGE: after Laurent Quetton St. George (1771-1821), an early trader at York and Niagara, and a partner of John Spread Baldwin, brother of Dr. William Warren Baldwin. (*See* Baldwin.)

ST. JOSEPH: after the convent of the Sisters of St. Joseph on the Elmsley estate. (*See* St. Alban.)

ST. LAWRENCE: after its location in old St. Lawrence Ward.

ST. MARY'S: (*See* St. Alban.)

ST. NICHOLAS: (*See* St. Alban.)

ST. PATRICK: after the ward of the same name. St. Patrick Street was formerly William Street and, before that, Dummer Street, both after Hon. William Dummer Powell, Chief Justice of Upper Canada 1815-1825. (*See* Powell.)

ST. PATRICK MARKET: after its location in St. Patrick's Ward.

ST. THOMAS: (*See* St. Alban.)

SACKVILLE: the street of that name in Dublin, Ireland. Sackville Street was formerly Pine Street.

SALEM: Salem, Massachusetts.

SALISBURY: the Marquis of Salisbury, Prime Minister of Great Britain, 1885, 1886-1892.

SARAH: Sarah Ellerbeck Playter, wife of John Playter (b. 1774). The land around this street was part of the original grant in 1793 to the Playter family. It is now Cambridge, north of Danforth. Playter Blvd. and Playter Cres. are nearby.

SAULTER: John Saulter, farmer on east bank of the Don River. (*See* Lewis.)

SAURIN: James Saurin McMurray (1840-1895), barrister and Alderman; secretary to the Hon. George Brown at a conference in Washington, D.C., in 1872. At the time of his death he was Vice-Consul to Norway and Sweden. His father was Archdeacon McMurray (1810-1894). Now Afton Ave.

SAYRE: the maiden name of Mrs. Christopher Robinson, mother of Chief Justice Sir John Beverley Robinson who laid out and named the street, now Chestnut Street. (*See* Robinson.)

SCADDING: John Scadding (1754-1824), who came to Canada with Gov. Simcoe in 1793 and returned to England with him. In 1818, he emigrated with his family and settled on his grant of 200 acres on the east bank of the Don River. The street is now the southern end of Broadview Ave. (*See* Amelia.)

SCARTH: after the family of William Bain Scarth, born 1837 in Scotland, Manager of the Scottish Ontario and Manitoba Land Company which developed an extensive tract in this vicinity. (*See* Binscarth.)

SCOLLARD: Maurice Scollard of the Bank of Upper Canada, whose name appears in the Directory of 1833-1834.

SCOTT: Chief Justice Thomas Scott, Chief Justice of Upper Canada 1804-1824, through whose estate the street extended.

SEATON: Lord Seaton, who, as Sir John Colborne, was Lt.-Gov. of Upper Canada 1828-1836, and the founder of Upper Canada College. (*See* Colborne.)

SELBY: Prideaux Selby, Receiver-General of Upper Canada from 1808 until his death in 1813.

SEVERN: John Severn, who built a brewery in Yorkville in 1835 and operated it until his death in 1888.

SHAFTESBURY: the 7th earl of Shaftesbury (1801-1885).

SHANLY: Walter Shanly, General Manager of Grand Trunk Railroad, *or* Francis Shanly, architect and City Engineer, 1875-1880. Both were sons of James Shanly who came to Canada in 1836. Shanly was formerly Durham Street.

SHAW: Major-General Aeneas Shaw (d. 1815), an officer of the Queen's Rangers under Simcoe during the Revolutionary War. His log cabin, called Oakhill after the ancestral home in Scotland, was built in 1793. It was succeeded by a larger house in 1797 which stood for over eighty years northwest of old Trinity College.

SHEPPARD: Harvey Sheppard's iron work establishment where he made axes and adzes.

SHERBOURNE: Sherbourne House, residence of Thomas Gibbs Ridout (1792–1861), cashier of the Bank of Upper Canada 1822–1861, and half brother of Samuel Ridout, Sheriff of the Home District 1815–1817. The Ridouts' home in England was at Sherborne, Dorsetshire. Sherbourne Street was formerly Caroline Street after the Princess of Wales, daughter-in-law of George III, and was also long known as Allan's Lane. (*See* Bleecker, Dorset.)

SHUTER: John Shuter, a director of the British American Land Co. and a Montreal friend of Captain John McGill, Receiver-General in 1813–1822. There is a Shuter St. in Montreal, transferred to the City of Montreal by the estate of his son Joseph in 1873, forty years after the naming of the Toronto Street. (*See* McGill.)

SIMCOE: John Graves Simcoe (1752–1806), first Lt.-Gov. of Upper Canada 1791–1796. Simcoe Street was formerly, until 1842–1843, called Graves Street. The original Simcoe Street, named in 1837, is now Richmond Street west of Spadina. (*See* John.)

SMITH: probably a John Smith who had property there, *c.*1884.

SOHO: the district in London.

SORAUREN: after the battle in Spain in 1815, the street so called by Col. Walter O'Hara who fought at the battle. (*See* O'Hara.)

SPADINA: "Spadina," the country home of Dr. William Warren Baldwin, to which it was the approach. The name is derived from Espadinong, an Indian word meaning a little hill. (*See* Baldwin.)

SPARKHALL: Cubett Sparkhall, born in Norfolk, England, in 1821, who emigrated to Canada in 1832 with his mother. In 1839 he opened a butcher shop.

SPENCER: Herbert Spencer (1820–1903), the English philosopher. So named by Dr. William Gwynne. (*See* Gwynne.)

SPRINGHURST: after the numerous springs in the vicinity. So named by Dr. William Gwynne. (*See* Gwynne.)

SPROAT: Charles Sproat, City Engineer 1883–1890.

STANLEY: Lord Stanley of Preston, Governor-General of Canada 1888–1893. (Also Stanley Barracks, built 1840, first called New Fort, renamed 1893.) (*See* New Fort.)

STEINER: N. L. Steiner, Alderman 1880, 1881, 1883–1886 and 1899. (*See* Bismarck.)

STEWART: Charles James Stewart (1826–1837), Anglican Bishop of Quebec. When the street was named in 1837, Toronto was in the Diocese of Quebec.

STRACHAN: the Hon. and Rt. Rev. Dr. John Strachan (1778–1867), Bishop of Toronto 1839–1867, founder of Trinity College in 1851. (*See* Ann, Bishop.)

STRANGE: Maxwell Strange, an auctioneer, who first appears in the directory of 1837.

SULLIVAN: Hon. Robert Baldwin Sullivan (1802–1853), Justice of the Queen's Bench in 1848, nephew of Dr. William Warren Baldwin, and Mayor of Toronto 1835. (*See* Baldwin.)

SULTAN: probably after the Sultan of Turkey, named at a time when that country was much in the public eye. (*See* Czar.)

SUMMERHILL: after the estate of Charles Thompson, who bought the stage service in 1840 from William Weller, and later of Dr. Larratt William Smith, Q.C. (1820–1905), Vice-Chancellor of the University of Toronto 1873.

SUNNYSIDE: from "my new villa, Sunnyside, on the Lake Shore Road." Sold by Mr. John G. Howard to Mr. George H. Cheney, merchant, for £1200 in 1853. This would appear to be a summer cottage or a speculation because Colborne Lodge (1836) continued to be the Howard home. (*See* Howard Park.)

SURREY: probably "Surrey Park," the home in England of Captain Benjamin Hallowell, R.N., father of Mary, wife of Chief Justice Elmsley who owned property here. (*See* Elmsley.)

SWORD: in 1856, Mr. P. Sword was proprietor of Sword's Hotel, later the Queen's, which stood on that site until Sept. 11, 1927, when it was replaced by the present Royal York Hotel which opened two years later.

SYDENHAM: Charles Poulett Thomson, first Baron Sydenham of Kent and Toronto (1799–1841), Governor-General of Canada 1839–1941. (*See* Poulett.)

SYMES PLACE: a Mr. A. Symes built houses in the area.

TATE: a Mr. Tate, contractor for the Grand Trunk Railroad.

TAYLOR: the Taylor family, who owned the Taylor Paper Mills in the Don Valley.

TECUMSETH: sometimes spelled Tecumseh; he was a famous Indian chief.

TEMPERANCE: named by Jesse Ketchum who built a Temperance Hall there. He was a leading temperance advocate. (*See* Ketchum.)

TERAULAY: a combination of the names of Elizabeth Hayter, and her husband Dr. James Macaulay, or solely from the Macaulay property, Ter Auly, land of Aulay. Dr. Macaulay's house on the site of the Church of the Holy Trinity was called Teraulay Cottage. (*See* Macaulay.)

THEATRE LANE: from the fact that it once led to the Royal Lyceum Theatre.

THORNWOOD: birthplace in Essex, England, of Jos. Price who owned from Yonge Street east to the Don and south from the C.P.R. tracks to Rowanwood. (*See* Price.)

TINNING: Richard Tinning owned a saw-mill and built houses on this street around 1852.

TORONTO: from an Indian word which some claim to mean "the meeting place of the waters." Correct or not, no more poetic derivation has been suggested.

TRAFALGAR: the naval battle of 1805.

TRINITY: after Trinity Church, the first city parish cut off from the original parish of York (St. James) in 1843. The church was built in the same year on King Street East at Trinity (near Parliament). Trinity Street was formerly Windmill Street because it led to the "Windmill" of Worts and Gooderham. (*See* Mill.)

TURNER: Frank Turner, C.E., who subdivided Bracondale, the home of his father Robert J. Turner, a solicitor from Yarmouth, England. Turner Avenue was originally West Street, and it is now Whittaker. (*See* Bracondale, Melita, Rains, Yarmouth.)

TYNDALL: John Tyndall, the natural philosopher (1820–1893). So named by Dr. William Gwynne. (*See* Gwynne.)

UNIVERSITY: originally (1829) College Avenue, it was laid out as a private tree-lined street from Queen Street to the future King's College (1843). In 1888 it was leased by the University of Toronto as a public street. (*See* College.)

VANAULEY: probably a combination of the names Vankoughnet and Macaulay. (*See* Macaulay, Vankoughnet.)

VAN HORNE: Sir William Cornelius Van Horne, born in Illinois in 1843, who became president of the Canadian Pacific Railroad. He refused a knighthood in 1891 and 1892, and finally accepted in 1895.

VANKOUGHNET: Philip Vankoughnet, Q.C. (1823–1869), Minister of Agriculture 1856, Chancellor of Upper Canada 1862–1867, and Chancellor of Ontario 1867–1869. (*See* Vanauley.)

VERMONT: for the first state received into the American Union after the adoption of the Federal Constitution.

VERRAL: George Verral, Alderman 1884–1891, 1892–1893.

VICTORIA: Queen Victoria; formerly known as Upper George Street. (*See* George.)

VINCENT: Anna Vincent Massey, wife of Chester D. Massey and mother of the Rt. Hon. Vincent Massey, C.H. (*See* Massey.)

VINE: after its location through an old vineyard.

VIRGIN: named after a Mr. Virgin by his close friend, Mr. Joseph Coatsworth. (*See* Coatsworth.)

WALKER: the family of Walter Walker, a carriage-maker and old resident who owned property here fronting on Yonge Street (1888).

WALMER: Walmer, in England, was the birthplace of James McQueen Baldwin who was born there in 1860; the street was named by his father Robert Baldwin. (*See* Baldwin.)

WALTON: Matthew Walton, in 1827, bought six acres here and laid it out in town lots. In 1834 he was appointed Chamberlain of the City, but held office only a few weeks.

WARDELL: O. Wardell, an auctioneer.

WATERLOO: the battle of 1815.

WAVERLEY: probably after Sir Walter Scott's novel.

WELLESLEY: the Duke of Wellington, formerly Arthur, Lord Wellesley. Was first Frank Street (after Castle Frank); then Charles Street after Charles Scadding, son of John Scadding, who bought the 200 acres of Castle Frank pro-

perty; then and finally, Wellesley. (*See* Wellington.)

WELLINGTON: the Duke of Wellington. Formerly called Market Street because it gave a direct approach to the market from the west in 1837. (*See* Douro, Wellesley.)

WELLS: Col. the Hon. J. Wells of Davenport who came here in 1821. (*See* Dartnell, Davenport, Dupont, Nina.)

WEST LODGE: "West Lodge" was the residence of Colonel Walter O'Hara. (*See* O'Hara.)

WEST MARKET: after its location bordering the west side of St. Lawrence Market.

WHITE'S PLACE: George White, tassel-maker, of 57 Sherbourne Street in the same district.

WHITESIDE: Thomas R. Whiteside, appointed collector of taxes in 1886. *Circa* 1897–1899 the system of appointing multiple tax collectors, one for each ward, was consolidated by the appointment of one tax collector with assistants.

WHITNEY: Sir James Pliny Whitney (1843–1914), D.C.L., LL.D., K.C.M.G., born at Williamsburg, Upper Canada, educated at Cornwall Grammar School, Prime Minister of Ontario, 1905–1908.

WICKSON: John Wickson, a butcher of Yorkville. Wickson Avenue is now called Alcorn Avenue.

WIDMER: Dr. Christopher Widmer (1780–1858), who was one of the first qualified medical practitioners in York. He was a member of the Upper Canada Medical Board from its inception in 1819 until his death, and its chairman from 1853. He was also one of the founders of the York General Hospital (*circa* 1818), a member of the faculty of King's College in 1842, and of the Legislative Council of Upper Canada in 1849.

WILLCOCKS: Col. William Willcocks (1736–1853), Judge of the Home District 1802, in whose name a large piece of property here was patented in 1798. His daugher Phoebe married Dr. William Warren Baldwin. (*See* Baldwin, Maria, Phoebe.)

WILKINS: Thomas Wilkins, a large property owner, founder of Wilkins Smallware, and builder of many houses in the vicinity of the Church of the Holy Trinity.

WILLIAM: Hon. William Dummer Powell (1755–1834), Chief Justice of Upper Canada, 1815–1825. (*See* Powell.)

WILMOT: Samuel Wilmot, Deputy-Surveyor in 1811.

WILSON: Sir Adam Wilson, K.C. (1814–1891). In 1859, he was the first popularly elected Mayor of Toronto and became Chief Justice of the Court of Queen's Bench in Ontario 1884–1887. He was knighted in 1887.

WILTON: after Sarah Lambert who married the Hon. George Crookshank, originally from Wilton, Conn. (*See* Crookshank.) Wilton Street was later called Crocker Avenue after James Crocker, Alderman for St. Stephen's Ward, 1875–1889. (*See* Crocker.)

WITHROW: John J. Withrow, of Withrow and Hillock, lumber dealers. Mr. Withrow was Alderman 1873–1878, a founder of the C.N.E. and its president 1879–1900.

WOLSELEY: Col. Garnet Joseph Wolseley (1833–1913), later

Lord Wolseley, who came to Canada in 1861 as Assistant Quartermaster-General. In 1870 he commanded the force sent west to the Red River to quell the Riel insurrection. Wolseley Street was formerly Monck Street. (*See* Garnet.)

WOOD: Alexander Wood in 1826 purchased from Mrs. Mary Elmsley 25 acres lying north of Carlton Street. (*See* Alexander.)

WOODBINE: name of the residence of Joseph Duggan, proprietor of Woodbine Park Hotel and, subsequently, the grounds of the Race Course.

WOODGREEN: WoodGreen Methodist Church founded in 1875. It was given the combined name in honour of Rev. Dr. Enoch Wood, President of the Toronto Annual Conference, and Rev. Anson Green, who conducted the opening services.

WOODLAWN: an estate of that name was owned by Mr. Justice Joseph Curran Morrison (1816–1885). Born in Ireland, came to Canada 1832; educated at Upper Canada College.

WORTS: James Worts of Gooderham and Worts. (*See* Gooderham.)

WYATT: Charles Burton Wyatt, third son of James Wyatt (1748–1813), architect. In 1904 he was appointed Surveyor-General of Upper Canada. He moved to York after a runaway marriage which alienated his father. He returned to England in 1807 after a "series of collisions" with Lt.-Gov. Francis Gore (1806–1817).

YARMOUTH: after Yarmouth, England, by Robert Turner (his birthplace), a large property owner in the Davenport Road district who emigrated to Canada about 1840. (*See* Turner.)

YONGE: named by Gov. Simcoe after Sir George Yonge, M.P. for Honiton, England, and Secretary of State for War, 1782–1794. One of the first streets laid out by Gov. Simcoe, it extended in 1794 from York at Bloor Street to Lake Simcoe.

YORK: probably because it presented a convenient way of entering the town of York from the northwest, Yonge Street then being in a deplorable condition.

YORKVILLE: after the Village of Yorkville, which extended from Sherbourne Street to a point opposite old McMaster University; and from Bloor Street north to approximately the former C.P.R. tracks. Yorkville was annexed in 1883.

Bibliography

I. Collections of Papers, Photographs and Drawings

METROPOLITAN TORONTO CENTRAL LIBRARY,
BALDWIN ROOM

Robert Baldwin Papers
W. W. Baldwin Papers
Copy-book of deeds . . . for the cession of lands in Upper Canada
John Elmsley Letter Book
J. G. Howard Collection of Architects' Drawings
Henry Langley Collection of Architects' Drawings
T. A. Reed Collection
J. Ross Robertson Collection
Peter Russell Papers
D. W. Smith Papers
Strachan Papers

ONTARIO DEPARTMENT OF PUBLIC RECORDS AND ARCHIVES
(P.A.O.)
Baldwin Papers

MCGILL UNIVERSITY, REDPATH LIBRARY
Collection of H. Notman Photographs

II. 18th and 19th Century Newspapers and Magazines

British Colonist
Canadian Architect and Builder
Canadian Correspondent
Canadian Freeman
Canadian Illustrated News
Canadian Review
Christian Guardian
Colonial Advocate
Courier of Upper Canada
Dominion Illustrated
Globe
Illustrated London News (London, England)
Leader
Loyalist
Mail and Empire
Observer
Patriot and Farmers' Monitor
Star
Telegram
United Empire Loyalist
Upper Canada Almanack
Upper Canada Gazette (or *American Oracle*)
York Gazette

III. Books and Articles

Publications of a general nature, such as biographical collections, encyclopedias, atlases, etc. (unless containing substantial text), are not listed. Publishers are not designated for any works previous to 1940.

ADAM, G. MERCER, *Toronto, Old and New* (Toronto, 1891).

ARMSTRONG, C. H. A., *The Honourable Society of Osgoode Hall,* with an essay on "The History and Architecture of the Fabric," by E. R. Arthur (Toronto: Clarke, Irwin, 1952).

ARMSTRONG, F. H., "The First Great Fire of Toronto, 1849," *Ontario History,* vol. 53, 1961, pp. 201-221.

"The Rebuilding of Toronto after the Great Fire of 1849," *Ontario History,* vol. 53, 1961, pp. 233-249.

BETHUNE, A. N., *Memoir of the Right Reverend John Strachan, First Bishop of Toronto* (Toronto, 1870)

BISSELL, CLAUDE T. (editor), *University College, a Portrait, 1853-1953* (University of Toronto Press, 1953).

BLAND, JOHN, "Osgoode Hall," *R.A.I.C. Journal,* July, 1959.

BONNYCASTLE, SIR RICHARD H., *The Canadas in 1841* (London, 1841-42).
Canada and the Canadians in 1846 (London, 1846).

BOUCHETTE, JOSEPH, *The British Dominions in North America* (London, 1832).

BRIDLE, AUGUSTUS, *The Story of the Club* (Toronto, 1945).

BULL, WILLIAM PERKINS, *Spadunk; or, From Paganism to Davenport United* (Toronto, 1935).

CARD, RAYMOND, *The Ontario Association of Architects, 1890-1915* (University of Toronto Press, 1950).

CARRE, W. H. & CO., *Art Work on Toronto* (Toronto, 1898)

City of Toronto Illustrated (Toronto, September, 1888).

CLARKE, C. K., *A History of the Toronto General Hospital* (Toronto, 1913).

COLGATE, WILLIAM, *Canadian Art* (Toronto: Ryerson Press, 1943).

COLLARD, EDGAR A., *Canadian Yesterdays* (Toronto: Longmans Green, 1955).

COLVIN, H. M., *A Biographical Dictionary of English Architects, 1660-1840* (John Murray, 1954)

Commemorative Biographical Record of the County of York, Ontario (Toronto, 1907)

CRUIKSHANK, E. A. (editor), *The Correspondence of the Honourable Peter Russell,* 3 vols. (Toronto, 1932-36).
The Correspondence of Lieut. Governor John Graves Simcoe, 5 vols. (Toronto, 1923-31).

CURRY, S. G., "Architecture: Looking Back," *Construction,* June, 1929.

DICKENS, CHARLES, *American Notes and Pictures from Italy* (London, 1842).

DUFFERIN AND AVA, Marchioness of, *My Canadian Journal* (London, 1891).

FIDLER, ISAAC, *Observations on the Professions, Literature, Manners and Emigration in the United States and Canada* (London, 1833).

FIRTH, EDITH G. (editor), *The Town of York, 1793-1815* (University of Toronto Press, 1962).

GALT, JOHN, *Autobiography* (London, 1833).

GOWANS, ALAN, *Looking at Architecture in Canada* (Toronto: Oxford University Press, 1958).

GRANT, G. M. (editor), *Picturesque Canada*, 2 vols. (Toronto, 1882)

GUILLET, E. C., *Early Life in Upper Canada* (Ontario Publishing Co., 1933; University of Toronto Press, 1963).
Toronto: From Trading Post to Great City (Ontario Publishing Co., 1934).
Pioneer Inns and Taverns, 4 vols. (published by the Author, 1954–58).

HAMILTON, JAMES CLELAND, *Osgoode Hall: Reminiscences of the Bench and Bar* (Toronto, 1904).

HERIOT, GEORGE, *Travels through the Canadas* (London, 1807).

Historical Atlas of the County of York (Toronto, 1878).

History of Toronto and County of York, Ontario, 2 vols. (Toronto, 1885).

HITCHCOCK, H. R., *Early Victorian Architecture in Britain*, 2 vols. (Yale University Press, 1954).

HOPKINS, J. CASTELL, *Toronto, an Historical Sketch* (Toronto, 1893).

HOWARD, JOHN G., *Incidents in the Life of J. G. Howard, Esq. of Colborne Lodge, High Park* (Toronto, 1885).

HUBBARD, R. H., "Canadian Gothic," *Architectural Review*, August, 1954.

HUMPHRIES, CHARLES W., "The Capture of York," *Ontario History*, vol. 51, 1959, pp. 1–21.

Illustrated Toronto: The Queen City of Canada (Toronto, 1890).

JAMESON, ANNA, *Winter Studies and Summer Rambles in Canada* (London, 1838).

LANGTON, JOHN, *Early Days in Upper Canada: Letters of John Langton*, edited by W. A. Langton (Toronto, 1926).

LIZARS, K. M., *The Valley of the Humber* (Toronto, 1913).

MACDONALD, EDITH, *Golden Jubilee, 1869–1919: The Fiftieth Anniversary of the T. Eaton Co.* (Toronto, 1919).

MACMURCHY, ANGUS and T. A. REED, *Our Royal Town of York* (Toronto, 1929).

MACTAVISH, NEWTON, *The Fine Arts in Canada* (Toronto, 1925).

MCEVOY, H., *The Province of Ontario: Gazeteer and Directory* (Toronto, 1869).

MASTERS, D. C., *The Rise of Toronto, 1850–90* (University of Toronto Press, 1947).

MEREDITH, A. G., *Mary's Rosedale and Gossip of Little York* (Toronto, 1928).

MIDDLETON, JESSE EDGAR, *The Municipality of Toronto: A History*, 3 vols. (Toronto, 1923).
Toronto's Hundred Years (Toronto, 1934).

MULVANY, C. PELHAM, *Toronto, Past and Present* (Toronto, 1884).

PEARSON, W. H., *Recollections and Records of Toronto of Old* (Toronto, 1914).

Picturesque Toronto (Toronto, 1885).

REED, T. A., "The Historic Value of Street Names," *Ontario Historical Society, Papers and Records*, 1929.
A History of the University of Trinity College, 1852–1952 (University of Toronto Press, 1952).
"The Story of Toronto, 1871–1958," *Ontario Historical Society, Papers and Records*, 1934.
"Records of Toronto," *Toronto Historical Society, Papers*, 1934.
"Toronto's Early Architects," *R.A.I.C. Journal*, February, 1950.
A History of the Church of Holy Trinity, 1871–1910, Ms, 1955, Metropolitan Toronto Central Library.
A Toronto Bibliography, Ms, Ontario Department of Public Records and Archives.

ROBERTON, T. B., *The Fighting Bishop* (Ottawa, 1926).

ROBERTSON, JOHN ROSS, *Landmarks of Toronto*, 6 vols. (Toronto, 1894–1914).
What Art Has Done for Canadian History (Toronto, 1917).

ROBINSON, BLACKETT C., *History of York County (Including Toronto)*, 2 vols. (Toronto, 1885).

ROBINSON, PERCY J., *Toronto during the French Régime* (Toronto, 1933; University of Toronto Press, 1964).

ROCHEFOUCAULD-LIANCOURT, Duke de la, *Travels through the United States of North America, the Country of the Iroquois, and Upper Canada, 1795–97* (London, 1799).

SCADDING, HENRY, *Toronto of Old: Collections and Recollections* (Toronto, 1873).
History of the Old French Fort at Toronto and its Government (Toronto, 1887).

SCADDING, HENRY and CHARLES DENT, *Toronto Past and Present* (Toronto, 1884).

SELZ, PETER and MILDRED CONSTANTINE, *Art Nouveau* (The Museum of Modern Art, 1959).

SHUTTLEWORTH, E. B., *The Windmill and its times* (Toronto, 1924).

SIMCOE, MRS. JOHN GRAVES, *The Diary of Mrs. John Graves Simcoe, 1792–96*, with notes and a biography by JOHN ROSS ROBERTSON (Toronto, 1911; rev. ed., Toronto, 1934).

SPENDLOVE, F. ST. GEORGE, *The Face of Early Canada* (Toronto: Ryerson Press, 1958).

SYLVESTER, ALFRED, *Sketches of Toronto*, with handwritten notes by the author (Toronto, 1858).

TAYLOR, C. C., *Toronto Called Back, from 1892 to 1847* (Toronto, 1947).

TIMPERLAKE, J., *Illustrated Toronto, Past and Present* (Toronto, 1876).

Toronto, Photographs in Black and White (New York, 1891).

Toronto Illustrated (Toronto, 1893).

Toronto in the Camera (Toronto, 1868)

TROLLOPE, ANTHONY, *North America* (New York, 1862).

WALKER, FRANK N., "Doorways That Welcome," *Canadian Banker*, Spring, 1959.

WALLACE, W. STEWART, *A History of the University of Toronto* (Toronto, 1926).

YEIGH, FRANK, *Ontario's Parliament Buildings, 1792–1892* (Toronto, 1893).

IV. Directories, Handbooks, Almanacs and Yearbooks

1833–62, York and Toronto City Directories
1834, Swift's Almanac
1851, The Canada Directory
1858, Descriptive Catalogue of the Provincial Exhibition
    The Handbook of Toronto. By a member of the
    Press (G. P. Ure)
1860–1900, Nelson and Sons, Handbooks
1874, The Toronto Illustrated Almanac for the Year 1874
1898, Fraser's Official Guide Book of Canada
    Official Guide and Souvenir of Toronto

Index

This Index is based on the text. For the Architects whose work is recorded in the book, the reader should also consult the biographical index provided in Appendix B. For the origin of street names in 19th century Toronto, the reader is directed to the alphabetical list in Appendix A.

This book is set in Monotype Bembo type, text size
12-point, leaded 2 points, with Bembo display. It is printed
on Provincial Georgian Offset Smooth and bound in
Holliston No. 3 Tag cloth

DESIGN: Paul Arthur and Associates Limited
PRINTING: Rolph-Clark-Stone Limited
TYPESETTING: University of Toronto Press